W9-ATS-708

America Had Never Known Crimes Like His . . .

Before Grace and the old man proceeded on their journey, he had a stop to make. At the corner of Fourteenth Street and Ninth Avenue, he retrieved his canvas-wrapped bundle and thanked the man inside the newsstand for watching it. Then he and Grace continued on their way, the old man cradling his bundle in his arms.

Wrapped inside were a butcher's knife, a meat cleaver and a small handsaw—the three items that the little gray man with the kindly eyes and friendly smile liked to think of as his "implements of hell."

Praise for Harold Schechter's National Bestseller, **Deviant** . . .

"In this grisly, wonderful book, Harold Schechter yields to no one . . . a scrupulously researched and complexly sympathetic biography of the craziest killer in American history. . . . A fascinating account."

—*Film Quarterly*

"A solidly researched, well-written account of the Gein story, told chronologically so that the mystery and horror unfolds just as it did 32 years ago. . . ."

—*Milwaukee Journal*

"Schechter . . . lets Gein's crimes speak for their gruesome selves. . . . [Gein was] arguably the most ghastly sociopath detected up until that time. . . . TOP-DRAWER TRUE-CRIME WRITING."

—ALA *Booklist*

Books by Harold Schechter

Deranged
Deviant

Published by POCKET BOOKS

Most Pocket Books are available at special quantity discounts for bulk purchases for sales promotions, premiums or fund raising. Special books or book excerpts can also be created to fit specific needs.

For details write the office of the Vice President of Special Markets, Pocket Books, 1230 Avenue of the Americas, New York, New York 10020.

DERANGED

THE SHOCKING TRUE STORY OF AMERICA'S MOST FIENDISH KILLER!

HAROLD SCHECHTER

POCKET BOOKS

New York   London   Toronto   Sydney   Tokyo   Singapore

An *Original* Publication of POCKET BOOKS

POCKET BOOKS, a division of Simon & Schuster Inc.
1230 Avenue of the Americas, New York, NY 10020

Copyright © 1990 by Harold Schechter

All rights reserved, including the right to reproduce
this book or portions thereof in any form whatsoever.
For information address Pocket Books, 1230 Avenue
of the Americas, New York, NY 10020

ISBN: 0-671-67875-2

First Pocket Books printing October 1990

10 9 8 7 6 5 4 3 2 1

POCKET and colophon are registered trademarks of
Simon & Schuster Inc.

Cover photo by Wide World Photos

Printed in the U.S.A.

O rose, thou art sick!
The invisible worm
That flies in the night,
In the howling storm,

Has found out thy bed
Of crimson joy,
And his dark secret love
Does thy life destroy.

WILLIAM BLAKE,
"The Sick Rose"

For
Linda Marrow

DERANGED

Prologue

On March 6, 1932, readers of *The New York Times,* sipping their breakfast coffee or settling back on the living-room sofa, were jarred from the enjoyment of their Sunday morning ritual by an alarming full-page feature, headlined "KIDNAPPING: A RISING MENACE TO THE NATION." Though the article was occasioned by the shocking abduction, just five days before, of Charles Lindbergh, Jr.—the infant son of America's most revered hero—it was not illustrated with a photo of the missing baby or a picture of his famous parents. Rather, the portrait that appeared on the top of the page was that of another, earlier kidnap victim, who had disappeared from her home in 1928, never to be seen again. This was a sweet-featured, ten-year-old girl with bobbed brown hair, a gentle smile, and a name which evoked such vivid images of tenderness and purity that no novelist would have dared to invent it: Grace Budd.

From the day of her disappearance, the mystery of little Gracie's whereabouts—and the efforts of the New York City Police Department to unravel it—had riveted the public's attention. What made the case so sensational was not simply the flowerlike innocence of the victim but, perhaps even more, the chilling circumstances of the

1

crime. The child had been lured from her home and family by an elderly, kindly-seeming gentleman who had offered to take her to a birthday party. Neither Gracie nor her grizzled companion—a figure of such cadaverous coloring that he came to be known in the tabloids as the "Gray Man"—returned that night. Or ever again.

The Budd kidnapping struck a powerfully disturbing chord in the hearts of parents throughout the country. In a way the crime was even more unsettling than the abduction of the Lindbergh baby. Because of the aviator's extraordinary renown, the theft of his child (whose corpse was eventually uncovered in a shallow grave not far from home) became the most infamous crime of the Depression. It was a deed that seemed not simply heinous but—given the worshipful regard in which the "Lone Eagle" was held by his countrymen—almost inconceivably wicked. As terrible as it was, however, the snatching of Lindbergh's twenty-month-old son was committed out of conventionally base motives. It was a straightforward (if appallingly cruel) kidnapping for ransom.

The abduction of the Budd girl was something else, a crime that couldn't fail to induce a shiver of dread in the parents of every young child. Only the rich, after all, had to worry that their offspring might be stolen for money. But no child was safe from the evil that had befallen Grace Budd—from the treachery of a smiling stranger, whose friendliness concealed a sinister intent. More than any other child-snatching of the Depression years, the Budd kidnapping brought home a terrible truth: that the world contains creatures who batten on innocence and that the trustfulness of children makes them frighteningly vulnerable to such beings.

In our own time, when child abduction has become epidemic and even our milk cartons are imprinted with the faces of the missing, that truth has been confirmed with dismaying regularity. To be sure, most kidnapped minors are the victims of broken marriages, of bitterly divorced spouses stealing their own children away from a hated ex-husband or wife. But the carrying off of young ones by predatory strangers happens often enough to be a legitimate fear. And, after all, it takes only a single outrage, like the 1979 disappearance of Etan Patz (the six-year-old Manhattan boy who set off for his school bus one Spring morning and was never seen again) or the slaying of little Adam Walsh (whose decapitated body was discovered shortly after he vanished from a Florida shopping mall in 1981) to poison the peace of mind of even the most carefree mother or father. Of all the evils that plague the modern world, none is more nightmarish from a parent's point of view than the crime we now call "stranger abduction."

For millions of Americans, the Budd case first gave birth to that nightmare. This is not to say that parents haven't always kept a close eye on their children or cautioned them to be wary of strangers. But the Budd kidnapping was one of the watershed crimes in American history. Before it happened, America was a more innocent place, a place where parents felt free to allow their young children to roam unattended, even in New York City, without fearing that they would disappear forever. Afterward, few parents would permit their sons or daughters to venture into the world without teaching them first that children who talk to, take candy from, or accept the generous offers of strangers sometimes come to very bad ends.

It would be six years from the day of Grace Budd's disappearance before the case was finally solved, and when it was, the truth turned out to be infinitely more horrifying than her parents' worst fears. The "Gray Man" would stand revealed as a creature of unimaginable perversity and evil.

Though his name has faded from public memory, his presence is inescapable. Behind the spectral features of the figure that haunts every parent's dreams—the fiend who lures children to destruction with the promise of a treat—lies the wizened face of the "Gray Man," whose name was Albert Fish.

PART 1

The Gray Man

elderly stranger, dressed in a dark suit and tie. A folded newspaper was tucked under one arm. In the

1

Great cities are not like towns, only bigger. They differ from towns and suburbs in basic ways, and one of these is that cities are, by definition, full of strangers.

JANE JACOBS,
*The Death and Life of
Great American Cities*

Every period is known not only by its heroes but by its killers as well. When we remember the late sixties, the Woodstock era, we think not only of Bob Dylan and Jimi Hendrix and the Beatles but also of Charles Manson—the drug-crazed demon-hippie, every grown-up's worst nightmare of the counterculture come true. The youth culture of the 1950s, whose icons were Elvis and Brando and James Dean, also produced Charlie Starkweather, the ultimate "JD," who imagined himself a romantic teen rebel as he hotrodded across the Nebraska badlands, leaving a trail of shotgunned corpses in his wake. And, whoever our heroes ultimately prove to be, our own age will forever be associated with figures such as David "Son of Sam" Berkowitz, Ted Bundy and Joel Steinberg, whose atrocities epitomize the nightmares of our time: urban terrorism, sexual violence, child abuse.

In May, 1924, a killing occurred in Chicago—a crime so sensational that it would come to be as closely identified with the twenties as flappers, the Charleston, and bathtub gin. Two brilliant and wealthy young men, Nathan Leopold, Jr., and Richard Loeb, the pampered scions of prominent Chicago families, concocted a plan

7

to carry out "the perfect crime." Its commission would confirm their image of themselves as Nietzschean supermen.

Cruising the streets of their exclusive South Side neighborhood, they selected a victim at random—a fourteen-year-old acquaintance named Bobby Franks—lured him into their car and, after bludgeoning him with a chisel, disfigured his corpse with hydrochloric acid and stuffed it into a drainpipe at the bottom of a remote railroad embankment.

The killing of little Bobby Franks by Leopold and Loeb (who, for all their arrogance, were easily captured less than two weeks after the murder) achieved instant notoriety as the "crime of the century." And their trial became the media event of the day. Defending them was the celebrated attorney Clarence Darrow, whose oratorical genius had saved 102 clients from execution.

During the month-long proceedings, the drama unfolding in the Chicago Criminal Courts Building overshadowed every other crime story in the country. For that reason, relatively little notice was taken when, in July, 1924, another child, a young New York City boy named Francis McDonnell, was brutally murdered. For sheer sensationalism, the McDonnell slaying, terrible though it was, simply couldn't compete with the Leopold and Loeb case, and the public quickly forgot it. Indeed, a full decade would pass before it burst back onto the front pages of the newspapers.

Only then would people realize that the death of little Francis McDonnell had not been a case of a single, depraved murder but an omen of more—and worse—to come.

Staten Island has always been the most sparsely populated of the five New York City boroughs, and in 1924, the section of Port Richmond where the McDonnell family lived struck first-time visitors as a particularly isolated place. Manhattan was only a short ferry-ride away, but the McDonnell's neighborhood—a scattering of modest, one-story houses surrounded by woods—

might have been located way out in the country. On sun-washed summer days, the streets seemed especially barren, their heavy silence broken only by the occasional shouts or laughter of a few neighborhood children at play.

Not far from the McDonnell home lay a place known locally as Charlton's Woods, a ten-acre tract belonging to the Charlton Nordling Fireworks Company. The area was a favorite haunt of neighborhood youngsters—a backyard wilderness with a little brook running through its center, where, in the summer months, the children came to swim, fish, and sail their toy boats.

Eight-year-old Francis McDonnell, the son of a Staten Island police officer, had spent the early afternoon of Monday, July 14, playing by himself on the front porch of his home. At around 2:00 P.M., his mother came out to join him, cradling her month-old daughter, Annabelle, in her arms. Shortly afterward, as she sat on the porch nursing her baby, Mrs. McDonnell caught sight of a strange figure making his way down the middle of the street—a stooped, elderly man, shabby in appearance, with gray hair, a gray moustache and a gaunt, gray-stubbled face.

His hands made a constant, nervous motion, clenching and unclenching, and he seemed to be mumbling to himself. As he passed down the street, the two German shepherds belonging to the McDonnell's next-door neighbor set up a howl. The gray-haired man turned to the woman on the porch, tipped his hat, then vanished down the road.

Later that afternoon, the stranger reappeared. By that time, Anna McDonnell had retired into her cottage with her infant daughter. Francis, accompanied by his little brother Albert, had gone off to join several playmates on the street—Eddie, Tommy, and Jimmy Donovan, the sons of a neighborhood fireman. The five boys were enjoying a game of catch with Francis's favorite plaything—a white rubber ball, printed with the silhouettes of circus animals—when they noticed an elderly man with a gray moustache standing a short distance away, beckoning to them. Little Francis walked over to see what the old man wanted, while the others turned their attention back to their game. When they looked for Francis a few moments later, both he and the stranger were gone.

The last person to see Francis McDonnell that day was a neighbor, George Stern. The time was roughly 4:30 P.M. Relaxing on his porch across the road from the McDonnell's place, Stern spotted the boy entering the grassy path that led to the little brook. Like other children from the area, Francis often played in Charlton's Woods and, ordinarily, Stern wouldn't have paid any attention at all. What caught his notice this time was a second figure—a gray-moustached "tramp," as Stern would later describe him—walking close behind the boy.

Nowadays, of course, the sight of a grubby, grizzled stranger following a young child into an isolated woodland would undoubtedly arouse suspicion, if not alarm, in the minds of most observers. And even in 1924, the residents of the Port Richmond area had been sensitized to crime. Not long before, a neighborhood woman, Mrs. Maud A. Bauer, had been shot and killed by a motion picture operator named Harry Hoffman. Even more dismaying to area residents had been the murder, a year earlier, of a young boy, whose body had been found hanging from a tree less than a mile from the McDonnell home.

Even so, in July, 1924, New Yorkers were less wary of certain perils than they soon would be. Clearly, George Stern couldn't imagine that, at the height of a sun-baked afternoon, on a lazy summer day, an eight-year-old boy could enter the woods that served as the neighborhood park and never come out alive.

When Francis failed to return home by suppertime, his parents became concerned. It was only then that Albert told them about the gray-haired old man who had called Francis away from their game. Immediately, Arthur McDonnell, still dressed in his police uniform, went out to scour the neighborhood. Unable to locate his son, he telephoned his colleagues at police headquarters. By the next morning, an alarm had gone out and a massive search was underway throughout Staten Island. Besides friends, neighbors, and police, a large volunteer force of Boy Scouts was involved in the hunt.

In the end, it was a trio of Scouts—Henry Laszarno, Thomas Passone, and Henry Wood—who found the missing boy. The three were passing through a clump of trees on the Charlton property when Wood, who was walking in front of his friends, literally stumbled upon the body.

It had been hastily concealed under a pile of branches and leaves. The clothes below Francis's waist—stockings and shoes, underpants, khaki knickerbockers—had been violently ripped from his body. He had been, as the newspapers would put it, "atrociously assaulted," then strangled with his suspenders, which were twisted so tightly around his neck that they seemed embedded in the flesh.

Within an hour of the discovery of the corpse, more than fifty police officers were on the scene, including Captain Ernest Van Wagner, Chief of Detectives on Staten Island; Deputy Chief Inspector Cornelius Calahan; and Captain Arthur Carey, head of the Homicide Bureau. Assistant Medical Examiner of Richmond County Dr. George Mord showed up shortly thereafter but was prevented from touching the victim's savagely mauled corpse until police photographers and fingerprint experts arrived from Manhattan. Much to Dr. Mord's dismay, it took nearly four hours for the Manhattan specialists to reach the scene.

By the next morning, July 16, an additional two hundred and fifty plainclothesmen had been assigned to the case. Arthur McDonnell, attached to a precinct in Manhattan, was officially transferred to Staten Island so that he could participate in the hunt for his son's murderer. "If I catch the killer," McDonnell assured reporters, "I'll turn him right over to Captain Van Wagner. I'll not harm a hair on his head. I want to see him punished as he deserves, but the law must take its course." A contingent of police guards was posted in Charlton's Woods to keep away the morbidly curious, who, as soon as the news of the murder was made public, began arriving in hordes to view the scene of the crime.

Hysteria swept across the borough. Police stations throughout Richmond were flooded with calls, most of them from young women, eager to report recent encounters with menacing-looking strangers. Typical was the story told by seventeen-year-old Jennie Carlson. According to the girl, she had been walking in Charlton's Woods the previous Saturday when she happened upon a man who looked to be in his late fifties, "unkempt, with gray hair and a thick growth of beard, about five feet six inches tall, and wearing blue trousers, a soiled white shirt and no coat." The man was eating something out of both hands, "with his face down and his body crunched over like an animal." As Jennie hurried past this sinister figure, he looked up and called out to her "in a foreign tongue which sounded like Italian." Terrified, the girl began to run, whereupon the stranger leapt up and began to chase her through the underbrush. When she reached a clearing not far from her home, however, he stopped, turned around, and melted back into the woods.

The police paid polite attention to this anecdote, but did not attribute tremendous significance to it, since they had already heard several dozen similar stories in the days since the discovery of the McDonnell boy's body. Indeed, if these tales were to be believed, there was scarcely a rock, tree, or bush on Staten Island without a murderous, gray-moustached derelict lurking behind it.

With the opening of the Leopold and Loeb trial still a few days away, the New York City news media had the opportunity to play up its own child-murder. The *Daily News* informed its readers that Staten Island was aswarm with sexual perverts—"overrun with old men, morons, degenerates of all types, men picked out of the gutters and bread lines of New York City and sent to the city farm colony on the island. At present, there are nearly five hundred men on the poor farm and many of them are known to be degenerates." According to *The New York Times,* "the sixty square miles of territory in Staten Island include large areas of uncultivated land, with woods and wild undergrowth, which are believed to be used as hiding places and meeting places by robbers, bootleggers, fugitives from justice, and criminals of various kinds."

Indeed, the lurid tales related by two men picked up as suspects in the case—Clyde Patterson and Jacob Gottlieb, orderlies at the Sea View hospital in New Dorp, Staten Island—seemed to confirm this grim picture. According to these "confessed perverts" (as they were characterized by the *Daily News),* the woods near the McDonnell residence concealed a small hollow known to its habitués as "Rattlesnake Nest," a place where child molesters gathered to engage in "wild orgies of degeneracy." This revelation not only made the two hospital employees the prime suspects in the case but also produced a public call for beefed-up police protection on Staten Island. When investigators went to check the place identified by Gottlieb and Patterson as "Rattlesnake Nest," however, they discovered not a rendezvous for sex fiends but an abandoned real estate shack used by local children as a playhouse. The two men were arraigned on sodomy charges but discounted as suspects in the McDonnell murder.

The manhunt went on. Scores of men were questioned and at least a dozen were taken into custody. Jacob Herman, an escaped inmate from a New Jersey insane asylum, provided police with a graphic description of the McDonnell boy's corpse, which he claimed to have chanced upon shortly after his getaway: "Tuesday, I was going through the woods. I stumbled upon the body. I touched it. It felt like putty. I was afraid. I ran." But investigators soon concluded that Herman's facts had been gleaned from newspaper stories—several clippings related to the case were found in his coat pocket—and that he had, in fact, been nowhere near Port Richmond at the time of the slaying.

Other suspects were grilled: a truck driver who had

been arrested in Brooklyn for impairing the morals of a minor; a middle-aged man charged with troubling little children in a playground; a male music teacher, accused of taking a young boy into the woods and talking to him about "sex psychology." But all of these individuals turned out to have solid alibis.

As their hopes for an early arrest evaporated, the police stepped up their search, canvassing the Port Richmond district door-to-door, questioning construction workers on the streets, stopping milkmen and ice-wagon drivers as they made their daily rounds. Tramps were rounded up from public parks across the city. Several promising suspects—a dishwasher discovered with a rubber ball like little Francis's in his possession, a paroled laborer who had been convicted of killing a dog in Charlton's Woods, an epileptic who displayed an "absorbing interest" in the crime—were arrested, interrogated, and, in the end, released for lack of evidence.

At Francis's funeral—attended by his parochial school classmates and a throng of curiosity seekers who had made their way to St. Mary's church from all around the city—detectives mingled with the crowd on the chance that, as Captain Van Wagner explained, the killer might put in an appearance, drawn to the scene by an "irresistible fascination." But no suspicious-looking strangers showed up. Dressed in his first communion suit, little Francis lay in an open white coffin, the terrible bruises on his face concealed by heavy makeup. Nearby, his stricken mother pillowed her head on her husband's shoulder and struggled to control her grief.

The autopsy report on the victim revealed the presence of undigested raisins in his stomach—the bait, the coroner theorized, which had been used to lure the boy into the woods. Because of the condition of the corpse, the medical examiner also speculated that the murderer couldn't have been as old as Mrs. McDonnell claimed. Only a man in his prime could have administered such a ferocious beating. Indeed, Dr. Mord suggested, there may well have been more than one killer involved.

In spite of these pronouncements, however, Anna McDonnell stuck to her original story. She knew exactly what the killer looked like, she insisted. She could see his features plainly, whenever she shut her eyes.

"He came shuffling down the street," she told reporters, "mumbling to himself, making queer motions with his hands. I'll never forgot those hands. I shuddered when I looked at them. I shudder every time I think of them—how they opened and shut, opened and shut, opened and shut. I saw him look toward Francis and the others. I saw his thick gray hair, his drooping gray moustache. Everything about him seemed faded and gray.

"I saw my neighbor's two police dogs spring at him, and I saw Philip, the hired man, call them off. The gray man turned to me and tipped his cap.

"And then he went away."

As she spoke, her husband sat by her side on their living-room sofa, one arm around his wife's shoulders. At their feet lay Francis's dog, Pal. "If Pal had only been with him," said the sorrow-worn father, "Francis would never have been killed. Pal would have chewed that man's leg off before he would have let him touch the boy."

As days passed and the police seemed no closer to a solution, the tabloids became increasingly shrill in their cries for retribution. "The fiend who attacked and killed Francis McDonnell seems to have gotten away," blared the *New York Daily News*. "But even if he should be apprehended—even if a confession should be wrung from his lips—there is little likelihood that the grim and merciless punishment that an outraged citizenry would look for could be inflicted by law!" "The chair," fumed the editor of another city paper, "will be far too good for the perpetrator of this atrocious deed."

Not long after these remarks appeared, some of the "outraged citizenry" of Staten Island had a chance to vent their wrath. The victim was a hapless drifter named John Eskowski, who had been squatting in an abandoned shack on the south shore of Staten Island, ten miles from the spot where Francis McDonnell was slain.

For several weeks, stories had circulated through the area—rumors of a sinister "hermit" who had been accosting local boys. Late one afternoon, a teenager named William Bellach happened upon Eskowski in the woods. Convinced that Eskowski was the child molester, Bellach ran to a nearby gas station and alerted the proprietor, Salvatore Pace, who armed himself with a pistol and followed the boy back to Eskowski's shack. Pace leveled his weapon at Eskowski and began to lead him from the woods, but the drifter—believing Pace to be a bandit—pulled his own gun from his coat pocket and ducked behind a tree.

The two men exchanged shots, but neither was hit. Beating a hasty retreat to his gas station, Pace called the police. Within minutes, a troop of mounted officers descended on the woods, followed by a mob of a hundred armed, enraged citizens, convinced that the killer of Francis McDonnell had finally been found.

Eskowski, who had taken cover behind some rocks, opened fire on his pursuers, who fired back. Hit in the side, Eskowski fell to his knees and, seeing the circle of men approaching, put his pistol to his temple and pulled the trigger. He survived only long enough to reveal that he was a farmer who had abandoned his home several weeks earlier after a bitter quarrel with his wife. Checking his story, the police confirmed that, at the time of the murder, Eskowski had been living in Radnor, Pennsylvania.

The Eskowski incident made it briefly into the headlines, but for most of the public, the McDonnell case was rapidly receding into the past. The Leopold and Loeb trial was well underway by then, and its irresistible mix of murder, money and courtroom melodrama made it the most popular show in America. The slaying of Francis McDonnell had become a matter of interest only to those most directly concerned with the crime—the police, the residents of Port Richmond, and, of course, the boy's parents. Just a few weeks after the discovery of her son's strangled and mutilated body, the heartbroken mother made one final appeal to a public that had already begun to regard her tragedy as yesterday's news.

"Help us catch the monster who murdered our little boy," Anna McDonnell implored. "Help us find the gray man."

2

"O come and go with me, no longer delay,
Or else, foolish child, I will drag thee away."
"O father! O father! Now, now keep your hold,
The Erl-king has seized me—his grip is so cold!"

JOHANN GOETHE, "The Erl-king"

There are certain wounds that time never heals. For the parents of Francis McDonnell, the savage murder of their child was an unabating horror, made even more unbearable by the escape of the creature who had committed it. The years went by, but—in spite of the ongoing efforts of the New York City police, who found it hard to swallow the unsolved murder of a fellow officer's son—the killer was still on the loose. To Anna and Arthur McDonnell, the gray man was as real as the grief that racked their hearts. But only their pain—and a small white coffin buried in the old Calvary cemetery—proved that he had existed at all. As far as the rest of the world was concerned, the gray man had vanished, seemingly forever.

And then, one day, on a mild afternoon in early 1927, he came back.

It had been an unusually temperate winter, and, by mid-February, people throughout New York State were already detecting the first signs of spring. Pussy willows were budding in Watertown, new grass had begun to sprout in Saratoga Springs, and, even in the northernmost reaches of the state, robins, starlings, and black-

18

birds had returned from their winter migrations. In New York City, at a time of the year when children could normally be found playing outside in the snow, the streets were full of lightly clad youngsters, skipping rope, shooting marbles, or clattering down the sidewalks on roller skates.

On Friday, February 11, the mildness of the weather was matched by the pleasantness of the local news. The metropolitan pages of *The New York Times* were full of sunny stories: the early coming of spring; the first, exciting demonstration, held at Manhattan's Rivoli Theater, of motion pictures with sound; the eightieth birthday of Thomas Edison, America's greatest inventor, who favored reporters with his "billion-dollar smile" and declared that work remained his greatest pleasure.

Even the day's top crime story was strikingly tame. The most sensational event in the city was the police raid on a trio of supposedly immoral Broadway shows, including a drama called "Sex," whose popularity had as much to do with its title as with the talents of its author and leading lady, Mae West.

In short, anyone reading the news of that Friday would have assumed that February 11, 1927, was a remarkably uneventful day in the city, a day when nothing very terrible had happened.

But—though it took a little while for the truth to sink in—something very terrible had.

It was the speed at which it happened that made the horror so hard to believe at first—that and the fact that the only witness was a child of three.

The Gaffney family occupied a small, sunless apartment on the second floor of 99 Fifteenth Street, one of several rundown tenements crammed between Third and Fourth Avenues in Brooklyn. Late in the afternoon of Friday, February 11, just around dusk, Billy Gaffney, a slender four-year-old with his mother's cornflower blue eyes and auburn hair, was playing in the dimly lit hallway outside his apartment. With him was his three-year-old neighbor, the Beaton boy, whose first name was Billy, too.

An older neighbor, twelve-year-old Johnny McNiff, who lived on the top floor of the tenement and who was home minding his baby sister, heard the sounds of the two friends at play and headed downstairs to join them, leaving the infant asleep in her crib. A few minutes later, however, the baby began crying. Johnny hurried back up to his flat to quiet her. When he returned to the second floor, no more than three minutes later, the two Billys were gone.

Just then, Billy Beaton's father, who was caring for his children while his wife was in the hospital, emerged from his flat and found Johnny in the hallway, looking puzzled. The boy explained what had happened. Mr. Beaton dashed to the Gaffney's apartment, but the children weren't there. Afraid that the boys might have wandered into the street, he ran down the two flights of stairs to the front stoop and began calling their names. But no one responded.

Mr. Beaton's apprehensions deepened by the moment. With Johnny at his side, he began a rapid search of the building, starting on the ground floor. But the two boys were nowhere to be found. As soon as they reached the top floor, however, Mr. Beaton heaved a sigh. There, alone by the ladder that led to the roof, stood his little boy.

Taking his child into his arms, he asked what had happened. "Where were you? Where did you go?"

Billy sounded excited. "We were on the roof," he said, pointing overhead. "We saw chimneys and buildings and steamships!"

Looking up, Mr. Beaton saw that the scuttle which opened to the rooftop had been shoved aside. He was baffled. The tenants of the building, most of whom had young children, were careful to keep the wooden hatch closed at all times, and no boy as young as Billy Beaton or Billy Gaffney could have possibly moved it aside.

"Where's Billy Gaffney?" Mr. Beaton asked. "Is he still up there?"

His son shook his head.

Mr. Beaton, who only a moment before had been

awash with relief, suddenly felt his throat tighten with anxiety. "Where is he then?"

Billy Beaton's reply, offered without hesitation, would be a source of continuing controversy in the days and weeks ahead. It was the sort of answer that a three-year-old could be expected to give and, for that reason, the authorities were inclined to discount it. Indeed, it would be six years before the world came to realize that the Beaton child had been right all along.

"The boogey man took him," Billy Beaton said.

By the following day, twenty-five detectives and patrolmen, under the command of Sergeant Elmer Joseph, had been assigned to the case. Little Billy Beaton, along with his father and Johnny McNiff—the last people to see the missing boy—were interrogated closely. Each time he was asked what had happened, the Beaton boy repeated his story, but Sergeant Joseph dismissed it as a three-year-old's prattle. "All children talk about the boogey man when they sense trouble," he explained.

A kidnapping made no sense to Sergeant Joseph. The Gaffneys were desperately poor. Edmund, the father, worked as a truck driver for a local stocking company, a job that barely paid him a living wage. Indeed, at the moment of her son's disappearance, Elizabeth Gaffney had been seated at the kitchen table, patching a pair of her son's tattered gray knickers. These and another equally shabby navy-blue pair were the only pants her child owned. He had been wearing the blue knickers, along with a gray middy, black stockings and black shoes (but neither hat nor coat) when he vanished into the gloom.

No one in his right mind, Sergeant Joseph reasoned, would kidnap the child of such penniless people in the hope of obtaining a ransom. It was the sergeant's opinion that the unsupervised boy had wandered out into the street and fallen into trouble. It was conceivable that he had taken it into his head to explore one of the many nearby factory buildings and had become trapped inside. Or—a much grimmer possibility—that he had made his way to the Gowanus canal, located less than five blocks from his home, and met with an accident. A police scow was dispatched to the canal, and two officers spent the day dredging its muddy bottom with grappling hooks. But they managed to bring up nothing except a sodden assortment of trash.

Over the days and weeks ahead, the tenement district surrounding Billy Gaffney's home was the scene of one of the most intensive hunts in New York City history. Before it was over, more than three hundred and fifty policemen, plus untold numbers of civilian volunteers— neighbors, school children, Boy Scouts, and others—had taken part. Every cellar, sewer, loft, factory, church, alleyway, lumber yard, coal bin, and crawlspace in the area was searched and searched again. But no trace of Billy could be found. As one dispirited detective put it, it was as if the earth had swallowed him up.

Throughout this period, Mrs. Gaffney remained sequestered in her dusky apartment, grieving and growing more haggard by the day. Her three married sisters had hurried to her side to offer what comfort they could, and it was only at their insistence that Mrs. Gaffney ate and slept at all. Though she remained firm in the conviction that Billy was still alive, the thought of her "candy boy" (as she called him) lost somewhere in the wintry streets was an unrelenting torment. "He was always so pale—in the house so much," she cried to reporters. "I can't bear to think how he looks now, without food and all."

To make matters worse, the Gaffneys—like other victims of highly publicized misfortunes—began receiving crank letters by the bundle. Some of these were nothing more than babble: "My dear friends, I will be fine to boy, my son in waters, rivers, cellars. Look out. My God, want back boy."

Others, such as the letter the Gaffneys received on February 16, were infinitely worse, impelled by an unimaginable sadism: "Wait! Do not appear too anxious. Your son is in safe hands. We fought for him, but I got him now. We will get the Beaton boy for Billy to play with, for Billy is lonesome. Do not show this letter to anyone if you know what is good for you. Again I say that Billy is safe and that we are experimenting on him."

But no matter how insane or incoherent these messages were, the police pored over all of them, in the desperate—and ultimately futile—hope that one might contain a clue to Billy Gaffney's whereabouts.

By this time, Billy Beaton had provided the police with a fuller description of the "boogey man." According to the three-year-old, the stranger who had taken Billy Gaffney away was a thin old man with gray hairs growing on his upper lip.

In spite of these specifics, Sergeant Joseph and his superiors remained skeptical. Of all the possible fates that could have befallen Billy Gaffney, kidnapping seemed the least likely. What could be the motive? A ransom was out of the question. The Gaffneys seemed to have no enemies. And it would be crazy for a childless adult to risk imprisonment by snatching someone else's son when city orphanages were packed with adoptable youngsters. "There is no reason why anyone should want to take this child," opined Inspector John J. Sullivan of the Missing Persons Bureau. "The kidnapper would have to be deranged."

Just a few years before, of course, a thin, gray-moustached and desperately deranged individual had snatched, sexually assaulted, and killed young Francis McDonnell. But—perhaps because so little weight was given to the three-year-old's testimony—no one connected Billy Beaton's "boogey man" to the "gray man" of the earlier crime.

As the investigation entered its second week, the police continued to pursue every lead, no matter how slender or farfetched it seemed. One of the countless crank letters mailed to the Gaffneys contained a crudely drawn map of an islet in the Bronx River where, according to the anonymous writer, the corpse of Billy Gaffney was buried. "I didn't mean to kill him. God forgive me!" When the police followed the map to the designated spot, however, all they found was a small strip of solid rock jutting out of the water.

Another letter indicated that Billy's corpse had been stuffed into a carton and left in an empty apartment on Alexander Avenue in Brooklyn. Police investigators hastened to the address, where they found a large cardboard box shoved into a corner of the abandoned flat. Inside was a mound of moldering rags.

In their growing frustration, the police began grasping at straws. At one point, Mrs. Gaffney revealed that, several years earlier, she had testified against two female cousins in a lawsuit involving a fiercely contested will. Because of the bitter enmity that had resulted, both cousins were brought in for questioning. They were released within the hour, however, when it became clear that they knew nothing whatsoever about the missing boy.

Even Billy Beaton's father came under suspicion for a short time. A neighborhood man named Gabriel Cardovez informed the police that, on the night of February 11, he had seen Mr. Beaton hurrying down the street with a bundle in his arms. Kings County D.A. Charles Dodd called Beaton in and questioned him about the incident. As it turned out, Cardovez's dates were off. Beaton had, in fact, carried a bundle from his apartment one evening. But the package contained freshly laundered underclothing for his recuperating wife, and—as hospital records confirmed—he had made the visit on February 16, five days after Billy's disappearance.

Hopes were raised and dashed with dismaying regularity. The day after Billy vanished, a truck driver named Edward Wisniski showed up at the Gaffney's apartment and explained that, on the previous evening, he had come upon a little boy, lost and crying on a nearby street corner, and turned him over to a passing patrolman. The news sent Billy's parents flying to the local precinct, where they discovered that the boy Wisniski had found belonged to someone else.

A day later, a Weehawken, New Jersey, policeman revealed that, on Saturday afternoon, he had observed a "short, swarthy woman" dragging a weeping little boy past his traffic post. This revelation set off a brief, frantic search for the woman, which came to an abrupt halt when Officer Martin was shown some photographs of the Gaffney boy and realized that the child he had seen bore no resemblance at all to Billy.

Anonymous tips continued to pour in by the dozen. One informant reported that Billy had been stolen by a "bereaved mother" and was living safely in Harlem. Another insisted that he was being kept by an old man in Roosevelt, Long Island.

One morning in early March, the Gaffneys received a special delivery letter which claimed that Billy was imprisoned in an old frame house in South Brooklyn. In three densely packed pages of handwritten script, the writer described in vivid detail how, while walking past the dilapidated house one recent morning, he had glanced up and seen, peering through the grimy panes of a second-story window, a wan child's face resembling newspaper photos of Billy. Suddenly, a man's hand appeared, clutched the boy by the shoulder, and jerked him from view. Then the blind had been hastily lowered. Inspector Sullivan immediately sent a dozen men to the address. But the house turned out to be empty.

Subsequent rumors placed Billy in increasingly far-flung locales. When an abandoned four-year-old was picked up on the streets of St. Louis, the police of that city believed that he might be the missing Brooklyn boy—until a frantic old lady showed up at the station house later that day, looking for her lost grandson. Some weeks later, Sergeant Joseph received a letter from a druggist's wife in Deadwood, South Dakota, who claimed that Billy was living on a ranch in Montana. Joseph immediately contacted the Deadwood Chief of Police, who dispatched a man to check out the story.

But like every other sighting of Billy, this one turned out to be a mirage.

The only solid lead that police investigators received came from a trolley car conductor named Anthony Barone who, after a period of what he termed "mental struggle" during which he agonized over the wisdom of getting involved, finally stepped forward to relate what he had witnessed on the evening of Friday, February 11.

It was shortly after 7 P.M.—not long after Billy's disappearance—when an elderly man with a heavy gray moustache boarded Barone's car at Prospect and Hamilton avenues in Brooklyn, just two blocks away from the Gaffney's tenement. Accompanying this man was a little boy, dressed in a gray blouse and blue knickers. Though the sun had set at 5:30 and the evening was raw, the boy wore neither hat nor coat. Barone had taken special note of that detail. And there was something else about the boy that caught the conductor's attention. He cried continuously, from the time he was led onboard until the moment he disembarked, in spite of the efforts of the wizened old man to hush him.

According to Barone, the pair rode to the end of Hamilton Avenue. "Before they got off the car," he explained to Inspector Sullivan, "the man asked me if they could get a ferry from there to Staten Island." Barone explained that the best way to reach Staten Island was to take the Hamilton Avenue Ferry to the Battery and then the municipal ferry to St. George.

Without another word, the old man—who seemed very jumpy, according to Barone—alighted from the trolley car, the little boy in tow. Instead of following Barone's instructions, however, he turned in the opposite direction. The last that Barone saw of the old man, he was hurrying along Sackett Street, away from the ferry, "half dragging, half carrying" the weeping little boy. For a few moments, Barone watched the strange duo, the hunched old man and the frightened child, as they made their way down the dimly lit street, their figures moving in and out of the shadows. Then they disappeared into the night.

Police investigators—who by this time had come to believe that Billy had, in fact, been the victim of a child-snatcher—attached considerable importance to Barone's story, particularly after they interviewed Joseph Meehan, the motorman on the trolley, who confirmed the conductor's account. Since there had been only one or two other passengers on the car at the time, Meehan recalled the man and boy clearly. Indeed, he had been struck by something Barone hadn't mentioned. Throughout the ride, the old man had kept his heavy overcoat wrapped around the underdressed boy, as if to keep him warm—or conceal him.

So important did Inspector Sullivan consider the testimony of the two transit workers that they were given a temporary leave of absence from their jobs and placed on the police payroll so that they could assist in the hunt. Meehan would prove to be a crucial eyewitness when it came time to identify Billy's abductor.

But that identification was still many years away.

The New York City tabloids had wasted no time in exploiting the melodramatic potential of the Gaffney case. The *Daily News* in particular did its best to transform the Gaffneys' personal tragedy into a shamelessly lurid soap opera, concluding each day's article on the case with a breathless "don't-miss-the-next-exciting-episode" tag:

> Somewhere in New York or nearby is little Billy Gaffney—or his body. An army of detectives, 350 strong, is hunting that somewhere. Watch for the results of that search in tomorrow's NEWS.
>
> Hoping against hope, police continue their search for missing Billy Gaffney. Follow the trail in tomorrow's NEWS.
>
> Will the seventh day bring joy or sorrow to the parents of little Billy? Read all the developments of the hunt in tomorrow's NEWS.

This kind of sensationalism not only sold papers but also had the effect of arousing the passions of many New Yorkers to a near-hysterical pitch. Within a single week in early March, on three separate occasions, mobs of enraged men and women attacked suspicious-looking strangers who were spotted in the company of neighborhood children.

All three incidents occurred in Brooklyn, close to the tenement district where the Gaffneys lived. In the first, a sixty-three-year-old salesman named Giles Steele was strolling down East 92nd Street when a four-year-old boy stepped into his path. "Move aside, son," Steele said, reaching down and taking the boy by the shoulder. At that moment, the child's mother, Mrs. Sadie Bernstein, came to the door of her house and, seeing a strange man with his hand on her son, began to scream for help. A crowd of neighbors immediately descended on Steele and began pummeling him. After being rescued by a passing patrolman, the hapless Steele was taken to the local stationhouse, where police quickly determined that he had no knowledge at all of the Gaffney crime. Even Mrs. Bernstein, once she calmed down, admitted that she might have overreacted. Nevertheless, Steele was arraigned on a kidnapping charge and held on $10,000 bail.

The other two men attacked by outraged mobs in Brooklyn that week were considerably more unsavory than Steele. Both of them—Louis Sandman, a forty-two-year-old waiter, and Samuel Bimberg, a dapper young man from Secaucus, New Jersey—were admitted pederasts with prior convictions for impairing the morals of minors. And both men were in the act of leading young victims into darkened tenement hallways when they were spotted and set upon by enraged neighborhood residents, who were prevented from beating the culprits to death only by the timely appearance of the police. Nevertheless, though detectives would have liked nothing better than to establish even a slender connection between one of these men and Billy Gaffney, Sandman and Bimberg —like Giles Steele—were quickly eliminated as suspects.

To the legion of New Yorkers who had been following every twist and turn in the search for little Billy Gaffney and sharing in the hope that the missing boy might still be found alive, the front-page headline in the Wednesday, March 9, edition of *The New York Times* was a shocker: "FEAR SLAIN CHILD FOUND IN CASK IS GAFFNEY BOY."

On the previous afternoon, in Palmer, Massachusetts, a high school sophomore named Chester Kolbusz had been scavenging at the town dump. Lying on top of a refuse pile was an old wine cask that appeared to be partially burned. Peering inside the cask, Kolbusz saw a lumpy, burlap-wrapped object. He reached a hand into the cask and pulled aside the fabric. What he saw sent him dashing in terror to the nearest police station. The object was the corpse of a child, its face horribly mutilated.

The police were on the scene within minutes. Nearly a month had now passed since Billy's disappearance and, by this point, a description of the kidnapped Brooklyn boy had been wired to policemen throughout the Northeast. By early Tuesday evening, Massachusetts state detectives had contacted their counterparts in New York with the details of the discovery. Inspector Sullivan broke the news to the Gaffneys as gently as possible, and arrangements were made at once for Billy's father to travel up to Palmer the following day.

By this point, of course, Billy's parents had suffered through a spate of false alarms—supposedly reliable (but invariably erroneous) reports that their son's body had been dumped in the East River or buried somewhere on Staten Island. Several weeks after Billy was stolen, a steam-shovel operator, digging up the grounds of a mental institution in Brooklyn for a new sewer line, turned up the body of a small boy wrapped in the remnants of a patchwork quilt. The police believed at first that the dead child was Billy Gaffney—until an autopsy revealed that the corpse had been in the ground for at least seven months. (The body turned out to be that of a neighborhood child, dead of natural causes, whose impoverished parents, unable to afford a funeral, had buried him by night on the hospital grounds.)

For the Gaffneys, however, the grisly discovery in the Palmer town dump was far more distressing than any previous scare. For one thing, a hasty postmortem by the medical examiner seemed to indicate that the murdered boy had been dead for just over three weeks—exactly as long as Billy had been missing. For another—as *The New York Times* reported—the corpse in the wine cask was that of a little boy "answering in almost every detail" to Billy's description.

Like Billy, the victim was a thin, pale child with brown hair and large blue eyes. Even more ominously, the killer had apparently taken pains to obliterate certain telltale features from the corpse, in places where Billy himself had identifying marks. The lower half of the murdered boy's face, for example, had been badly disfigured, his jaw crushed by a series of savage blows. Billy had a scar on his lower lip, the token of a bad spill he had taken as a baby. And the skin of the dead boy's stomach had been slashed with a sharp object. Billy had a distinctively shaped birthmark on his stomach, precisely where the corpse's abdomen had been carved up.

The following morning, in the company of Detective James Dwyer, Mr. Gaffney—whose employer had given him a paid leave of absence until the kidnapping was solved—took the train up to Palmer. During the entire ride, he sat in an agonized silence, praying for a miracle. The thought of his son, his "candy boy," dying so grotesquely was more than he could stand. He stared out the window at the bleak late-winter landscape and did his best to steel himself for the dreadful confrontation that awaited him in a small-town Massachusetts mortuary.

That confrontation never took place. Even before Mr. Gaffney arrived at Palmer, the police had discovered that the murdered child was not his missing son.

He was, in fact, a local child, the son of twenty-five-year-old Ida Kelly, who worked as a housekeeper for a farmer named Albert Doe. Shortly after Christmas, Doe had lost his temper at the four-year-old boy and beaten him brutally while his mother looked on. The child died two days later. Doe hid the body in the cellar of his farmhouse for a few days, then stuffed it into a wine cask, drove it to the dump, and tossed it on a garbage heap, which he attempted—unsuccessfully—to set on fire. By the time Mr. Gaffney and Detective Dwyer showed up, Doe had already been arrested and charged with first-degree murder.

The Gaffneys felt badly, of course, for the victim's mother, but their overwhelming emotion was sheer gratitude and relief. "Thank God it wasn't my son!" Mr. Gaffney exclaimed to reporters as he started back to New

York. Though their prayers had been answered at another parent's expense, Billy's mother and father could only interpret the Palmer episode as a hopeful sign—an affirmation of their faith that their own child would yet be found alive.

By this point, however, the Brooklyn police were rapidly approaching the end of their rope. It was a measure of their increasing desperation that, by early March, they had begun welcoming the assistance of various cranks. One of these was a crackpot inventor, who showed up at the Gaffney home one day with a contraption he described as a "mechanical bloodhound." In effect, the apparatus was nothing more than an elaborately tricked-out divining rod with a rubber tube at one end, into which a strand of Billy's hair was inserted. With the device vibrating in his hands, the inventor led a dozen policemen to a nearby varnish factory, which they spent the next several hours searching—in vain.

Even more bizarre was a séance conducted by a building contractor and part-time hypnotist named Harry Culballah one evening in late March. As Billy's parents, along with two New York City detectives—William Casey and Fred Shaw—looked on, Culballah put a cousin of Mrs. Gaffney's, a man named Bill Hersting, into a deep trance. Culballah asked Hersting what he saw.

"I see Billy in the spirit world," Hersting replied in a heavy, drugged voice.

"Look further!" Culballah commanded.

"I see a man," Kersting continued. "He is leading Billy by the hand."

"Where are they going?"

The spectators stood transfixed as Hersting proceeded to give a highly detailed, and increasingly animated, recitation of Billy's fate:

"The man is taking Billy to 286 Sixteenth Street. This is a red brick building, three stories, with a bakery on the ground floor. They go into the bakery and the man asks for a cup of coffee. He buys Billy some buns and has difficulty getting him to eat them, but Billy finally eats them.

"The man and Billy now walk down Sixteenth Street, across Fifth Avenue. When they reach Fourth Avenue, the man seems to fade out of the picture. Billy continues to Third Avenue, then up Fifteenth Street. He stands at the curb. A woman appears and takes him by the hand, then leads him across the street and leaves him. Billy goes north on Third Avenue, walks to Twelfth Street, turns west and passes some factory buildings, then a gas tank.

"He reaches water. My God! He's going into the canal! He's disappeared!"

At this point, Hersting leaped from his chair, his hands outstretched as if to grab the drowning boy. Then, with a terrified scream, he slumped back into his seat and awoke seconds later, deeply shaken.

The detectives were so impressed by this performance that they immediately ordered a new search of the Gowanus Canal. A police diver spent much of the following day searching the muddy bottom of the waterway.

But like every other source that claimed to know the whereabouts of Billy Gaffney, the spirit that had spoken through the mouth of William Hersting had been wrong.

By early spring, the Gaffney story, which had been covered more extensively by the city's newspapers than any kidnapping in recent memory, had begun to disappear from their pages. Even the tabloid audience was growing tired of it. The drama simply refused to arrive at a satisfyingly happy—or tragic—conclusion. Small news items about Billy continued to appear from time to time, but they were relegated to the back pages. Soon, the flood of letters that had poured into the Gaffney home since the tragedy began had slowed to a trickle. By mid-April, even the cranks had lost interest.

On July 7, 1929—more than two years after Billy's

disappearance—a small article appeared in *The New York Times*. Mrs. Elizabeth Gaffney, her health broken by her unrelenting grief, had been taken to Bellevue Hospital with severe chest pains. Never a heavy woman, Mrs. Gaffney had lost forty-six pounds since that terrible day. Besides heart trouble, she had also developed a severe infection of her tear glands—a consequence of her chronic sleeplessness and uncontrollable bouts of weeping.

She was released several weeks later, but her life remained dominated by her loss. Often, in her fitful sleep, she would dream of Billy. In the middle of the night, she would awaken her oldest daughter, Irene, to tell her of an especially wonderful dream—of Billy running up the steps, hammering on the door, crying, "Mamma, mamma, let me in!"

On special holidays she always set a place for Billy. "I know he will come back some day," she told reporters, who visited her apartment at Christmastime in 1930. "There is nothing a mother can do but hope."

For the rest of her life, Elizabeth Gaffney would never reconcile herself to the loss of her son. Even after the truth came to light, years later, she refused to accept it—an understandable act of denial, given how appalling the truth turned out to be.

3

_. . . horrid king, besmeared with blood
of human sacrifice, and parents' tears._

JOHN MILTON, _Paradise Lost_

He had always been a man of passion. Now, his lust
had become even stronger, a terrible appetite that
seemed to grow more ravenous with each new feeding.

In the beginning, he had craved only the pain. It wasn't
until later that the blood-hunger had possessed him. He
remembered the first time he had sought to satisfy it. He
had cut off a piece of the monkey—just the tip—with a
pair of scissors. But the little one had set up such an
awful howl, even through the gag, that he had taken pity
on it and run away, leaving it bleeding and moaning on
the bed.

Afterward, though, he couldn't get the picture out of
his mind—the cropped and bleeding monkey, the agony
on the little one's face. Even now he stiffened at the
memory.

Sometimes, he felt overcome with contrition. At such
moments, the urge to atone for his sins by butchering one
of Christ's lambs was impossible to resist. A verse floated
into his head: "Happy is he that taketh Thy little
ones/And dasheth their heads against the stones."

The latest sacrifice had been the sweetest. It, too, had
made pitiful noises—from the moment he had led it
from the roof until its final seconds, when its dying bleats
truly sounded like those of a bleeding little lamb.

The commandments came more frequently now. He

34

would need another victim soon, another Isaac offered as a sacrifice for his own iniquities, sins, and abominations in the sight of God.

His work had always made it easy for him to find, and snare, his prey. But he was often without work nowadays and had to depend on other tricks. There were many of them, and by now he knew them all.

His hungry eyes never stopped scanning the world for the signs that would lead him to his preordained prey.

He had found them everywhere—on the streets, in the churches, in the houses of the poor and the insane.

A message might arrive at any time, from any place.

It was only a matter of knowing where to look.

4

What ugly sights of death within mine eyes!

SHAKESPEARE, *Richard III*

Edward Budd was a short but powerful eighteen-year-old, built like a bantamweight. Square-jawed and square-shouldered, he had the cockiness of the young Jimmy Cagney. Even standing still, he seemed tensed for motion, charged with the buzzing energy of the New York City streets.

In this respect, he differed markedly from his parents, who seemed to have been defeated, if not crushed, by the hardness of their life. Albert Budd, a head taller than his son, seemed like a wisp in comparison. A porter for the Equitable Life Assurance Company, he had a hapless air about him and a look of perpetual bewilderment that was partly the result of a flagrantly phony glass eye. By contrast, his wife, Delia, was a mountainously large woman with an underslung jaw that added to her look of stubborn immobility. Seeing the oddly matched pair together, more than one observer was reminded of the old nursery rhyme about Jack Sprat and his wife.

Besides Edward, Mr. and Mrs. Budd had four other children: Albert Jr., George, baby Beatrice, and—the flower of the family—little Grace, a sweet-tempered ten-year-old, strikingly pretty in spite of her city-child's sallowness.

All seven Budds inhabited a cramped apartment at the rear of 406 West 15th Street at the edge of Manhattan's Chelsea district. The apartment was overheated in the

36

winter and—in the pre-air-conditioned days of 1928—
unbearably oppressive in the summer. Young Edward
had resolved to spend the summer outside of the city,
away from its ceaseless clatter, rotting-garbage smells,
and deadening heat. He had been working part-time as a
truck driver but had no regular job. What he wanted
most was a few months of fresh country air and a chance
to work his muscles. He wanted to spend the summer on
a farm. The question was how to secure such a position.
And the answer, proposed by his mother, was to take out
a classified ad.

And so, on Friday, May, 25, 1928, the teenager rode
the subway to the offices of the *New York World,* where he
arranged to have a one-line classified inserted into that
Sunday's edition: "Young man, 18, wishes position in
country. Edward Budd, 406 West 15th Street."

Two days later, his notice appeared in the "Situations
Wanted" section of the newspaper's morning edition,
and Edward, after satisfying himself that his ad had been
printed as scheduled, went off to spend the day with his
buddies, confident that his classified would do the trick.

On that same Sunday, in a different part of the city, an
elderly man sat at a rickety kitchen table, studying, as he
did every day, the classifieds in the *New York World*.
When he got to Edward Budd's ad he stopped and read it
again. And then again.

To anyone else's eyes, there would have been nothing
notable about the ad, except, perhaps, for its simple
reflection of old-fashioned American virtues—industry,
youthful ambition, a feel for the outdoors.

It took a mind already hopelessly lost to sanity to
attach a very different meaning to it and to feel, at the
sight of those innocent words, an overpowering thrill of
malignant desire.

5

~~~~~~~~~~~~~~~~~~

The soul of the wicked desireth evil: his neighbors findeth no favor in his eyes.

PROVERBS 21:10

At around 3:30 in the afternoon of the following day—Monday, May 28, 1928—someone knocked on the door of the Budds' apartment.

Seated on the creaky double bed she shared with her husband, Delia Budd was folding up underwear from a shapeless pile of freshly washed laundry that sprawled at her side. The day was warm and muggy, and Mrs. Budd, whose bulk made the heat even harder to bear, had undone the top few buttons of her tentlike cotton housedress. Even so, she found herself pausing every few moments to swab the sweat from her neck with a balled-up hanky. Through the plaster wall behind her, she could hear the muffled squeals of her youngest daughter, Beatrice, playing in the adjacent bedroom. The rest of the family was away from home, at work or with friends.

At the sound of the knock, Mrs. Budd raised herself with a little groan from the buckled mattress and made her way slowly to the door. Before she reached it, the rapping began again.

"Just a minute," she called.

Rebuttoning the top of her flower-printed housedress, Mrs. Budd pulled the door open. There stood a small, elderly stranger, dressed in a dark suit and black felt hat. A folded newspaper was tucked under one arm. In the

38

dusk of the tenement hallway, he looked impressively well-to-do and dapper. Mrs. Budd was unaccustomed to such nicely dressed callers. Instinctively, she reached up and patted at her shapeless hair.

"Can I help you?" Mrs. Budd asked.

The elderly gentleman reached under his arm, removed the newspaper, and held it out to Mrs. Budd, as though he had dropped by to deliver it.

"I am looking for a young fellow named Edward Budd. I read his ad in yesterday's paper."

"You come to the right place. I'm his mother."

The little man removed his hat and bowed slightly, a gesture that, in Mrs. Budd's eyes, seemed as courtly as a kiss on the hand. "Good day to you," he said. "My name is Frank Howard. I'm here with an offer that might be of interest to your son."

Stepping back from the doorway, Mrs. Budd held out a welcoming hand. "Come on in. Eddie's over to a friend's, but I'll have my little girl fetch him for you."

The old man nodded again and, walking with a slightly bowlegged gait, followed Mrs. Budd into the living room, where she invited him to have a seat. As carefully as a convalescent, Mr. Howard lowered himself into a chintz-covered armchair.

Calling Beatrice from the bedroom, Mrs. Budd told the child to run around the corner to the Korman apartment and tell her brother to come home immediately. As the five-year-old passed the stranger in the easy chair, the old man reached out a bony hand and took her by the wrist.

"You remind me of my own granddaughter. What do they call you?"

The little girl, who had just turned five, stared shyly at her feet. "Beatrice," she said after a moment.

Reaching into his pocket, the old man came up with a shiny coin. "Here's a five-cent piece for your trouble," he said, placing the nickel in her palm.

Beatrice held up the coin for her mother to see.

"What do you say to the man?" Mrs. Budd asked reprovingly.

"Thank you," said Beatrice, then dashed out the door.

"You'll spoil the child," Mrs. Budd said with a smile. "Would you care for some lemonade? I got some fresh-made in the ice box."

"That would be nice."

The windows of the Budds' apartment faced a back alley, and even at the height of a bright spring afternoon, the rooms were filled with shadows. After returning with the drink, Mrs. Budd switched on a table lamp next to her guest, and in its yellow glow, she took a better look at him.

It was hard to tell his age, though he seemed dried-up and shrunken, one of those wizened old men whose hollow faces look like parchment-covered skulls. He had a sharp, beaked nose, watery blue eyes, a thatch of gray hair, and a gray moustache that drooped over the corners of his mouth. Gazing up at Mrs. Budd, he smiled benignly, revealing a set of moldy teeth. His top incisors protruded slightly, giving him the look of a kindly old rodent.

His navy blue suit, Mrs. Budd could now see, was shabbier than it had seemed in the hallway—its jacket cuffs frayed, its pants worn to a shine at the knees. Still, he looked respectable enough, and when he raised his left hand to lift the lemonade glass to his mouth, a large diamond pinky ring glittered in the lamplight.

The old man had just set his empty glass down on the side table when Beatrice returned with her brother Eddie and his best friend, Willie Korman, another compactly built teenager with an impressive set of shoulders. Mrs. Budd introduced the boys to the elderly visitor, who half-raised himself from his seat to shake hands, then settled back onto the cushion with a wince.

As Mrs. Budd made room for the boys on the sofa, the old man proceeded to describe his situation. For many years, he explained in a quiet, almost whispery voice, he had worked as an interior decorator in Washington, D.C. He had done very well for himself. He had a good marriage and six wonderful children. Then, his eyesight began to fail. Taking the money he had made from his business, he had indulged a lifelong dream by purchasing a "nice little farm" out in Farmingdale, Long Island.

His wife, however, had hated country living from the start, and within a year she had abandoned him, leaving him with the care of their children. He had been both mother and father to them for a dozen years. Life had been hard for them during that time, but his children, thank God, had all turned out well. "One of my boys is a cadet at West Point," he said proudly.

Moreover, he had managed to make the farm a go. With three hundred chickens and a half-dozen milk cows, the place provided him with a good steady income. At present, he was able to employ a full-time Swedish cook and five farmhands.

One of his most dependable workers had decided to move on, however, and Howard was looking to replace him. Edward's ad had appeared at a most propitious time. He smiled up at the boy. "You look strong enough to work."

"Yes, sir," Eddie answered, leaning forward eagerly. "And I ain't afraid of hard work, either."

Howard nodded approvingly. "I am prepared to pay fifteen dollars per week for as long as you can stay with me."

"That sounds good to me," Eddie said, turning to his mother, who was sitting beside him with a look of perfect satisfaction on her face.

A moment of silence passed, during which Eddie and his friend exchanged a glance. "We was wondering, Mr. Howard," Eddie said, pointing a thumb at his friend. "My chum Willie here is also looking for summer work."

Howard turned his gaze to Willie, then asked if he would mind standing for a moment. The boy got to his feet, drawing himself up to his full height, while the old man looked him up and down.

"All right," he said after a moment. "I can use a fine, big fellow like you on my farm."

Grinning broadly, Willie plopped himself back onto the sofa.

Reaching a finger into his vest pocket, the old man

fished around for a moment, then pulled out a big stemwinder. He snapped open the lid and held the timepiece close to his face. "I must be on my way. I have a business engagement out in New Jersey."

Lifting himself gingerly from his seat, he told the boys to pack the "oldest clothes you have." He would return on Saturday afternoon with a car and drive them out to Farmingdale.

The boys, followed by Mrs. Budd and Beatrice, escorted their benefactor to the door, where Howard shook hands all around, thanked Mrs. Budd for her hospitality, and patted the little girl on her head. Then he was gone.

No sooner had the door shut behind him than Edward and Willie began doing a little dance around the living room, as tickled as a pair of ten-year-olds who have just received a particularly profitable visit from Santa Claus. The classified that Eddie had invested in had paid off in spades. Mr. Howard's offer seemed too good to be true.

And so, over the next few days, Edward Budd and William Korman excitedly began making their preparations, while the little gray man who called himself Frank Howard set about, in a state of even greater excitation, making his.

6

~~~~~~~~~~~

Workers of iniquity, which speak peace to their neighbors, but mischief is in their hearts.

PSALMS 28:3

Eddie and Willie passed most of the appointed day—Saturday, June 2—inside the Budds' apartment, impatiently awaiting Frank Howard's arrival. A pair of canvas duffel bags, crammed to capacity with well-worn but freshly washed work clothes, lay in a corner of the living room.

The two teenagers had spent the week crowing to their acquaintances about their good fortune, about the "gentleman farmer" from Long Island who had offered them summer jobs in the country and fair wages to boot. Now Eddie and Willie were eager to get going. But the day wore on with no sign of Frank Howard.

Late in the afternoon, someone finally knocked on the door, and Eddie hurried to open it. Much to his disappointment, he found himself face-to-face with a Western Union delivery boy, who handed him a message and hovered in the doorway until Eddie forked over a dime.

With Willie peering over his shoulder, Eddie read the terse, handwritten note: "Been over in New Jersey. Call in morning." The message was signed "Frank Howard." The boys exchanged a brief, crestfallen look. Then Eddie shrugged. By now, it was four o'clock. Evening was just a couple of hours away. They had managed to wait this long. Waiting another day wouldn't kill them.

* * *

43

Though he had decided, for reasons of his own, to delay his plans until Sunday, the old man, too, had been impatient for the week to pass. True, neither the Budd boy nor his friend was exactly what he'd had in mind when he first came upon Eddie's classified in the newspaper. In spite of the enthusiasm he'd found it necessary to feign, he had been disappointed by their appearance.

But—aflame with a passion he could barely contain—he was in no position to pick and choose. Eddie Budd and Willie Korman might not have been his ideal choices. But they would do.

He had, in fact, spent much of the week in an agony of anticipation, so intense at times that it felt almost paralyzing. Still, he had not allowed himself to be idle. There were important things to be done, and he had attended to them promptly and efficiently.

The first order of business had been his shopping. On Tuesday, the day after his visit to the Budds', he had strolled over to a hock shop called Sobel's on 74th Street and Second Avenue. There, for less than five dollars, he had bought three of the items he would need. The three most essential items.

Carrying them back to his apartment at 409 East 100th Street, he had carefully opened the brown paper package and, after briefly admiring his purchases, placed them in a neat row on the floor underneath his bed.

As it turned out, he had cause to regret removing them from their wrapping. Later that week, shortly before noon on Thursday, he had gone out to buy a newspaper and had run into a twelve-year-old acquaintance named Cyril Quinn, who was playing boxball on the sidewalk with another boy the old man recognized, the son of the burly Italian who delivered coal to his building.

For several months, the old man had been cultivating the Quinn boy's trust by giving him small gifts—candy, ice cream, pieces of change. He had particular plans for the lad, which he had been waiting for the right moment to implement. Now, seeing the boys playing on the street and thinking about his new acquisitions resting on the floor beneath his bed, he was seized by a sudden inspiration. He would test out his new purchases on Cyril Quinn.

Greeting the boys, the little man asked if they had eaten lunch. When they shook their heads, he invited them to his apartment for a bite. As soon as they were all inside, the old man repaired to the kitchen, pointing to his bedroom and telling the boys to wait for him there.

The old man was at the sink, slicing bread and cheese for sandwiches, when the accident occurred.

Cyril—who had visited the apartment before and felt at home there—began wrestling with his friend on the old man's creaky mattress. The rough-housing grew wilder. Suddenly, locked in a bear hug, the two boys slid to the floor, laughing raucously. Their laughter died abruptly, however, when they looked over and saw what was lying under the bed.

Before the old man could stop them, the boys had jumped up and rushed from the apartment.

Not a word had been spoken. But the old man knew exactly what had occurred. Through the wall that separated his bedroom from the kitchen, he had heard the sounds of the horseplay, the thump of the bodies tumbling onto the floor, then the sudden, charged silence. And as the two boys hurried past the kitchen on their way to the door, Cyril Quinn had shot the old man a look that spoke more eloquently than any words.

It had been a look of pure fear.

7

~~~~~~~~~~~~~~~~~~

Childhood is the kingdom where nobody dies.

EDNA ST. VINCENT MILLAY

Sunday, June 3, was one of those gray, dreary days in the city when the sky seems less cloudy than smudged. At around 10:30 in the morning, Frank Howard, dressed in the same slightly scruffy blue suit he had worn the previous Monday, disembarked from the subway at 14th Street and began making his way toward the Budd residence, several blocks away.

Cradled in one arm was a compact bundle, tightly wrapped in a piece of red-and-white-striped canvas. A small white enamel pail—purchased the previous morning from a peddler named Reuben Rosoff, who sold sundries from a pushcart on the corner of 100th Street and Second Avenue—dangled from his other hand.

On the way to the Budds' apartment, the old man made several stops. At a small German delicatessen, he had his pail filled with fresh pot cheese. Across the street, at a fruit-and-vegetable stand, he purchased a small carton of plump strawberries. Then he continued west-ward along Fourteenth Street. Managing the box of berries, the pailful of cheese, and the canvas-wrapped bundle was a slightly awkward business, but the old man was more dexterous—and far less feeble—than he looked.

Still, when he stopped to buy a paper at a newsstand on the corner of Ninth Avenue and Fourteenth Street, just a block away from the Budds' apartment building, he made a show of fumbling with his packages as he fished for a coin.

"You going to be able to manage the paper, too, Pops?" asked the news seller.

"I'm not so sure," said the old man. Then, nodding at the canvas-covered parcel under his arm, he asked if he could leave it at the newsstand for a little while. He would return for it in an hour or so.

"Sure," said the newsy, reaching for the bundle, which he placed inside his stand.

Frank Howard thanked the man for his trouble. Then he picked up his paper and turned the corner toward the Budds' apartment.

It was a few minutes before eleven when Frank Howard knocked on the door of the Budds' ground-floor apartment. The family had been to church that morning. Mr. and Mrs. Budd, still dressed in their Sunday best, were relaxing in the living room, listening to Gene Austin croon "My Blue Heaven" on the Victrola, while little Beatrice sat cross-legged on the carpet, leafing through the pages of a picture book. The rest of the Budd children were outside on the street with their friends.

Mrs. Budd greeted the little man warmly, then led him into the living room, where she introduced him to her husband.

"These are for you," said Howard, handing the woman the berries and cheese.

Mrs. Budd exclaimed over the gifts, while the two men shook hands.

"You'll never taste creamier pot cheese than that, I can guarantee it," said Howard. "Nor sweeter strawberries." He reached down and petted Beatrice on the head. "I bet you like strawberries, don't you?" he whispered.

Beatrice, embarrassed, looked down at her feet and shrugged.

"This come from your farm, Mr. Howard?" asked Albert Budd, moving closer to his wife and squinting at the fruit and the little white pail with his one good eye.

Frank Howard smiled often enough, but he didn't

seem to know how to laugh. Instead of opening his mouth, he would tighten his lips together and make a faint snuffling sound through his nose, like someone clearing his sinuses. He did this now in response to Albert Budd's question.

"That's right," he said happily. "Those products come direct from my farm."

Howard was invited to stay for a potluck lunch. Eddie was over on Seventeenth Street, Mrs. Budd explained, playing stickball with some friends, but he had promised to be home by noon. Removing his hat, the old man said he would be pleased to join the family for their meal. Mrs. Budd excused herself and bustled off to the kitchen, carrying the treats that Howard had brought.

"I'd be interested to hear more about that farm of yours, Mr. Howard," said Albert Budd, motioning his visitor toward the sofa.

"I hope the boy wasn't too disappointed about yesterday," the old man said. "I was over in New Jersey buying horses." He was about to seat himself on the sofa when he stopped, as if struck by a sudden thought. "That message I sent," he asked. "Do you know if the boy threw it away?"

Why no, replied Mr. Budd. It hadn't been thrown away. Eddie had stuck it over there, on the mantelpiece.

Frank Howard nodded, then did something that would stick in Mr. Budd's mind, though at the time he didn't attach much significance to it. Stepping over to the mantel, the little man picked up the message, glanced at it for a moment, then casually slipped it into the pocket of his suit jacket and walked back to the sofa, where he carefully lowered himself onto the cushion with a sigh.

Mr. Budd settled into the easy chair facing the sofa. Then, as he listened raptly, Frank Howard proceeded to paint the same beguiling picture he had evoked for Delia Budd the previous Monday—a vision of his twenty fertile acres, his teeming colony of fat Rhode Island Reds, his fecund dairy cows, his lush fields of produce, his crew of happy workers, his Swedish cook. Poor and uneducated, a simple man who had spent his life toiling at the most menial jobs, Albert Budd could only shake his head and make admiring sounds.

This Frank Howard, thought Budd, might not look like much. With his stooped and shrunken frame, he certainly didn't look like a successful farmer. But clearly he was a man of substance. Albert Budd—accustomed in his work life to assuming a submissive manner in the presence of the businessmen and financiers he served—responded to his visitor with a deeply ingrained and automatic deference.

A short time later Mrs. Budd appeared in the doorway, announced that lunch was ready, and ordered little Beatrice to go and wash her hands. The men retired to the kitchen, a clean but dingy-looking room, illuminated by a single bare bulb that tinged the whitewashed walls a sickly yellow. The long wooden table, covered with a plaid oilcloth, held a big cast-iron pot full of ham hocks and sauerkraut—the warmed-over remains of the previous night's dinner. The sharp, briny odor of the cabbage filled the room. Arranged around the pot were platters of pickled beets and boiled carrots, a basket of hard rolls, and two ceramic bowls into which Mrs. Budd had transferred Frank Howard's pot cheese and strawberries.

The Budds and their guest had just seated themselves at the table when they heard the front door open and somebody enter the apartment and proceed down the hallway to the living room. The person was humming a sweet, buoyant tune, and the voice, fragile and bright, clearly belonged to a young girl.

"That'll be Gracie," said Mrs. Budd, and called her daughter's name.

A moment later, Grace Budd stood in the kitchen doorway.

Everyone who set eyes on little Grace for the first time was struck by two things: her prettiness and her pallor. She had an invalid's complexion, the look of a child who had spent too much of her life surrounded by concrete and brick and was in need of some sunlight. (The previous summer, Grace had, in fact, managed to get out of the city for a short time, courtesy of the *New York*

Tribune's Fresh Air Fund, a charitable program that arranged for underprivileged children to spend a week or two in the country.) But her anemic coloring couldn't obscure her loveliness. With her big, dark eyes, her lustrous brown hair—cut in a fashionable bob—and her radiant smile, she seemed destined to blossom into a beauty.

She was still dressed for church—in the white silk dress she'd been confirmed in a month earlier, white silk stockings and canvas pumps, and a string of imitation pearls. The outfit made her look surprisingly grown up. But her pose, as she stood in the doorway—hands clasped behind her back, right foot pointed like a fledgling ballerina's—was unmistakably that of a little girl.

The old man lowered his fork and stared. He smiled his rabbit-toothed smile. "Come here, child," he said, patting his leg.

"This is Mr. Howard," Delia Budd explained. "The man Eddie's going to work for. Come say hello."

Gracie lingered in the doorway a moment longer, regarding the stranger. Then she walked to the table and stood by his knee.

So intent was the old man's gaze as he took in the child that it was as if her parents had simply vanished from the room. Speaking in a soft, wheedling voice, he told her how slender and pretty she was. He asked her questions about her friends, her favorite pastimes, her school. As he talked, he reached up a hand—mottled with liver spots but surprisingly powerful-looking, a laborer's hand —and began to stroke her hair. Gracie squirmed a bit under the stranger's touch and cast a questioning look at her mother, who smiled back in encouragement. Catching the wordless exchange, Howard let his hand slip down to the girl's flank and nudged her onto his lap.

"Let's see how good a counter you are," he said, leaning backward in his chair so that he could stick one hand deep into his pants pocket. He pulled out a thick wad of bills, which he set on the table before him. Then, reaching back into his pocket, he came out with a handful of coins. At the sight of the overspilling money pile, Mrs. Budd lifted her eyebrows appreciatively, while her husband gulped down a big swallow of sauerkraut and smiled vacantly.

At Howard's prodding, Gracie picked up the stack of bills—so thick that she needed both hands to hold it—and counted them back onto the table, one at a time, adding aloud as she did so. Then she scooped up the coins and counted those. The total came to $92.50.

"What a bright little girl," said Howard. Plucking a few nickels and dimes from the table, he held her hand open, placed the coins into her upturned palm, then folded her fingers over the money and patted her fist. "Here is fifty cents. Go out and buy some candy for you and your sister."

"Thank you," sang Grace as she slid from his lap, grabbed her sister's hand, and sped from the room.

"If you see Eddie," Mrs. Budd shouted after her older daughter, "tell him Mr. Howard's come for him!"

"Well," said Mr. Budd, chuckling softly. "You've made them children happy."

But the old man seemed lost in thought.

Grace had heeded her mother's instructions. Just a few minutes after she disappeared out the door, Eddie showed up with Willie Korman at his side. The boys, breathless from running, burst into the kitchen, where Mr. Howard greeted them warmly. But after apologizing for the previous day's delay, the old man made an announcement that took the two friends by surprise.

"Edward," he said. "I am not going to take you to the job right at the present. I received a letter from my sister yesterday, and she is throwing a birthday party for one of her children, which I'm obliged to attend." Howard, who had replaced his money in his pocket after Gracie's departure, now pulled out the wad again and peeled off a couple of bills. "Here's two dollars. You and Willie and some of the boys go take in the moving pictures. Later on this evening, after the party, I will pick you up on my way home."

Eddie and Willie took the proferred singles with thanks.

"Before you two run off," Mrs. Budd said, "why don't you have a bite of lunch?"

Eddie and his friend seated themselves at the big kitchen table, heaped their dishes with food, and began to shovel it in. Their plates were clean in minutes. Shoving their chairs away from the table, they thanked Mr. Howard again, told him that they would see him that evening, and headed back onto the street to round up some friends.

By that time, Grace and her little sister had returned with their treats. Mrs. Budd had just stood up to pour the coffee when the old man consulted his pocket watch. "It's almost time for me to be on my way," he said, then paused as if considering a possibility.

Something had just occurred to him, he said. He wondered if Gracie would like to come with him to his niece's birthday party. It was going to be quite a bash. Lots of children and games. He would take good care of her, he assured the Budds, and bring her home no later than nine.

Mr. and Mrs. Budd found themselves in a delicate position. They were reluctant to offend their guest by suggesting that they couldn't trust him with their daughter. And with Howard sitting right there, they didn't feel free to discuss their doubts with each other. But after all, what doubts could they have about their son's kindly new employer, the well-to-do, grandfatherly man who had treated them all with such generosity?

Mrs. Budd hesitated for a moment, but her husband cleared his throat and said, "Let the poor kid go. She's always cooped up here in this dungeon. She don't see much good times."

There was one important fact the Budds had neglected to ascertain. Where, Grace's mother wondered, did Mr. Howard's sister live?

The old man answered without hesitation. In a nice building on 137th Street and Columbus Avenue, he said.

New Yorkers like to think of themselves as streetwise and worldly. But many New Yorkers are as provincial as any small-towners. Both Delia Budd and her husband had lived their whole lives in Manhattan. But like many working-class housewives of her time, Mrs. Budd rarely ventured out of her neighborhood, and her husband's world was only slightly less circumscribed, its boundaries defined by the Midtown office building he worked in and his Fifteenth Street home. For that reason, no alarm bells rang in their heads when the little man told them where the party was taking place. The Budds simply didn't know that Columbus Avenue ends at 110th Street—that the old man had given them a nonexistent address.

By the time they found out, it was already too late.

Mrs. Budd helped Gracie into her dress-up spring coat with fur-trimmed collar and cuffs. A fake pink rose was pinned to the lapel. On her head, the girl wore a gray hat with blue streamers. With her little brown leather bag clutched in her hand, she was the picture of a proper young lady, dressed for a Sunday stroll.

The old man bid goodbye to Gracie's parents and little Beatrice, who was still munching candy from a small paper sack.

Mrs. Budd followed the pair outside and stood on the front stoop of her apartment building, watching them walk up the street, the bowlegged old man in his dusty, dark suit with her pretty ten-year-old daughter beside him. A few of Gracie's friends, playing on the street and spotting the girl in her holiday finery, began to shout at her in razzing tones: "Gracie's a swell! Gracie's a swell!" The little girl ignored them for a moment before turning her head quickly and sticking out her tongue.

Then, with Mrs. Budd still watching, the couple turned the corner and disappeared.

Before they proceeded on their journey, the old man had a stop to make. At the corner of Fourteenth Street and Ninth Avenue, he retrieved his canvas-wrapped bundle and thanked the man inside the newsstand for watching it. Then he and the girl continued on their way, the old man cradling his bundle in his arms.

Wrapped inside were a butcher's knife, a meat cleaver, and a small handsaw—the three items that had come from Sobel's hock shop and that the little gray man with the kindly eyes and friendly smile liked to think of as his "implements of hell."

PART 2

King of the Missing

8

~~~~~~~~~~~~~~~~

*He looked like a meek and innocuous little old
man, gentle and benevolent, friendly and polite.
If you wanted someone to entrust your children
to, he would be the one you would choose.*

FREDERIC WERTHAM,
The Show of Violence

There is a type of optical illusion known, in its more
pretentious manifestations, as "camouflage art." These
are paintings, generally of wilderness landscapes, that,
viewed up close, look like simple, picturesque scenes—a
mountain lake with a snow-covered slope reflected on its
surface, a field of wildflowers, a forest of birch trees.

Take a few steps back, however, and the picture
changes. The mirrored rock assumes the shape of an
eagle in flight, the flowers form themselves into a rearing
stallion, the boles of the birch trees become the profile of
an Apache warrior. The myriad details resolve themselves into a single, unmistakable image, previously
hidden from sight—but only when they are seen from a
distance.

So it was with that terrible sequence of crimes that
commenced with the killing of Francis McDonnell and
climaxed, several years later, with the kidnapping of
Grace Budd. Overwhelmed with a welter of tips, leads,
rumors, and clues—countless bits and pieces of information and hearsay—the police failed to perceive a
connection among the three cases. It was only from the
distance of years that those scattered facts came together

and formed themselves into a single, distinct identity, and the shadowy figures of the "gray man," the "boogey man," and the "gentleman farmer," Frank Howard, merged into the same monstrous individual.

For the present, in early June, 1928, all the police—and the city—knew was that another child was missing.

Early Monday morning, after a torturous night of sleeplessness and mounting alarm, Grace's parents had sent Edward off to the West 20th Street stationhouse to report their daughter's disappearance. A short time later, Lieutenant Samuel Dribben and three of his men—Detectives Jerry Mahar, James McGee, and James Murphy—arrived at the Budd's apartment, where they questioned the distraught couple closely about Frank Howard of Farmingdale, Long Island, who had promised to bring their daughter home from his niece's birthday party by nine o'clock Sunday night and never returned.

Lieutenant Dribben, after inquiring where the party was supposed to have taken place, informed Grace's parents that 137th Street and Columbus Avenue was a fictitious address. Dribben's news hit the Budds like a physical blow.

Dribben did what he could to comfort Mr. and Mrs. Budd—who seemed to have passed beyond panic into a state of glazed stupefaction—then ordered Maher and McGee to make a thorough search of neighborhood rooming houses.

Meanwhile, Detective Murphy escorted young Edward and his chum Willie Korman back to the stationhouse, where the boys spent an hour or so searching through the rogue's gallery in the hope of identifying Gracie's abductor.

Two more detectives were put on the case that day. One was dispatched to the main office of the Motor Vehicles Bureau to check its records for Howard's name and address.

Another was assigned the task of tracing the Western Union message that the old man had sent to Edward Budd on Saturday and whose contents Grace's parents had detailed for Lieutenant Dribben. Mr. Budd remembered something else about the message, too. He described the way Howard had asked about and then pocketed the telegram virtually the moment he arrived —an act which Albert Budd had noted with only casual curiosity at the time but whose full, ominous import had suddenly become all too clear.

The news broke on Tuesday, June 5—"HUNT MAN AND CHILD HE TOOK TO 'PARTY,'" read the headline in *The New York Times*. During the next few weeks, the public must have experienced a disconcerting sense of déjà vu, since the story was, in so many respects, a grim replay of the Gaffney abduction, which had dominated the news the year before. The Budd case contained all the ingredients of the earlier tragedy—the clues that led nowhere but to blind alleys and dead ends, the suspects hauled in and promptly released, the well-meaning tipsters and anonymous cranks, the kidnap-hysteria that swept through the boroughs, the cheap melodrama of the tabloid press ("Follow the search for little Grace Budd and her kidnapper in tomorrow's DAILY NEWS!").

There were, however, a few elements peculiar to the Budd case that, right from the start, made it even more gripping—and sensational—than the snatching of little Billy Gaffney: a fiend in the guise of a benevolent old man; a trusting mother and father beguiled by a smooth-talking tempter; and, most riveting of all, a lovely little girl in a communion dress, a victim whose very name seemed emblematic of her unprotected innocence and who—believing she was being taken to a birthday party —was lured to a nameless fate.

Assisted by Gracie's older brothers, officers from the West 20th Street precinct conducted an exhaustive search of the Budds' Chelsea neighborhood—cellars and rooftops, alleyways and empty lots, lodging houses, movie theaters, subway stations, and garages. But no trace of the girl could be found.

At the same time, several detectives traveled out to Farmingdale, Long Island, in an attempt to locate the truck farm supposedly owned by Grace's abductor. But that effort, too, proved fruitless.

A more promising lead turned up in another town called Farmingdale, this one located in New Jersey. Because Howard had telegrammed that he had "been over in New Jersey" on Saturday, Lieutenant Dribben—determined to pursue every possibility—dispatched Detective Jerry Maher to the little town across the Hudson River. Sure enough, Maher discovered that, some fifteen years earlier, a man named Frank Howard, who answered in a general way to the description of Grace Budd's abductor, had owned a small chicken farm in the town. Maher was also able to obtain the name of one of Howard's relatives, a woman named Low, who had recently moved to Weehawken.

In Weehawken, Maher quickly located the woman—Mrs. Birdsall Low of 508 Park Avenue—who confirmed that she was the niece of a farmer named Frank Howard. Her uncle, Mrs. Low explained, had lived in Farmingdale until 1913, at which point he had sold his farm and moved his family to Chicago.

Maher was heartened, but his hopes were exceptionally short-lived, nipped by Mrs. Low's next piece of intelligence. Her uncle was clearly a most promising suspect—a farmer named Frank Howard who had lived in the town of Farmingdale and whose appearance conformed in important ways to the physical characteristics of Grace Budd's kidnapper. There was only one problem. As Mrs. Low informed Maher—and as a quick phone check with the Chicago police confirmed—her uncle had died ten years before.

On the evening of Tuesday, June 5, police at the West 20th Street precinct received a frantic call from one of the Budds' neighbors, a woman named Juliette Smith, who reported that an elderly man had just attempted to lure her ten-year-old son, Arthur, into a tenement hallway. Within a short time, several officers arrived on the scene and quickly arrested fifty-nine-year-old Joseph

Slowey of 86 Eighth Avenue on a charge of impairing the morals of a minor.

Interrogated at the stationhouse, Slowey admitted that he had approached the boy, though he denied having harmed him in any way. As for his involvement in the Budd case, Slowey was so clearly ignorant of the crime that—though police would have liked nothing better than to have a suspect in custody—they quickly discounted him as a possibility.

The charge against Slowey was reduced to disorderly conduct. Two days later, he appeared before Magistrate Stern of the Jefferson Market Court, who dismissed the charge against him and ordered his immediate release.

Juliette Smith, Slowey's accuser, was not the only mother in the Budd's neighborhood whose fears had been raised to a high pitch by Grace's disappearance. Canvassing the area in the days immediately following the kidnapping, the police heard the same story again and again. According to various women, who swore that they had observed the individual in question with their own eyes, an elderly man with gray hair and a neatly trimmed moustache had been "loitering around" the neighborhood for several weeks, casting suspicious looks at their children as though sizing up prospects.

The police were well aware that "sightings" like this often occurred in the aftermath of serious crimes. But they couldn't afford to dismiss these reports as just the products of overheated imaginations. It was likely that the old man spotted in the neighborhood was nothing more than an innocent passerby—assuming that he existed at all. But slim as it was, there was always a chance that the women were right. If they were, the police had to assume that the Budd crime had been the work of a coolly premeditating individual—very possibly a professional kidnapper.

The possibility that the Budd girl had been the victim of a carefully planned and executed abduction was given added credibility by the testimony of several residents of her block, the last of her acquaintances to see her on the day she disappeared.

DERANGED

According to Loretta Adaboy, Jimmy Kenny, George Barrins, and Phillip Gully—the neighborhood children who had shouted taunts at Gracie when she passed them on Sunday in the company of her grizzled escort—a second man was involved in the crime.

All four of these small witnesses told police that, when the couple reached the corner, the girl had been ushered into a waiting automobile—a mud-spattered blue sedan with a yellow Pennsylvania license plate—which then sped away from the curb and down Ninth Avenue, a young straw-hatted man behind the wheel. Another eyewitness, a teenager named Margaret Day, who had been working at a candy store on the corner of Ninth Avenue at the time Gracie left home, corroborated the children's account.

By the morning of Wednesday, June 6, investigators had learned of the existence of a second purported accomplice, this one a woman.

A Brooklyn mother, Mrs. Harold DeMille of 981 East Fifteenth Street, told police that at around 6:30 Sunday evening she had gone inside her house to fix supper, leaving her four-year-old son, Desmond, to pedal his tricycle up and down the block. No sooner had she left than a mysterious couple—an elderly fellow in a dark business suit and a handsomely dressed woman—strolled up to little Desmond and, after speaking to him briefly, helped him off his tricycle and led him up the street. A second man, much younger than the first, followed close behind, the tricycle in tow.

Mrs. DeMille had just begun her dinner preparations when a neighbor—a woman who lived across the street and had been relaxing on her front stoop when the boy was taken away—rushed into the kitchen with the news. Dashing onto the street, Mrs. DeMille ran up the block in the direction indicated by her neighbor, finally catching up with the foursome on 13th Street and Avenue U. Snatching little Desmond up into her arms, she began screaming at the old man—the obvious leader of the band—who calmly protested that he and his friends had only meant to buy the child a new bell for his tricycle.

Where, shouted the agitated mother, did they expect to

find an open store on Sunday evening? The old man and his companions exchanged an anxious look; then, without another word, they hurried away. Mrs. DeMille, winded and shaken, conducted Desmond back home, scolding him for having given her such a scare and admonishing him to be more careful of strangers.

It wasn't until Tuesday, when the story of the Budd girl's disappearance hit the newsstands, that Mrs. DeMille suspected she had rescued her son from the clutches of the very criminal who had snatched little Grace. Contacting the police at once, she provided them with a description of the old man that, as the *Daily News* put it, "tallied exactly" with that of Frank Howard.

The police, who had been operating under the assumption that they were hunting for a single kidnapper, a "lone hand" in Detective Dribben's words, were suddenly faced with a new and even more unsettling possibility —that somewhere, loose in the city, was a ruthless band of professional child-snatchers, consisting of at least three individuals and headed by a cunning old man, who had masterminded and carried out the abduction of little Grace Budd.

The Budd kidnapping was big news and, predictably, the plight of the family drew the poisonous attention of the usual collection of cranks. Crude handwritten messages—ranging from lunatic ramblings to the cruelest of taunts—came pouring in through the mail. Typical of this warped correspondence was a postcard that arrived at the Budds' apartment on Wednesday morning, less than twenty-four hours after the story broke, and that seemed almost identical to one of the many crazed communications that had been sent, a year earlier, to the grief-racked parents of Billy Gaffney: "My dear friends. All little girl is to cellar and into water."

Before long, the Budds were receiving dozens of crank notes a day, though few of them were more vicious than the one that read, "My Dear Mr. and Mrs. Budd. Your child is going to a funeral. I still got her. HOWARD"

Of all the letters mailed to the Budds, one, at least, had been written out of genuinely charitable impulses. Sent by a woman named Martha Taggart, who had been appalled to read of the horror that had descended on the Budd family as a result of Edward Jr.'s innocent classified ad, the note contained a small but concrete form of consolation—an offer of a summer job for young Edward on her husband's farm in the Bronx. But Edward's summer, like that of his family and a sizable contingent of New York City police detectives, would be occupied with another, far more urgent matter—the search for his missing sister.

On Thursday morning, June 7, one thousand circulars —containing detailed descriptions of Grace Budd and Frank Howard, along with a black-and-white photo of the missing girl in a plaid dress, puffy bonnet, and gray cloth coat—were mailed to police departments throughout the United States and Canada. By the middle of the following week, several thousand more had been printed up and posted around New York City—in subway stations and ferry terminals, bank lobbies and barber shops, post offices, grocery windows, and corner luncheonettes.

The immediate result of this massive publicity effort was a rash of false sightings. Dribben's office was flooded with reports—that Howard and his captive had been spotted in Stroudsburg, Pennsylvania, Monmouth, New Jersey, Mineola, Long Island, Niagara Falls, New York, and dozens of other locales. In the weeks following the Grace Budd kidnapping, any gray-haired old man out for a stroll with his granddaughter was in danger of being identified as a child-snatcher. Each of these stories was scrupulously checked out by one of the two dozen detectives that, by this point, had been assigned to the case (some from the West 20th Street Precinct, others from the Bureau of Missing Persons). Ultimately, each story turned out to be completely worthless.

There was, however, one solid lead which the police had received even before their search had entered its second week. Thanks in part to a public "Notice to Telegraphers"—a printed plea for information run by the editors of the New York *Daily News* in the June 6th edition of the paper—investigators had been able to trace the source of Howard's telegram to the Western Union office at Third Avenue and 103rd Street in Manhattan.

An intensive search of the surrounding neighborhood quickly turned up a second important clue. Armed with the small enamel pail that had held the pound of pot cheese Howard had brought to the Budds, supposedly from his farm, Detectives Jerry Maher, Charles Reilly, and John McGee managed to locate the man who had sold it to Howard—the pushcart peddler Reuben Rosoff, who identified the handwritten price inscribed on its underside *("40¢")* as his own printing.

The address of the telegraph office along with the location of Rosoff's pushcart—100th Street and Second Avenue—strongly suggested that the elusive Frank Howard was, if not a resident, certainly a habitué of East Harlem. Detectives and patrolmen of the East 104th Street Station were put on alert and, along with Dribben's men, they organized a dragnet of the area, checking rooming houses, restaurants, barber shops, newsstands, and any other place that Howard might be known.

In the meantime, Captain John Ayres of the Missing Persons Bureau had obtained a copy of the Western Union blank on which Howard had written out his telegram. After studying it closely, Ayres met with reporters to describe its content and style. According to the captain, Howard "wrote a good, quick, clear hand and wasted no words in sending his message." He seemed to be a man of some sophistication and schooling. For this and other reasons, investigators had concluded that, in Captain Ayres' words, "Howard's occupation was not that of a farmer."

The captain's announcement was certainly newsworthy, though not exactly startling. By this time, it could have come as no surprise to anyone following the case that, like everything else about Grace Budd's shadowy abductor, his story of owning a lush twenty-acre farm on Long Island was nothing more than an elaborate—and diabolical—lie.

* * *

In an effort to locate the blue sedan with yellow plates that had—according to the eyewitness testimony of Gracie's playmates—whisked the girl away on the day of her abduction, Dribben had contacted his counterparts in Pennsylvania. But investigators in that state were no more successful in tracking down the alleged getaway car than the New York City police.

A week after the abduction, however—on the morning of Monday, June 11—several of the Budds' neighbors contacted Dribben and informed him that on the previous evening they had spotted a mud-spattered blue sedan cruising up and down their block. Its driver, they reported, was a young man dressed in a brown suit.

Dribben didn't know what to make of this story. Like the site of other highly publicized crimes, the Budd home had drawn its share of curiosity seekers, and the driver of the blue sedan might simply have been another of that morbid breed. On the other hand, it was also conceivable that the young man was a conscience-stricken member of Howard's kidnapping ring, impelled by guilt to revisit the crime scene but afraid to surrender.

Whatever the case, Dribben did not intend to take any chances. A guard was posted in front of the Budds' apartment building to keep watch on the street. But this measure, too, proved fruitless. The young driver in the suspicious blue sedan never returned—assuming he had ever been there at all.

Wildly conflicting rumors and reports continued to pour in. On Thursday, June 14, for example, the Budds received a letter which boosted their spirits, filling them with the hope that Grace was being well cared for. "Dear Mrs. Budd," the letter began:

I have Grace. She is safe and sound. She is happy in her new home and not at all homesick.

I will see to it that Grace has proper schooling. She has been given an Angora cat and a pet canary. She calls the canary Bill.

I am a keen student of human nature. That was

why I was attracted to Grace. She seemed like a girl who would appreciate nice surroundings and a real nice home.

I drove with Grace past your house in an automobile several days ago. I saw several persons standing in front of the house and did not stop, as it looked as though they were waiting for me. I will see to it in the near future that some arrangements are made so Grace will be able to visit you for a short time.

The letter, which struck some of the detectives as authentic, was signed "J.F.H."

Later that day, however, the police received a far different, though equally compelling report, this one from a Brooklyn man named Nicholas Grimaldi, an employee of the New York City sanitation department. According to Grimaldi, he had gone down into the cellar of his building at 5:30 A.M. the preceding Monday and had been startled to find a young girl asleep on a burlap-covered board supported by two ash cans.

"What are you doing here?" Grimaldi demanded, nudging the girl awake.

Leaping from her crude, makeshift bed, the girl—whose age, Grimaldi judged, was somewhere between ten and twelve—shook her head and answered, "Nothing."

Grimaldi ordered the child to wait for him while he fetched his wife, but the girl—crying "Don't tell my brother!"—dashed up the cellar steps and vanished down the street, just as Mrs. Grimaldi appeared at the doorway. Though Mrs. Grimaldi got only a fleeting glimpse of the skinny, pale-faced waif, she was convinced that the frightened child was none other than Grace Budd, whose description she had read in one of the city's Italian newspapers.

These reports left the police more confused than ever. If the letter from the mysterious "J.F.H." was to be believed, Grace Budd was living in luxury. On the other hand, if Mrs. Grimaldi was right, Gracie had become a street urchin, living among ash cans in tenement cellars.

As the police were painfully aware, however, there was another, far more terrible possibility: that Grace Budd was no longer living at all.

Mrs. Budd's nightmare was a tabloid editor's dream, since few things sold more papers than the heartrending spectacle of a sorrowing mother praying for the safe return of her kidnapped daughter. A simple, uneducated woman—grateful for any publicity that might aid the police in locating her child—Mrs. Budd dutifully posed for press cameramen, dabbing tears from her eyes or staring mournfully at photographs of her lost little girl.

Her state of mind was subject to wild fluctuations. At first, though no demand for money was forthcoming, she shared Lieutenant Dribben's belief that Grace had been stolen for ransom by a kidnapping gang, who—in spite of their cunning and professionalism—had seriously miscalculated the Budds' ability to pay. Perhaps, Mrs. Budd told reporters, the kidnappers were hoping that "a newspaper or some charitably inclined person" would post a reward for Grace's return.

Before very long, Mrs. Budd's hopefulness evaporated. Unlike Elizabeth Gaffney, who never ceased to believe that she would one day be reunited with her stolen child, Mrs. Budd suddenly became certain that her daughter was dead. Lieutenant Dribben continued to express his conviction that, within a short time, Grace would be recovered, healthy and unharmed. But his faith failed to reassure the disconsolate mother.

Two weeks after Grace's disappearance, however, Delia Budd experienced an abrupt and dramatic mood swing—a powerful premonition that her daughter was, after all, safe and sound. "I seem to feel," she told reporters, "that Grace is alive. I am almost sure of it. I think that when this excitement dies down, the man who took her from here will return her to me. I don't think any harm has come to her."

Ironically, at the very moment that Mrs. Budd was inspired with renewed optimism, Lieutenant Dribben was beginning to feel the first real stirrings of doubt. The Budd kidnapping, he told reporters, was the "most baffling" case he'd ever encountered. Two weeks of the most arduous detective work had turned up nothing. Every lead had been illusory, every clue a will-o'-the-wisp. The police felt farther from a solution than they had at the start of their investigation. They were completely at a loss.

Dribben couldn't conceal his frustration. What he did conceal, particularly from Grace's mother, was his growing fear that Delia Budd's former belief—her despairing sense that her child was no longer alive—might have been correct after all.

9

~~~~~~~~~~~~~~

*"Kidnapping is the feature crime of the present
time. . . . It is one of the newest crimes. It is a
crime that men with some of the best brains in
this country have gone into, because it offers big
returns and reasonable safeguards."*

WALTER B. WEISENBERGER, President of
the St. Louis Chamber of Commerce,
in a statement to the House
Judiciary Committee, March, 1932

Throughout the summer of 1928, New Yorkers
broiled, occasionally collapsed, and, in a number of
cases, perished in the blast-furnace heat. On one day
alone—Monday, July 9—six people died and twenty-
five more suffered prostration in the airless swelter of the
city. But as the weeks wore on, the trail of Grace Budd's
elusive kidnapper only grew colder.

Even before June ended, the Budd case had largely
disappeared from the city's papers, displaced by more
thrilling, momentous or simply more novel events. Aviation was much in the news. Amelia Earhart, accompanied by two male pilots, flew a multiengine Fokker from
Boston to South Wales, thus becoming the first woman to
cross the Atlantic in an airplane. Her triumph, however,
was offset by a tragedy that occurred less than a month
later, when a monoplane piloted by Captain Emilio
Carranza was hit by a bolt of lightning during a nonstop
flight from Long Island to Mexico City and crashed in a

New Jersey woodland, killing the "ace of Mexican fliers."

Beginning in mid-June and continuing for the next several weeks, the public was riveted by the high drama taking place in the Arctic Circle, where the dirigible *Italia,* commanded by the Italian explorer and aviation pioneer Umberto Nobile, crashed on an ice pack in the frigid waters north-northeast of Spitsbergen. An international rescue effort was immediately launched, and eventually, Nobile and seven of his crew members were plucked from the ice. But before the incident was over, nineteen men had lost their lives, including famed Norwegian explorer Roald Amundsen, discoverer of the South Pole, who set off in a seaplane to hunt for the downed airship and was never seen again.

In national politics, the big event of the summer was the nomination in Houston, Texas, of New York Governor Al Smith as the Democratic party's presidential candidate. On Wednesday, June 20, just as convention delegates and party leaders were pouring into the city, a young black man named Robert Powell, who had been wounded in a shoot-out with police, was snatched from his bed in the Jefferson Davis Hospital by a band of five vigilantes, driven six miles into the countryside, and lynched under a wooden bridge.

Across the border, in Mexico City, President-elect Alvaro Obregon was assassinated during an official luncheon on the afternoon of July 18. Another political assassination—this one dating back to the sixteenth century—also made news when the members of Madrid's Academy of Spanish History announced plans to exhume the centuries-old corpse of Don Carlos, Prince of the Asturias, in order to check the truth of the controversial legend that he had been poisoned by his father, King Phillip II, in 1568. In London, Sir Arthur Conan Doyle, creator of the arch-rationalist Sherlock Holmes and (paradoxically enough) a devout believer in the occult, appeared at the trial of a London medium to testify on the legitimacy of Spiritualism. And on July 10, in New York City, the stock market suffered its worst decline since 1914—a portent of the economic catastrophe that was soon to overtake the country.

There were amazing feats and remarkable finds. A daredevil named Jean A. Lussier of Springfield, Massachusetts, became the third man to conquer "the mighty Niagara" when, on July 4, he plunged over Horseshoe Falls while strapped inside a giant rubber ball. The very next day, the world was startled by the announcement that an archaeological expedition to the Aleutians had stumbled upon the mummified remains of four Stone Age humans—three adults and an infant—perfectly preserved in the ice.

As always, sports made up a healthy chunk of the summer's news. Johnny Weissmuller, future Tarzan of the movies and head of the U.S. Olympic swim team, took the gold medal in the men's 100-meter freestyle at the VIIIth International Games in Amsterdam. At Wimbledon, Rene Lacoste defeated Henri Cochet for the men's singles championship. And Gene Tunney held onto his championship by flooring New Zealander Tom Heeney in the eleventh round of their heavyweight title bout at Yankee Stadium. Two days later, on July 29, Tunney announced that he was quitting boxing to study philosophy at the Sorbonne.

By the time July, 1928, drew to a close, the Budd story had been off the front pages for so long that the public had, by and large, put it out of mind. And so it must have come as a surprise to many New Yorkers when they opened their papers on the morning of August 2 and discovered headlines announcing that, according to police, the case of the Grace Budd kidnapping had finally been solved.

Like hundreds of other law enforcement officials and prison personnel throughout North America, J. S. Blitch, warden of a prison farm in Raiford, Florida, had received a copy of the flier describing the victim and suspect in the Budd kidnapping. Studying the circular, Blitch was struck by the similarities between Frank Howard and a man the warden knew well, a former inmate of the farm who had been released in 1926 after serving four years for embezzlement.

Albert E. Corthell was the prisoner's name, though he was also known by several aliases: Charles Parker, A. Edward Drawfell, J. W. West. A glib, gray-haired con artist, slight of build and in his early fifties, Corthell was a Midwesterner who had spent much of his adult life in and out of prisons throughout the U.S., serving time for a wide range of felonies from swindling and forgery to car theft. But there was nothing crude about Corthell. A sharp-witted smoothie with an ingratiating manner and a smattering of medical knowledge (during one of his many jail stints, he had worked as an orderly in the prison hospital), he was able to pass himself off as a Harvard-educated physician from St. Petersburg, who had practiced medicine in Manhattan from an office in the Astor Court Building. To give himself an added touch of respectability when pulling off a scam, he often hired preadolescent girls to pose as his daughters.

Certainly, Blitch thought, Corthell's practice of exploiting young girls could explain his interest in Grace Budd. And there was something else about the ex-convict which made him a plausible suspect in the Budd case. The way Blitch figured it, after having spent so much time at Raiford, Corthell would have had no trouble at all in conjuring up a very convincing picture of his mythical farm on Long Island to beguile the impressionable Budds.

The more he thought about the parallels, the more convinced Blitch became that Howard and Corthell were the same individual. Pulling out his file on Corthell, Warden Blitch forwarded it, along with the most recent mug shot of the gray-haired con man, to the New York City Police Commissioner, Joseph A. Warren.

Shortly after Corthell's photograph had been received and added to the Rogue's Gallery at police headquarters, William L. Vetter, the assistant superintendant of the Brooklyn branch of the Society for the Prevention of Cruelty to Children, contacted the police with an interesting story. According to Vetter, he had been visited just a few days before the Budd kidnapping by a slightly built, gray-haired man seeking to adopt a six-year-old girl. The fellow was well-dressed and soft-spoken, but something about his manner struck Vetter as suspicious. Vetter had spoken to him briefly and set up a date for a second, more exhaustive interview. But the gray-haired stranger had never returned.

Like most New Yorkers, Vetter had followed the Budd story with grim fascination, but only recently had it occurred to him that there might be a connection between the gray-haired man and the mysterious Frank Howard. It had taken him nearly two months to make that connection. Now he wasted no time in getting in touch with the police.

Vetter was invited to headquarters, where he was asked to go through pictures from the Rogue's Gallery. He pored over scores of photos before he came upon one that looked exactly like the face he remembered—the face of the man who had visited the S.P.C.C. at the beginning of June.

It was the face of Albert Edward Corthell.

Lieutenant Dribben had every reason to feel pleased. For the first time in weeks, his optimism—which was becoming increasingly hard to sustain—seemed justified. But before he would let himself believe that the kidnapper had finally been identified, he needed some key corroboration.

The Budd family was brought down to police headquarters and shown the photograph of Corthell. Albert Budd, half-blind and still stupefied with grief, thought the man in the picture looked like Frank Howard but couldn't say for sure. Nor could his son. But Grace's mother was adamant. The man in the photograph was Frank Howard, all right. Mrs. Budd was ready to swear to it. She'd know that monster's face anywhere.

By the beginning of August, rumors had reached the press that a big break in the Budd case was about to be announced—rumors that were confirmed on Friday,

August 3, when the grand jury returned an indictment against Albert E. Corthell and General Sessions Judge Koenig issued a bench warrant for the ex-convict's arrest.

This sudden turn of events was a boost for the Missing Persons Bureau, whose men were still smarting from their failure to solve the mystery of Billy Gaffney's disappearance. And it was enormously heartening to Mr. and Mrs. Budd, who were infused with fresh hope that their daughter would be recovered safely after all. Whatever else Corthell might be, he was no murderer. And if Warden Blitch was right about Corthell's motives for snatching the girl, then Grace was sure to be alive and even well cared for.

Finally, after two dispiriting months of dogged but fruitless detective work, everything seemed to be falling into place. The police had a positive identification, an indictment, and a warrant for the suspect's arrest. True, they didn't have the suspect himself—or his young victim—but Dribben had received reliable tips that Corthell had been spotted in Toledo, Ohio. According to Assistant District Attorney Harold W. Hastings, detectives from the Missing Persons Bureau were "hot on the trail" of the kidnapper. It was only a matter of days, Hastings assured reporters, before Corthell would be in police custody—and little Grace Budd restored, at last, to the bosom of her family.

10

~~~~~~~~~~~~~~~

A hero is a man who does what he can.

ROMAIN ROLLAND, *Jean Christophe*

Among the detectives assigned to the Budd case was a member of the Missing Persons Bureau named William F. King. A tireless and resolute lawman with gunmetal eyes and the leathery mug of a Marine drill sergeant, King conformed so closely, in both appearance and manner, to the popular image of the tough, big city "dick" that he could have been dreamed up by Dashiell Hammett. Only King was no Hollywood crimebuster, no make-believe hero with a hardboiled style and the soul of a crusader. He was the real thing.

King possessed several qualities which made him particularly well suited for his job. To begin with, he was a man of action, a former locomotive fireman who became a cop in 1907, quit a decade later to fight in the Great War, then rejoined the department in 1926 after working for a number of years in the private sector. At the time of the Budd kidnapping, he had risen to the rank of detective lieutenant in the Bureau of Missing Persons.

Besides determination and toughness, King was renowned for his tenacity. He was a man of supreme patience, dogged in his refusal to give up on a case until it was solved. This attribute would stand him in especially good stead in the case of the Budd abduction. In the late summer of 1928, King was one of several detectives dispatched to the Midwest to follow the trail of "Dr." Corthell. As it turned out, the trip would be only the first

76

leg of a journey that would eventually cover many thousands of miles and span several years. King wouldn't rest until Corthell was in custody, and, in the end, he would get his man.

But before that day arrived, the search for Grace Budd's kidnapper would take a sudden and wholly unexpected twist.

Two years had passed since Assistant D.A. Hastings had made his hopeful pronouncement that Corthell's arrest and Grace Budd's recovery were only a few days away. In spite of such official optimism—and the un-flagging efforts of Detective King and his colleagues to track down the suspect—the slippery con man re-mained at large and little Gracie's whereabouts a mys-tery.

Intermittently during those two years, the police would uncover clues that sent the hopes of the Budd family soaring. But inevitably, each of these leads would fail to pan out. In March 1930, for example, the Budds received a strange packet in the mail. By this time, the family had moved to even cheaper quarters, a base-ment apartment at 404 West 15th Street, several doors away from their former address. (The Depression was now in full swing, and though Albert Budd was better off than millions of his countrymen, having managed to hang onto his job, his salary remained pitifully small.)

Inside the packet was a copy of *The Christian Science Monitor,* dated March 21. The paper itself, mailed anonymously from Portsmouth, New Hampshire, con-tained nothing of apparent significance. But Delia Budd's attention was instantly caught by the penciled address. It was written in a hand that looked remarkably like her daughter's.

Pulling one of Grace's schoolbooks out of the bureau drawer where she had carefully stored them, Mrs. Budd compared the two samples of handwriting. To her eager eyes they looked the same. She quickly called in a few of her neighbors, who confirmed the similarity. At that point, Mrs. Budd threw on her overcoat and, packet in hand, made her way to the West Twentieth Street precinct.

The packet was turned over to Detective King, who had by this point become the primary investigator in the Budd case. Indeed, the Budd girl's kidnapping had become more than the focus of King's professional life. It had become a personal obsession.

Carefully examining the envelope and its contents, King discovered a small mailing label affixed to a corner of the newspaper. It bore the name of Herbert J. Sherry, U.S. Navy, Portsmouth. The following day, King, accompanied by Detective Jerry Maher, was on a train headed for New Hampshire.

Meanwhile, Delia Budd met with reporters to announce the good news. "I am certain that the writing is in the hand of Grace," she proclaimed, "and so are the neighbors. I am very hopeful that something may come of it. It is the first word of any kind we have had since Grace went away."

Even as she was speaking, however, King and Maher were reluctantly coming to a very different conclusion. They had already surmised that, since Sherry was in the U.S. Navy, he was undoubtedly too young to be the kidnapper himself. But perhaps he might be the mysterious accomplice who, according to various eyewitnesses, had driven the getaway car.

No sooner had they arrived in Portsmouth than the two detectives discovered that Sherry—who was doing time in the brig for desertion—couldn't possibly have been involved in the abduction. Sherry's service record showed that he had been in trouble before and that, at the time of the girl's disappearance, he had been confined to the naval prison at Parris Island, South Carolina. King and Maher remained in Portsmouth for a few days, hoping to locate the person—presumably Grace herself—who had addressed the envelope to the Budds.

As it turned out, the two men could have saved themselves the effort. Shortly after they returned empty-handed to New York, a report from a police graphologist revealed that the handwriting on the mysterious packet was not, in fact, Grace Budd's—though who the writer was, and why the newspaper had been sent to the Budd family in the first place, no one could say.

Several months after the Sherry incident, in early June, 1930, Detective King was traveling again—this time on a train headed south, in pursuit of a man who called himself Charles Howard.

A fifty-year-old Floridian, Howard had married a vacationing New York City woman in May. Immediately after the wedding, the happy couple returned to the city, where they moved into an apartment belonging to the bride's aunt at 2410 Second Avenue. Exactly eight days later, Charles Howard disappeared, absconding with $2,800 of his wife's cash, plus $1,000 more of her aunt's.

The hoodwinked bride rushed to the police and lodged a complaint against Howard. She also suggested that the two-faced reprobate might well be the other Howard the police had been searching for, the one who had kidnapped little Grace Budd.

The claim seemed plausible, assuming that Charles Howard was simply another alias of the notorious Albert Corthell. Corthell, after all, had plied his criminal trade in Florida for many years. And the deception that had been practiced on the hapless New York woman was just the sort of swindle that a con man like Corthell would be liable to pull.

This time, King seemed to get lucky. Almost immediately upon his arrival in Florida, he managed to locate his quarry. On June 10, Charles Howard was arrested in Belvedere, Florida. A slight, stooped, prematurely grizzled man, he matched the description of Grace Budd's abductor. Howard was brought back to New York City, where he was arraigned on a charge of grand larceny.

One fact immediately became evident—Charles Howard was not Albert Corthell. Indeed, Charles Howard was the man's true name, not an alias at all. Still, King clung to the hope that his prisoner might be implicated in the Budd mystery.

A lineup was arranged. Delia Budd and Willie Korman (now a young man of twenty) were brought down to police headquarters to view the suspect.

Korman couldn't identify the man with any certainty, but Delia Budd seemed to harbor few doubts. "He looks like the man," she insisted.

In the end, however, Howard was able to provide an airtight alibi. He was living in a completely different part of the country at the time of Grace's disappearance. He remained locked up on the grand larceny charge but was cleared as a suspect in the kidnapping.

As it happened, this wouldn't be the only time that Delia Budd would identify the wrong man as her daughter's abductor. (In fact, she had already pointed the finger at several other individuals, including a detective from the Missing Persons Bureau, who had been recruited to fill out a lineup on an earlier occasion.) Nor would this be the only time that an incensed wife would accuse her husband of being the man who had stolen Grace Budd. Just a few months later, the same situation would figure in the most sensational—and surprising—development in the Budd case up to that point.

That development came about as a direct result of the Charles Howard episode. A woman named Jessie Pope had been reading newspaper accounts of Howard's arrest as a suspect in the Budd case and his subsequent exoneration. The seed of an idea was planted in her mind, germinated there for several months, and finally came to fruition at the tail end of the summer.

On September 3, 1930, Mrs. Pope appeared at the West Twentieth Street station to inform the police that her estranged husband—a sixty-seven-year-old janitor named Charles Edward Pope—was the man who had snatched Grace Budd.

Mrs. Pope had an amazing story to relate. At the time of the kidnapping, she explained, she was separated from her husband and living with her sister, Mrs. Margaret McDougal, at 314 High Street in Perth Amboy, New Jersey. On June 3, 1928—the day of Grace Budd's disappearance—a Western Union boy arrived with a message from her husband, asking her to meet him at the corner of High and Smith Streets, just a few blocks away.

Mystified but intrigued by the telegram, Mrs. Pope proceeded to the spot, where she found her husband waiting. With him was a sweet-faced, brown-haired girl, dressed up in her Sunday best.

Pope asked his wife if she would mind taking care of the girl for a few days while he went off on some unspecified business. The girl, he explained, was the daughter of a friend, and it would be "a great favor" to everyone if Mrs. Pope consented to look after the child.

Mrs. Pope had no idea what sort of funny business her husband was up to, but she refused to have any part of it. "Then I'll have to take her back home with me," Pope grumbled. After a brief but bitter exchange of words, Pope stormed away, leading the little girl off in the direction of the Perth Amboy–Tottenville ferry. Before they disappeared from view, the girl turned and gave Mrs. Pope a look that "she would never forget."

Almost immediately after this strange incident, Mrs. Pope continued, she had become "seriously ill." By the time she recovered, months later, the excitement over the Budd case had died down and the memory of that day had faded from her mind. Only recently, after reading about Charles Howard in the newspapers, had it all come back to her. Throughout the summer, her suspicions had mounted, until, just the day before, she had finally taken it upon herself to visit the Budds. Delia Budd had shown her photographs of the missing ten-year-old. As soon as Mrs. Pope laid eyes on them, she recognized who her husband's mysterious, brown-haired companion had been.

The detectives were impressed by Mrs. Pope's story— so much so that on the following day, September 4, 1930, at the East 78th Street apartment he shared with his widowed sister, Charles Edward Pope was arrested for the kidnapping of Grace Budd.

Once again, Delia Budd was called down to the stationhouse to pick out the suspect from a lineup. And once again, she provided a positive identification. "That's the man who stole my Gracie," she declared, pointing directly at Pope. And there was no doubt that the old janitor—a wizen-faced codger with a bushy gray moustache and a shriveled physique—bore a vague resemblance to the man who had called himself Frank Howard.

The next morning, the tabloids trumpeted the news: "BUDD KIDNAP SUSPECT CAPTURED AFTER TWO YEARS!"

As an angry crowd—consisting mostly of neighborhood mothers and assorted friends of the Budd family—gathered outside the police station, Pope tearfully protested his innocence. He shook his head in amazement as his wife told police that Pope was "a dangerous man" who had once been confined to a mental institution in Gowanda, New York.

It was true, Pope admitted, that he had been locked up in Gowanda for a few months. But he had been sent there by his wife, who had conspired to commit him in order to get her hands on some money his father had left him. His only crime, Pope insisted, was a weakness for the game of "Klondike crap." Questioned at police headquarters by King, Maher, and a third detective, Samuel Ryan, Pope explained that he was the son of a steamboat inspector and the executor of his father's $30,000 estate, though he himself had only come in for a pittance of that inheritance. He had been trained as an engineer, but he had not practiced that profession for many years. Now, with the Depression underway, the only work he had been able to find was as the superintendant of an apartment building on Madison Avenue. He lived with his sister, an elderly spinster, and supported them both on his meager salary.

Ada Pope, the suspect's sister, confirmed every part of his account. Though her brother and his estranged wife had been married for forty-two years, their relationship had always been difficult. Indeed, over the course of those decades, they had been separated more than twenty times. Her brother, Ada Pope tearfully told the detectives, was a hard-working but soft-hearted man who had fallen victim to the malice of a spiteful woman. "I do not know why she hates Charlie and me so much. Charlie has not been able to give her much money these past few years. He does not make very much, and he is looking out for me."

Investigating Pope's story, King discovered that it checked out in every detail. The old man had no police record. And though it was true that he had been institutionalized for eight months between September 1924 and July 1925, the superintendant of the asylum, Dr. E. H. Mudge, affirmed that Pope's ailment was of "a mild nature." There was nothing violent or dangerous about the man at all.

Reluctantly, King and his colleagues were beginning to conclude that their elation over the capture of Grace Budd's kidnapper had been premature. What they had on their hands, it seemed, was not the long-sought solution to the girl's disappearance but a sordid squabble, motivated by rankling resentments over money, between a pathetic old man and a bitterly vindictive woman. It was true that Delia Budd had unhesitatingly picked Pope out of the lineup. But Mrs. Budd had already proved herself a notoriously unreliable witness.

From the moment of Pope's arrest, the city's papers, from *The New York Times* to the *Daily News,* had been running major stories about the successful climax of the two-year manhunt for the Budd kidnapper. But just two days after Pope was arraigned before Magistrate Anthony Burke—who set his bail at $25,000—reporters learned that King and his fellow investigators now had serious doubts about Pope's guilt and were on the verge of dropping all charges against him.

Before that could happen, though, events took a sudden and very dark turn for the unhappy Mr. Pope.

During his initial two-hour interrogation of the suspect, King had learned that Pope owned an old farmhouse on an acre of land in Shandaken, New York, a small town in the Catskills. A search order was put through to the State Police base at nearby Sidney, New York. Early the next morning—Sunday, September 7—a contingent of troopers, led by Lieutenant Matthew Fox, arrived at Pope's place and proceeded to ransack the two-story farmhouse from basement to attic. There was nothing even remotely suspicious inside the house. Concluding that they had been sent on a wild goose chase, Lieutenant Fox and his men made ready to leave.

Determined, however, to "leave no stone unturned" (as Fox later told reporters), they decided to take a look inside the small garage at the rear of the farmhouse.

Inside was an old Dodge touring car bearing 1929 license plates. But what caught the lieutenant's eye were three small trunks lined up against the far wall of the little building. Dragging them out into the sunlight, the troopers swung open the lids. The contents of the first two seemed innocent enough—newspaper clippings and old magazines, used clothing, and "assorted odds and ends."

The third, however, was filled with more provocative material—pictures and postcards of women and girls, many of them in alluring poses. There were also various bundles of letters. Undoing the ribbon around one of the packets, Fox scanned a few of the letters and discovered that they had all been written by women and were of a most personal nature—"mushy notes," as he described them.

Though the postcards and letters shed new light on the private life of the elderly caretaker, they weren't especially incriminating in themselves. But that couldn't be said of the other items in the trunk. Three strands of deep brown hair, tied with white ribbon, lay concealed beneath the letters. Judging by their color, length and texture, Fox concluded that the strands had been clipped from the head of a young girl.

Back in New York City, the news of the discovery hit like a bombshell. "RIBBONS, CURLS FOUND IN TRUNK IN BUDD SUSPECT'S OLD HOME," blared the headline of the next morning's *Daily News*. Suddenly, Charles Edward Pope no longer seemed like the put-upon victim of a termagant wife. A new and sinister light had been cast on the old caretaker. Perhaps he was the Budd kidnapper after all.

The discovery of the hair clippings set off an intensive search of the Shandaken property. Troopers from the Sidney base swarmed over the premises, digging up the entire yard in an effort to uncover more clues. The contents of the three trunks were carefully removed and closely analyzed. Tucked among the old clothes in one of the trunks was a box of revolver ammunition. Even more significantly, troopers found a pair of white child's stockings with darned heels—similar, according to Mrs. Budd's testimony, to the ones that her daughter had been wearing on the morning she left home forever.

By Wednesday, September 10, things were looking grim for Charles Pope. "NEW CLEWS TIGHTEN BUDD KIDNAP NET," the *Daily News* reported. According to the article, the police, in searching Pope's property, had found a file of letters covering the period from 1891 to 1929. Suspiciously, one entire year's worth of correspondence was missing. That year was 1928. Grace Budd, of course, had been abducted in June, 1928.

Investigators also learned that Grace had spent a few weeks in the vicinity of Pope's farm during the summer of 1927, when she had been sent to live with a local family under the sponsorship of the *New York Tribune's* Fresh Air Fund.

And then there was the story told by Albert H. Kilner, a Phoenicia, New York, radio mechanic. According to Kilner, he was called to the Pope farm to repair a radio in the late summer of 1928. "I happened to stop my car at some little distance from the house," Kilner told police.

I reached the front door without seeing anyone. I went around to the back and while there I heard the sound of wood splitting. I pushed the door open. Inside, to the right, I saw another closed door. I opened it. It was a bedroom. Pope was inside. I had a quick glance at what he had been doing. The floor boards were ripped up and I saw several piles of earth. Pope turned red in the face and snarled at me: "What do you mean by entering the house this way? Get out!" He forced me to leave without fixing the radio. Later I went back and did the job.

Checking Kilner's story, state troopers discovered that the ground beneath Pope's bedroom did indeed show signs of digging. They announced plans to excavate the spot to a depth of five feet in an effort to unearth more evidence—perhaps even the remains of the missing girl herself.

* * *

Though the tabloid press had been doing its best to convict Pope without a trial, the preliminary hearing held on September 11 made it clear that there were still serious reasons to question his guilt.

Jessie Pope—the suspect's main accuser—proved to be a highly dubious witness. Under cross-examination by Pope's lawyer, James A. Turley, she admitted that she had schemed to have her husband committed to an insane asylum in order to get her hands on the money willed to him by his father. And her recollection of the clothing worn by the little girl she had supposedly seen with Pope in Perth Amboy—a blue dress and a blue hat with a red band—didn't gibe at all with the description of the confirmation outfit Grace had been wearing at the time of her disappearance.

Mrs. Budd's testimony was equally suspect. She admitted that the white stockings found on Pope's farm were not, in fact, very much like her daughter's (though she stoutly maintained that another item uncovered by the police—a clasp made of imitation pearl—was identical to an ornament on Grace's handbag). And she acknowledged that, before she came down to view Pope in the lineup, his wife had already provided her with such a minutely detailed description of the old man that it would have been next to impossible *not* to recognize him.

Pope himself had perfectly reasonable explanations for the pieces of evidence that had been made to seem so incriminating by the press. The stockings and other items of children's clothing were hand-me-downs, passed along to Pope by tenants of the Madison Avenue apartment house he superintended. Pope collected them for his son, who had five young children of his own.

As for the three mysterious curls (which, as Turley pointed out, were much longer and wavier than Grace Budd's straight, bobbed hair), they were, according to Pope, family keepsakes—snipped from his son's head many years before and stored away in the trunk as mementos.

In spite of the questions that Turley had managed to

cast on Jessie Pope's motives and Delia Budd's credibility, Magistrate George De Luca felt justified in holding Pope for the grand jury. Bail was continued at $25,000. Unable to raise that sum, the old man was returned to the Tombs.

On Monday, September 15, 1930, the grand jury indicted Charles Edward Pope for the kidnapping of Grace Budd, and a trial was scheduled for December.

In its excitement over Pope's arrest, the press seemed to have forgotten all about the man who had been the primary suspect in the Budd case for two years—Albert E. Corthell. But Detective King, who was finding it increasingly difficult to believe in Pope's guilt, hadn't forgotten, and during the months that the old man languished in jail, awaiting his trial, King continued to pursue every lead.

In early December, just two weeks before the start of Pope's trial, King finally got his man. Corthell, going under the name of J. W. West, was arrested in St. Louis, Missouri, where he was trying to cash a certified check in the amount of $15,000 made out to the treasurer of the Park Board of Joliet, Illinois. Under questioning by police, he finally admitted his true identity.

Extradition papers were quickly prepared, and on Wednesday, December 3, Detectives King and Maher set off for St. Louis. Four days later, on Sunday, December 7, they were back in New York City with Corthell in custody at last. The prisoner was booked at the East 51st Street station, then removed to Police Headquarters, where, early Monday morning, both Delia Budd and her husband picked him out of a lineup, acknowledging that Corthell "might be" the man who had stolen their daughter.

Suddenly, after two fruitless years of searching for the Budd kidnapper, the New York City police found themselves with two suspects on their hands.

But not for long.

The trial of Charles Edward Pope, began on Monday, December 22, 1930, and lasted only long enough to qualify as farce. Delia Budd, the first witness called to the stand, retracted her identification of Pope, admitting that she had "made a mistake in saying he was the man." She had only accused him, she confessed, because Pope's wife had persuaded her of his guilt. Both her husband and Willie Korman were even more emphatic in denying that Pope was Frank Howard.

Only Jessie Pope persisted in her denunciation, but Attorney Turley quickly undermined her testimony by establishing that she had been hounding her estranged husband for years. Judge William Allen put a few sharply worded questions to Mrs. Pope, then directed the jury to return a "not guilty" verdict.

After three-and-a-half months of imprisonment, Charles Edward Pope was a free man.

With Pope's acquittal, Corthell resumed his status as the primary suspect in the Budd case. But—though he admitted to having spent some time in New York City during the summer of 1928—he fiercely maintained that he knew nothing at all about the kidnapping. And while Corthell was a thoroughgoing fraud and professional liar, it seemed as if he might actually be telling the truth.

Over the course of the next few months, the police made every effort to connect Corthell to the Budd crime. But they couldn't come up with a single shred of evidence. And after her humbling experience with the Pope episode, even Delia Budd was unprepared to make a positive identification.

On Friday, February 6, 1931, following the recommendation of Assistant District Attorney John MacDonnell, Judge William Allen discharged Albert E. Corthell without a trial.

Corthell's release was a devastating setback for the detectives involved in the Budd case. Not only had they wasted two years searching for the wrong man, but they were now left with no leads at all—not a single clue to the fate of little Grace Budd or to the identity of her kidnapper. Detective King, who had devoted the most time and energy to the hunt for Corthell, felt especially embitterred by the outcome of the affair. But for all his frustration, he remained undeterred. Holed up somewhere in the world was the cunning old fox who had made off with Grace Budd. And King was determined to sniff him out, no matter how long it took.

11

~~~~~~~~~~

Q. Do you call a man who drinks urine and eats human excretions sane or insane?
A. Well, we don't call them mentally sick.
Q. That man is perfectly all right?
A. Not perfectly all right. But he is socially perfectly all right.

> from the testimony of Dr. Menas S. Gregory,
> Head of the Psychiatric Department,
> Bellevue Hospital

On December 15, 1930, exactly one week before the Pope travesty finally fizzled to an end in court, another elderly man—who bore such a strong resemblance to the forlorn janitor that they could have been fraternal twins —was committed to the psychiatric ward at Bellevue Hospital for a ten-day observation period. Withered and frail-looking, with watery eyes and a drooping gray moustache, the old man had been arrested earlier that fall for sending "non-mailable matter" through the U.S. Post Office—specifically (in the words of his indictment) a "letter of such a vile, obscene, and filthy nature that to set forth the contents thereof would defile the records of the court."

This was not the first time that the old man had gotten into trouble for sending obscene material through the mails. Nor would it be the last.

His name, though he conducted his rank correspondence under many different aliases, was Albert Fish.

He was a member—or so he believed—of one of

America's most eminent families. Indeed, "Albert" itself was an assumed name, adopted many years before, during his adolescence. His parents had christened him "Hamilton," in honor of his putative ancestor, who had been the Governor of New York in the early 1850s, and later, during the eight years of the Grant Administration, the U.S. Secretary of State. At the time of the old man's commitment in late 1930, another Hamilton Fish—the grandson of the illustrious statesman—was serving in the U.S. House of Representatives, utterly unaware of the gray-headed reprobate in Bellevue who shared his name and claimed a distant kinship.

There is reason to doubt the validity of that claim. But, if true, it can confidently be stated that, of all the black sheep ever to tarnish the names of old and distinguished American families, the blackest of all was Albert Fish.

Fish had been arrested before. His criminal record dated back to 1903. And during a brief, frenzied period in the summer of 1928, he had been arrested three times for larceny in a span of six weeks. Since that time, he had been making an effort to steer clear of the police. He had compelling reasons to avoid them, besides his growing arrest record. But he was subject to demons beyond his control, and among his many aberrations, he was a habitual—indeed, compulsive—writer of obscene letters.

Beginning in the spring of 1929, Fish mailed a series of such letters to women whose names he had gotten from various sources. Some names were secured from matrimonial agencies. Others came from newspaper classifieds, which Fish studied raptly in his constant search for innocent prey.

Indeed, it was a classified ad that had led the old man to one of his most memorable experiences. But that had been several years before.

In his letters, Fish often presented himself as a successful Hollywood producer, ready to offer large sums of money (as well as his undying affection) to women willing to perform certain services either for himself or, at times, for a fictitious teenage son, generally identified as "Bobby." The letters were a delirium of violent, sadomasochistic fantasies, involving some (but by no means all) of Fish's favorite activities—bondage, flagellation, and coprophagy.

"I wish you could see me now," Fish wrote in a typical passage. "I am sitting in a chair naked. The pain is across my back, just over my behind. When you strip me naked, you will see a most perfect form. Yours, yours, sweet honey of my heart. I can taste your *sweet piss,* your *sweet shit.* You must *pee-pee* in a glass and I shall drink every drop of it as you watch me. Tell me when you want to do #2. I will take you over my knees, pull up your clothes, take down your drawers and hold my mouth to your *sweet honey fat ass* and eat your sweet *peanut butter* as it comes out *fresh* and *hot.* That is how they do it in Hollywood."

To another woman, he explained that his "only son" Bobby—who had been crippled at nine by "an attack of infantile paralysis"—required frequent spankings with a cat-o'-nine tails "for his own good." Bobby, Fish assured his correspondent, "does not wet or muss his clothes or the bed. He will tell you when he has to use the toilet, #1 or #2. For #1 his pants must be unbuttoned at the crotch and *his monkey* taken out. His pants and drawers are all made with a drop seat. All you have to do is loose three buttons in the back and down they come. Saves a lot of undressing. Handy when you want to spank him, just drop the seat of his pants and drawers. You don't have to strip him except at night for bed, or to give him a bath (or a switching). The Doctor says three or four good spankings a day on *his bare behind* will do him good as he is nice and fat *in that spot.* It will be an aid to him. When he don't mind you, then you must strip him and use the Cat-o-nine tails. Say *you won't hesitate* to use the Paddle or Cat-o-nine tails on him when he needs it."

In September, 1930, Fish mailed one of these scatological ravings to a professional housekeeper, whose name he had found in the "Situations Wanted" section of the *New York World.* The woman—a Mrs. E. Solarid of 245 East 40th Street—promptly turned the letter over to the police. Though Fish had signed it with a pseudonym— "Robert Fiske"—he had included a return address in the hope that the recipient would warm to his advances and respond in kind. It was a routine matter, therefore, for the police to locate and arrest him. He was picked up shortly before Thanksgiving, and—after an examination by a court social worker, who diagnosed the old man's mental condition as "questionable"—Fish was delivered to Bellevue for psychiatric observation.

Fish had been on the ward for just over a week when he was interviewed by Dr. Attilio La Guardia, a young physician on Bellevue's psychiatric staff. La Guardia began by asking the wizened old man when he had first started writing obscene letters.

"Last year, about June," Fish replied, keeping his eyes averted and picking at a sore spot on his scalp, just above the hairline.

"How did you come to write these letters?"

Fish explained that, during the summer of 1929, he had been working as a handyman and painter at a Harlem sanitarium run by one Dr. Robert B. Lamb. One day, according to Fish, Dr. Lamb's chauffeur discovered a cache of dirty letters in the sanitarium garage and, that night, read them aloud to a group of men—Fish among them—who had gathered for their evening card game in the chauffeur's room. Hearing them had put the idea into Fish's head.

"Before that," asked Dr. La Guardia "you never had any desire for anything of this sort?"

Fish shook his head emphatically. "No, sir, not at all."

La Guardia jotted down something on his notepad. "When you wrote these obscene letters," he asked, "how did you feel?"

"I had no particular feeling," Fish replied in his whispery voice.

"Did you feel that you *had* to write these letters?"

The old man shrugged and said, "It was just sort of a habit."

La Guardia went on to question Fish about his marital status, his previous troubles with the law, and his memory, asking him at one point to count backwards from one hundred by deducting seven each time. Fish rattled off the sequence without a mistake.

La Guardia made more notes. There were just a few more questions he wanted to ask. "When was the last time you had intercourse?"

Fish seemed to ponder for a moment before responding. "Two years ago," he said.

"Have you had any desire since that time?"

"No," said Fish, his eyes still downcast.

"Have you been a steady churchgoer?" La Guardia asked.

Fish smiled, his front teeth protruding slightly through his tightly drawn lips. For the first time during the interview he looked directly at his questioner. "Yes, sir," he said proudly. "Episcopal church."

"How can you reconcile the things you do with the church?"

Fish's smile evaporated and was replaced by a solemn frown. "There is no comparison," he said.

The examination was over. Dr. La Guardia shook the old man's hand and left.

Later, after senior members of the staff had met to evaluate Fish's case, La Guardia's handwritten notes were assembled into a formal report by Dr. Menas S. Gregory, head of the hospital's psychiatric department. The report was forwarded to Judge Frank J. Coleman of the U.S. District Court, Southern District of New York.

During Fish's observation period in Bellevue, Gregory noted, the inmate had been "quiet and cooperative" and had "conducted himself in an orderly and normal manner." There had been "no evidence of delusional notions or hallucinatory experiences. It is true that he shows some evidence of early senile changes; this condition, however, is quite slight at the present time and has not impaired his mentality. His memory, particularly for a man of his years, is excellent."

The old man was certainly suffering from some sort of "sexual psychopathy." The contents of the letters Fish had mailed to Mrs. Solarid and others offered sufficient proof of that. "Such conduct," Gregory explained, "frequently is the result of Senile Dementia and is observed in men of advanced years, but in this particular case we believe it has not the same significance, for the reason that this man, according to the history as well as our examination, has manifested sex perversion from early life."

In short, Dr. Gregory wrote, though Fish might be a sexual pervert, he showed no signs of "mental deterioration or dementia."

"As a result of our psychiatric examination," he concluded, "we are of the opinion that this man at the present time is not insane."

Though Gregory's report would come back to haunt him, he wasn't the first—and wouldn't be the last—to misjudge the depths of Fish's derangement. For one thing, Fish looked so harmless—a shriveled and decrepit old-timer, as menacing as Whistler's mother—that it was hard for anyone, even experienced mental health specialists, to conceive of him as dangerously insane. And in spite of his tenuous hold on reality, he retained enough cunning to conceal his true nature.

At the time of his arrest he had recently turned sixty (though he looked so infirm that Gregory had taken him for a much older man). For close to fifty years, he had engaged in the most appalling deeds, committed crimes of such an atrocious nature that they were nearly impossible to credit, even after Fish made a full confession and provided incontrovertible proof.

But those disclosures were still several years away.

In the end, Fish remained in Bellevue for close to thirty days. To the nurses who observed him on the ward, he seemed polite and cooperative—though as the weeks wore on, Fish felt increasingly desperate for freedom. On January 5, he mailed a letter to his eldest daughter, Mrs. Anna Collins of Astoria, Queens. "Why do none of you write to me," the letter began in the whiny, self-pitying tone he often took with his children.

I am the only one here who does not receive a letter or a visitor. I have written to you, to Gertrude, Gene, Henry—none of you answer. I am three weeks here today. Now Annie, do this for your poor old father. Write a letter to Dr. Gregory, Bellevue Hospital, as soon as you get this. Ask him in God's Name to send me back to court. You know the sooner I get my sentence, the sooner I am back home . . . . Don't fail me now. Love to you all from Papa.

Shortly afterward, the old man got his wish. On January 16, Fish was discharged from Bellevue. Several days later, Judge Coleman put the aged defendant on probation and released him into the custody of his daughter Anna.

Once again, Albert Fish was on the loose.

12

You all know his father, he flew across the sea.
You all know his mother, she's famous as can be.
They all lived together in a big white house,
But now the baby's gone.
Oh sorrow! sorrow!

ANONYMOUS, "Ballad of the Lindbergh Baby"

During the early years of the Depression, kidnapping became such a common criminal enterprise that, in July, 1933, *The New York Times* began running a regular front-page feature covering the latest developments in what had come to be known as the "snatch racket." The column, called "The Kidnapping Situation," provided readers with periodic updates on recent abductions—identities of victims, ransom demands, and so on—as well as on the progress of the government's all-out war against kidnappers, which President Roosevelt had declared earlier that month.

The appearance of this column—which resembled nothing so much as the capsule summary of weekend sports results that appeared on page one every Sunday—was a striking sign of the sudden, shocking prevalence of the crime. By the summer of 1933, kidnappings were occurring so frequently that news readers required a scorecard to keep track of them.

In July alone, *The New York Times* reported on over a dozen cases, including the actual or attempted abductions of John J. O'Connell, Jr., scion of one of New York State's most powerful political families; August Luer, a seventy-eight-year-old banker from Alton, Illinois; John "Jake the Barber" Factor, a Chicago "stock promoter" wanted in England on swindling charges; Dr. Walter Hedberg, a prominent Minnesota chiropractor; two well-to-do Brooklyn residents, Dr. Jacob Wachsman and bakery owner Harry Pechter; Charles F. Urschel, millionaire oil man from Oklahama City; William Hamm, Jr., St. Paul brewer; Miss Edia Neumoegen of Mahopac, New York; Miss Mary McElroy, daughter of City Manager H. F. McElroy of Kansas City, Missouri; two infant grandchildren of Park Avenue attorney Henry W. Taft; and an unnamed motion picture actress targeted for abduction by the Oklahoma gangster, Charles "Pretty Boy" Floyd.

Though all of these were highly publicized cases, the attention they received was negligible compared to the notoriety of a 1932 crime that had first brought the "kidnapping situation" to the forefront of the national news. This was, of course, the abduction and murder of twenty-month-old Charles Lindbergh, Jr. Though public concern with kidnapping had been growing since the late 1920s, it was the tragedy which had befallen America's golden couple—"Lucky Lindy" and his lovely young wife, Anne—that transformed concern into national obsession.

On the evening of March 1, 1932, Colonel Lindbergh was chatting with his wife in the living room of their sprawling new house near Hopewell, New Jersey, when he heard a sudden crack, like the snapping of a tree branch, outside the window. His wife had heard nothing except the ordinary noises of a gusty night. They listened a moment longer, then returned to their conversation.

Sometime later, at around ten o'clock, Betty Gow, the nursemaid, entered the baby's second-story bedroom to take him on his nightly trip to the toilet. Bending over the crib, she discovered that he was missing. The blankets, affixed to the mattress by a pair of large safety pins, were undisturbed, as if the child had been carefully extracted from his bedding.

The Lindberghs and their help made a frantic search of the premises. On the radiator grill in the nursery, beneath the corner window, lay a white envelope. Lindbergh ordered the servants not to touch it.

The Hopewell police were notified and arrived minutes later. Outside the house, directly beneath the nursery window, Police Chief Harry Wolfe discovered two holes in the dirt, evidently formed by a ladder. About sixty feet away, he came upon the ladder itself, a crude homemade affair with a single splintered rung—the source of the snapping sound Lindbergh had heard several hours earlier.

The white envelope was opened. Inside was a ransom note, badly misspelled and ungrammatical, as if its author had only a rudimentary command of English. The note demanded $50,000 in cash for the safe return of the baby.

The weeks that followed were a nightmare of false leads, dashed hopes, wild rumors, and cruel hoaxes. In the course of that time, the distraught parents received over one hundred thousand letters offering comfort, advice, and a staggering quantity of well-intentioned but thoroughly useless information.

President Hoover issued a statement deploring the crime. Will Rogers wrote columns conveying the shock of the nation. William Green, president of the American Federation of Labor, called on his entire membership to help track down the perpetrator. From a holding cell in the Cook County jail, where he was awaiting transfer to the Atlanta penitentiary to begin an eleven-year sentence for income-tax evasion, Al Capone offered a reward of $10,000 for the return of the child. "It's the most outrageous thing I ever heard of," Capone declared. "I know how Mrs. Capone and I would feel if our son were kidnapped, and I sympathize with the Lindberghs. If I were out of jail, I could be of real assistance. I have friends all over the country who could help in running this thing down."

While Mrs. Lindbergh issued heartbreaking bulletins to the kidnappers, detailing the baby's dietary needs, her husband broadcast a fervent appeal over the radio, offering not only the ransom money but full immunity from prosecution in exchange for his unharmed child. In desperation, he enlisted two notorious bootleggers to serve as go-betweens with the underworld.

Finally, through another intermediary, a retired Bronx schoolteacher named John Condon who had managed to make contact with the abductor, the ransom was paid in $50,000 worth of marked bills. But the kidnapper's claim that the child would be found safe onboard a sailing boat lying off Martha's Vineyard proved to be a vicious hoax. Five weeks after the snatching, the whereabouts of the Lindbergh baby remained an agonizing mystery.

Its terrible resolution, a month later, sent the country into a paroxysm of outrage and grief. On the afternoon of May 12, a gray, drizzly Thursday, a forty-six-year-old laborer named William Allen was driving down a deserted stretch of road a mile from the village of Hopewell. Pulling his truck off to one side, he slid out of the cab and entered the woods to empty his bladder. Fifty feet from the roadside, in a thicket of maple and locust, he suddenly came upon the half-buried remains of what he took, at first, to be an animal. Peering closer, he saw a tiny human foot protruding from the shallow grave.

The drama of the hunt for the missing Lindbergh baby, which had kept the American public spellbound for seventy-two days, had come to a devastating climax in a dreary clump of woods less than five miles away from the slain child's home.

The snatching and murder of the Lindbergh baby (for which a German-born carpenter named Bruno Richard Hauptmann would eventually be arrested, convicted, and electrocuted) made the magnitude of America's kidnapping crisis stunningly clear. Kidnapping—once a crime so uncommon that the legal codes of many states (including New Jersey) did not define it as a felony—had spread through the land like a plague, a full-blown epidemic from which no one, no matter how revered or lucky, was immune.

As a reporter for *The New York Times* named R. L. Duffus put it, "No conceivable event, unless it were an invasion of the White House itself, could have so dramatized the crime of kidnapping as did the carrying off of the infant son of Colonel Charles A. Lindbergh." Appearing just a few days after the abduction, Duffus's article, "Kidnapping: A Rising Menace to the Nation," traced the recent evolution of the crime from a practice largely confined to members of the underworld—gangsters snatching other gangsters for extortion or revenge—to a highly professional operation "organized on an unprecedented scale and with unheard-of extremes of cruelty and audacity."

True, abductors had been plying their trade since the days of Joseph and his brethren. And famous kidnappings had occurred throughout American history. But in terms of cunning and sophistication, Duffus wrote, present-day kidnappers were as far removed from their predecessors as "the airplane from the one-horse shay."

Because of legal loopholes (soon to be sewn up in the wake of the Lindbergh outrage), it was virtually impossible to prosecute a criminal who transported a kidnap victim across state lines. As an activity involving minimal risks and potentially great rewards, kidnapping had become the crime of choice for the "best brains" in the business. In 1932 alone, there were 282 reported kidnappings in twenty-eight states. And all but sixty-five of the perpetrators had gotten away scot-free with their crimes.

Duffus's article was illustrated with photographic portraits of four well-known kidnap victims, all of them children. There was Jackie Thomas of Detroit, looking glum in his little boy's sailor suit. There was Edward Cudahy of Omaha, posing stiffly in a starched, high-collar shirt. There was Marion Clarke of Manhattan, a curly-haired two-year-old sporting a big floppy bow.

But the most arresting image of all was the first in the series. It was a picture of Grace Budd, smiling winsomely at the camera, her big dark eyes alight with intelligence and pleasure.

The four innocent faces made a poignant group. But though Duffus didn't stress it, there were significant differences between Grace Budd and the rest. In contrast to the other cases, no ransom demand had ever been made in the Budd kidnapping. Moreover, whereas

Clarke, Cudahy, and Thomas had all been restored to their parents in fairly short order, no trace of Grace Budd had so far been found.

And on the day Duffus's article was published, March 6, 1932, Grace Budd had been missing for close to four years.

13

"I am not insane. I am just queer."

ALBERT FISH

Late one muggy afternoon in midsummer 1934, Albert Fish, Jr., then thirty-five years old, returned unexpectedly to the four-room apartment he shared with his father. The two men were living together at 1883 Amsterdam Avenue on Manhattan's Upper West Side, one of three buildings on the block that they had been hired to superintend.

Because of his age and infirmity, the elder Fish—a prematurely decrepit sixty-four-year-old at the time—took responsibility for the lighter chores, such as sweeping the rear alley and keeping the vermin in check, while his son handled the more strenuous ones like painting, plumbing repairs and carpentry work.

On this particular afternoon, sometime around four, the younger man was painting the lobby of 1887 Amsterdam when a tenant in one of the top-floor apartments ran downstairs to tell him that a pipe in the bathroom sink had burst and the room was flooding with water. Albert dropped what he was doing and hurried to his apartment to fetch his tools.

His father was often home during the day, so Albert wasn't surprised to hear noises from inside the apartment as he opened the front door. What did surprise him was the source of the sounds. They were coming, not from his father's bedroom, but from his own. And the sounds themselves were very strange—thuds, slaps, and muffled cries.

He walked quietly down the corridor and peered inside his room.

The window shades had been drawn, but enough light filtered through the fabric for Albert Jr. to see clearly. The old man was standing in the center of the room, completely nude, stroking his swollen member with one hand while, with the other, he reached behind and smacked himself with a nail-studded wooden paddle. Wild-eyed and panting, he jumped and cried out with every blow. His skin was soaked with sweat, and his face looked almost as red as his raw and bloody buttocks.

Lost in some unimaginable ecstasy of voluptuousness and pain, the old man continued his self-flagellation, completely oblivious to his son's presence. For a few moments, Albert simply stood there and stared, too paralyzed by embarrassment and dismay to say or do anything. Then, shaken and confused, he backed away from the doorway, retrieved his toolbox from the hallway closet, and crept out of the apartment.

As disconcerting as this episode was to Albert Fish, Jr., it was not the first time that he had come upon evidence of his father's weird proclivities. For as long as he could remember, his father had displayed certain extreme peculiarities of behavior.

He clearly recalled the time back in 1922, for instance, when he and his brothers, Henry and Gene, had been kicking around a football outside the old cottage they used to rent up in Worthington. Albert had just bent down to catch a low kick, and as he straightened up to boot the ball back to Henry, he caught sight of his father standing in the apple orchard on the little hill behind the bungalow. The old man had his right hand raised high in the air and was shouting something over and over. Albert had strained to listen. The old man was shouting, "I am Christ."

And as for this paddle business, Albert had known about it for at least five years—since an evening in 1929, when he was living with his father in a little flat on 74th

Street. The old man had gone off for the day, leaving his son with a few dollars to buy food. Albert—who was unemployed at the time—had spent most of the afternoon at the movies, returning home around six to prepare supper.

He was standing at the kitchen sink when his foot struck something concealed in the shadowy corner behind the pipes, something that made an odd-sounding clatter. Albert crouched to take a closer look.

There, leaning against the wall, were a pair of crude, homemade paddles, each about two feet in length and bristling with finishing nails, which protruded about one and a half inches from the wood. The nails seemed stained with dark paint. Reaching under the sink, Albert removed one of these strange instruments and looked at it closely in the light. He was taken aback to see that the nails were covered, not with paint, but with blood.

A short time later, at around six thirty, the old man returned to the flat. No sooner had he walked through the door than his son confronted him with the paddles. What was the idea of these damned things? he demanded.

At first the old man was flustered and refused to speak, but when Albert persisted, his father—eyes flicking nervously from side to side—finally responded. Albert would never forget the old man's words. "I use them on myself," he had said in his soft, raspy voice. "I get these feelings that come over me, and every time they do, I have to torture myself with those paddles."

That was the last word the two ever exchanged on the subject. Albert Jr. couldn't think of a single thing to say, and he was too ashamed to confide in anyone else, even his brothers and sisters. Throughout his life, he had seen his father do many strange things. And he had learned long ago that it was best just to shut up about them.

Given the old man's increasingly strange behavior, it had embarrassed but not surprised Albert when his father had ended up in Bellevue the following year. Even the old man's subsequent run-in with the law hadn't come as much of a shock.

That one had happened in the summer of 1931, just six months after his father had been discharged from Bellevue. Fish, who was working at the time as a dishwasher and handyman at the Steeplechase Hotel in Rockaway Beach, Queens, had been picked up by the police for sending obscene mail to the proprietor of a local boarding school.

Searching the old man's room, the officers had discovered additional letters stuck under his mattress. They also found a homemade cat-o'-nine-tails and, tucked inside a dresser drawer, a frankfurter and a carrot, both fetid with decay—and with something worse.

One of the arresting officers, John P. Smith, picked up the little wood-handled whip and asked Fish what he used it for. The old man shrugged. He liked to whip himself with it, he replied, though he didn't suppose that was anybody's goddamned business but his own.

Using his thumb and his forefinger as a pincers, Smith gingerly lifted the frankfurter by one end and held it at arm's length. And what the hell did the old man use the carrot and this damned thing for? he demanded—though the feculence of the two objects made the answer revoltingly clear.

The old man's sneering reply confirmed what Smith already knew. "I stick 'em up my ass," said Albert Fish.

Fish was arrested and shipped off to King's County Hospital, where he underwent another period of observation. This time, he was held for just ten days. He was interviewed only once by a staff psychiatrist, who never bothered to ask him about the whip, carrot, or frankfurter and who concluded his written report by describing the patient as "quiet, cooperative, and oriented." On the fifth of September, 1931, Fish was set free.

Since then, he had stayed out of trouble with the law. For a long time—at least as far as Albert Jr. could see—the old man had acted almost normal. Maybe those ten days in the mental ward had done him some good after all. Or maybe he was just mellowing with age. Albert had allowed himself to hope that, at close to sixty-five years old, his father had finally managed to lay his demons to rest.

And then, beginning in June, 1934, the craziness had

flared up again. This latest scene with the nail-studded paddle was by no means the first indication that his father was getting worse. There had been the business with the black cat, for example. And those needles Albert had found hidden inside that book by Edgar Allan Poe. And the odd newspaper clippings.

And then there was his father's ferocious craving for raw meat, which seemed to come upon him only at certain times of the month, when the moon was full.

Something bad was going on inside the old man's head. And Albert Jr. didn't know how much longer he could take it. He was already thinking of splitting with the old man when the summer was over, of finding his own place and letting his father manage by himself.

It was even becoming hard for him to get a decent night's sleep, what with all the nightmares the old man suddenly seemed to be having. Just a few nights ago, Albert had been awakened by fearful sounds—violent thrashing and terrified gasps—coming from his father's bedroom. He had gone in and shaken the old man awake.

Panting and sweating, his father had sat up and looked around wildly. The light from the streetlamp outside the bedroom window spilled across his face. His features were contorted with horror. Staring down at the tormented old man, Albert wondered what kind of dream could have produced such a look.

He couldn't begin to imagine.

14

⚉⚉⚉⚉⚉⚉⚉⚉⚉

*The merciful man doeth good to his own soul: but
he that is cruel troubleth his own flesh.*

PROVERBS 11:17

She haunted his dreams. In his sleep, she would rise
from the depths and come at him, her small face twisted
with terror and fury, her fingers curled into claws, her
little girl's voice shrill with her final cry. "I'll tell mama!"

He would wake in a puddle of sweat, heart racing,
God's own words ringing in his ears, demanding atonement, mortification of the flesh. He would leap from his
sodden bedclothes, strip to his skin, and fetch his needles
and thimble.

He would squat, reach under, find the place, shove,
shove harder, until it was all the way in. The torture was
white-hot, agonizing, but the pain made him stiffen, and
he would pull at himself savagely, seeing the girl's face
swim before him, hearing the booming voice inside his
head: "O ye Daughter of Babylon!"

Afterward, after his suffering, after his release, he
would lie on the floor, breathing raggedly, savoring the
burning soreness between his legs. Cleansed and clear-
headed, he would be filled with a deep sense of his own
justification. After all, hadn't he rescued the girl from the
ultimate violation? Her virginity had remained intact.
And if the sacrifice had been unrighteous, would not the
angels have intervened to save her, as Isaac had been
saved?

He thought about her all the time now. Not one of all

the other children he had known in his life—how many had there been?—were like her.

There had, of course, been many thrilling experiences since that June day. His marriages, to begin with. And the good times he'd had with little Mary Nichols and her family. He had such fond memories of the games they had played. "Sack of Potatoes Over," "Buck, Buck, How Many Hands Up?" and the others. She was as dear to him as one of his own children. He still wrote to her whenever he could.

But the Budd girl was different from the rest. Lying in bed sometimes, thinking back to that day and the frenzied week of pleasure that had followed, he could still recall her taste.

On several occasions, he had made his son drive him back to the cottage. But the last time, remorse had overwhelmed him at his first glimpse of the place, and he had been unable to get out of the car. He was beginning to doubt that he would be able to take his secret to the grave.

From time to time, a story about her would turn up in the newspapers. He searched their pages eagerly for these items. Whenever he encountered one, he tore it out and stored it with his other special clippings.

Just this June—exactly six years since the incident— several interesting articles about her had appeared. He couldn't help snickering at the stories, they were so far from the truth. Poor Mrs. Budd had had her hopes dashed once again. But he had learned an interesting fact from the articles: the Budds had moved to a new address, 135 West 24th Street. He wasn't sure how or when he might use that bit of information. But he felt certain it would come in handy.

Maybe he'd write to Mrs. Budd one of these days and tell her what had really happened to her daughter. At least that would spare her the pain of future disappointments. After all, she had treated him so nicely, inviting him to Sunday dinner, giving little Gracie permission to go with him to the party.

The least he could do was let her know the truth.

15

*The miserable have no other medicine
But only hope.*

SHAKESPEARE, *Measure for Measure*

On the afternoon of Thursday, May 30, 1934, a mighty armada—the entire U.S. naval fleet, "the united sea power of the nation"—steamed into New York City's harbor. It was a stirring spectacle with eighty-one warships, including dreadnoughts, destroyers, cruisers, and aircraft carriers sweeping up the river in a twelve-mile procession.

Overhead, a squadron of planes, 185 strong—"the sky talons of the American fighting eagle," as the New York *Daily Mirror* proclaimed—roared above the fleet, wheeling and swooping in a breathtaking demonstration of aerial prowess.

It was the most spectacular display of naval might in U.S. history. Nothing like it had ever been seen before, and the citizens of New York turned out by the hundreds of thousands to cheer the awesome pageant. From Coney Island to Yonkers, Sandy Hook to Hoboken, they thronged the shoreline and waterfront, shouting and cheering as the stately procession cruised past.

From the forward gun turret of the heavy cruiser *Indianapolis,* anchored close by Ambrose Lightship, President Roosevelt reviewed the fleet with unconcealed pride. At the conclusion of the one-and-a-half hour review, he directed that three pennants be raised on the forward mast of the cruiser, spelling out in naval code the words "Well done."

For eighteen days, the men-of-war remained anchored in the harbor, drawing massive crowds of sightseers. On Sunday, June 3, more than a quarter of a million people turned out to see the ships. Half that number waited for hours in slow-moving lines for a chance to get aboard. Others viewed the fleet from nearby pierheads, sightseeing buses, or hired boats. Before that sun-baked day was over, nearly forty people had been felled by heat prostration, and a seven-year-old girl had drowned after tumbling over the side of a sightseeing boat. Her father, Arthur Hallowell, the captain of the boat, also perished when he plunged overboard in an effort to save her.

Meanwhile, the city rolled out the red carpet for the men of the fleet. The officers and their wives were welcomed, wined and dined at receptions arranged by Mayor LaGuardia and Mrs. William Randolph Hearst. Special Sunday services were conducted at St. Patrick's Cathedral and the Cathedral of St. John the Divine. At the Episcopal Church on Fifth Avenue, Bishop Manning denounced pacificism as incompatible with Christian doctrine, a position shared by Cardinal Hayes, who deplored the "supreme folly" of "military unpreparedness." From pulpits all over the city, speakers bestowed their blessings on the fleet and its men, though at least one dissenter decried the gathering of warships as nothing more than a show of "brute force."

While the officers mingled with the city's social elite, 22,000 enlisted men swarmed ashore on overnight liberty. A thousand of them spent Sunday afternoon at the Polo Grounds, watching the Giants game as guests of the National League. Others headed directly to Times Square, Chinatown, and Coney Island, determined to make the most of their holiday.

For the next two and a half weeks, the fleet was the biggest attraction in town, and the newspapers covered it accordingly, with daily features and dozens of photos of battleships, cruisers, teeming crowds of tourists (more than 1,400,000 people would eventually visit the fleet), and beaming "tars" enjoying the hospitality of the city.

On Monday, June 4, the *Daily Mirror* ran a special section of photographs related to the fleet as it had every day since the warships put into port. There were shots of the battleship *Colorado,* of the sightseers lined up behind police barricades, of the blue-jacketed ranks posed at attention on the steps of St. Patrick's Cathedral. And at the very top of the spread, there was a photograph of two young couples—a pair of smiling sailors and their smartly dressed dates—having their picture snapped on Riverside Drive by a "tintype man," who was apparently instructing them to "watch the birdie." All of them were obeying his directions, except for the girl on the far right, who was looking not at the tintype man but straight into the camera of the news photographer. She was a dark-haired teenager, wearing a full dress, a big-brimmed hat, and a charming half-smile.

Millions of people saw this photograph when it was published on Monday. And one of these people was a well-meaning soul, a Brooklyn housewife named Adele Miller who, perhaps even more than most New Yorkers, had been engrossed by the drama of the Budd abduction. Contemplating the picture of the two young couples on Riverside Drive, this woman was gripped by an absolute certainty. She became convinced that the dark-haired girl staring back at her was none other than Grace Budd herself, grown into a teenager.

Scissoring the photo from the paper, she drew an arrow pointing to the girl in the big-brimmed hat and in the margin above it wrote, "This is the girl, Grace Budd." Then she stuck the photo in an envelope and sent it off to the Budd family.

Though the Budds had been inundated with crank letters six years earlier, it had been a long time since they had received mail from a stranger, and they examined the clipping with keen interest. Grace's mother found a magnifying glass and studied the dark-haired girl's face. She showed the picture to her family and friends. No one could make a positive identification. But they all agreed that the girl in the picture did, in fact, look like an older version of Gracie.

The following day, Mrs. Budd, accompanied by her

husband, took the subway to the Missing Persons Bureau and showed the photograph to Detective King. Within twenty-four hours, the city's papers were reporting that a girl, tentatively identified as the grown-up Grace Budd, had been spotted in a news photo in the company of two sailors from the fleet. The photo itself was reprinted along with the stories. For the first time in years, the Budds allowed themselves to feel a spark of hope.

It didn't take long for that spark to be extinguished. On Thursday, June 14, a sixteen-year-old named Florence Swinney of 541 East 150th Street appeared at the Morrisania police station in the Bronx and identified herself as the girl in the news photo. The other girl, she said, was her friend, Lillian Hagberg, and the two sailors were young men they had met in the city and spent the day with.

That evening at around six o'clock, Deputy Chief Inspector Francis J. Kear climbed the stairs to the Budds' apartment at 135 West 24th Street to break the bad news to the family. He found Delia Budd clearing the dinner dishes from the kitchen table. "That's another hope gone," Mrs. Budd said, sighing. Her husband simply stared into space and said nothing.

At first, the Florence Swinney episode seemed to be just another dead-end lead in a six-year string of disappointments. But as it turned out, the stories about the mistaken identification of the dark-haired girl in the news photo would have dramatic consequences. For it was from one of these stories that Albert Fish learned the Budds' new address. And armed with that information, the diseased old man would find himself impelled, six months later, to commit one last outrage against the Budds—an outrage that would finally solve the mystery of the missing girl's fate.

16

~~~~~~~~~~~~

"His Gossip of Today is the Headline of Tomorrow!"

slogan for the Walter Winchell column
"On Broadway"

In the years since Albert Corthell had been captured and released, the police had been unable to come up with a single plausible suspect in the Budd kidnapping. Officially, the case was still open. But no one in the Bureau of Missing Persons had much faith that it would ever be solved. No one, that is, except William F. King.

For over six years, King had continued to pursue the case. During that period, he had been involved in other investigations, including the search for Joseph Force Crater, the New York Supreme Court Justice whose disappearance in August, 1930, was one of the major mysteries of the Depression (and remains unexplained to this day).

But King had never abandoned his hunt for the missing Budd girl and her elderly abductor. By the fall of 1934, he had traveled over fifty thousand miles on that quest, running down rumors, following dead-end leads, chasing phantoms. He had done everything possible to flush his quarry out of hiding.

One of his ploys was to plant phony news items about the Budd case in the New York City papers. He didn't want the public to forget about the case. Each time one of these stories appeared, the police would receive dozens of phone calls and letters from people who claimed to know something about the missing girl. None of these tips had ever panned out. But there was always the chance that someone might yet come forth with a key piece of information. The newspaper gambit was a long shot, King knew. But he was willing to give anything a try.

The main outlet for King's plants was Walter Winchell's enormously popular gossip column, "On Broadway," the pride of William Randolph Hearst's brassy tabloid, the New York *Daily Mirror*. Winchell was unquestionably the most influential newspaper columnist of his time and on close terms with everyone from J. Edgar Hoover to the mobster Owney Madden. He was always happy to do the police a good turn.

On November 2, 1934, the following newsflash appeared in Winchell's column:

> I checked on the Grace Budd mystery. She was eight when she was kidnapped about six years ago. And it is safe to tell you that the Dep't of Missing Persons will break the case, or they expect to, in four weeks. They are holding a "cokie" now at Randall's Island, who is said to know most about the crime. Grace is supposed to have been done away with in lime, but another legend is that her skeleton is buried in a local spot. More anon.

There was no factual basis at all for this story—no cocaine addict on Randall's Island with inside knowledge of Grace Budd's death. But by a strange turn of events, this fabrication would prove to be uncannily prophetic and come to be chalked up as another major coup for Winchell.

17

"I write as a habit—just can't seem to stop."

ALBERT FISH

Ten days after Walter Winchell reported an imminent break in the Grace Budd case a letter arrived at the home of the missing girl's family. It had been mailed the previous night, November 11, from the Grand Central Annex post office in Manhattan and was addressed to Delia Budd.

Though Mrs. Budd was functionally illiterate, she could make out her name—written in a neat, bold script—on the front of the envelope. Seating herself at the kitchen table, she carefully tore open the top of the envelope and removed the folded sheet inside. But she had trouble reading what the letter said.

It was the one time in her life that her illiteracy proved to be a blessing.

Her son Edward was at home, relaxing in his bedroom. Mrs. Budd called him into the kitchen and handed him the letter. The young man began to read it silently. Almost immediately, the color drained from his face.

Mrs. Budd stared at him, alarmed. "What's wrong?" she demanded "What does it say?" Edward Budd didn't answer; he was already on his way out the front door.

116

18

~~~~~~~~~~~~

The wicked is snared by the transgression of his lips.

PROVERBS 12:13

By 10:30 that morning, the letter was in Detective King's possession.

Over the years, King had read countless pieces of crank mail—inhumanly cruel letters full of vile taunts. But for sheer viciousness and depravity, nothing he had ever seen could begin to match the letter that Edward Budd had just delivered into his hands:

My dear Mrs. Budd,

In 1894 a friend of mine shipped as a deck hand on the Steamer Tacoma, Capt. John Davis. They sailed from San Francisco for Hong Kong China. On arriving there he and two others went ashore and got drunk. When they returned the boat was gone. At that time there was a famine in China. *Meat of any kind* was from $1--to 3 Dollars a pound. So great was the suffering among the very poor that all children under 12 were sold to the Butchers to be cut up and sold for food in order to keep others from starving. A boy or girl under 14 was not safe in the street. You could go in any shop and ask for steak— chops—or stew meat. Part of the naked body of a boy or girl would be brought out and just what you wanted cut from it. A boy or girls behind which is the sweetest part of the body and sold as veal cutlet

117

brought the highest price. John staid there so long he acquired a taste for human flesh. On his return to N.Y. he stole two boys one 7 one 11. Took them to his home stripped them naked tied them in a closet. Then burned everything they had on. Several times every day and night he spanked them—tortured them—to make their meat good and tender. First he killed the 11 yr old boy., because he had the fattest ass and of course the most meat on it. Every part of his body was Cooked and eaten except head—bones and guts. He was Roasted in the oven (all of his ass), boiled, broiled, fried, stewed. The little boy was next, went the same way. At that time, I was living at 409 E 100 st., near—right side. He told me so often how good Human flesh was I made up my mind to taste it. On Sunday June the 3—1928 I called on you at 406 W 15 St. Brought you pot cheese—strawberries. We had lunch. Grace sat in my lap and kissed me. I made up my mind to eat her. On the pretense of taking her to a party. You said Yes she could go. I took her to an empty house in Westchester I had already picked out. When we got there, I told her to remain outside. She picked wildflowers. I went upstairs and stripped all my clothes off. I knew if I did not I would get her blood on them. When all was ready I went to the window and Called her. Then I hid in a closet until she was in the room. When she saw me all naked she began to cry and tried to run down stairs. I grabbed her and she said she would tell her mamma. First I stripped her naked. How she did kick—bite and scratch. I choked her to death, then cut her in small pieces so I could take my meat to my rooms, Cook and eat it. How sweet and tender her little ass was roasted in the oven. It took me 9 days to eat her entire body. I did *not* fuck her tho I could of had I wished. She died a *virgin*.

So monstrous was this letter that it was hard to conceive of the mind that could have produced it. Still, it had a strangely authentic quality. Though clearly deranged, it was far more coherent than the foul ravings of most hate letters. And the details it described—the strawberries and pot cheese, for example—were completely accurate.

True, those details had been reported in the papers. But there was a piece of information that hadn't. The writer had supplied a specific address—409 East 100th Street, located in the very neighborhood where the police had concentrated their search in the weeks immediately following the abduction.

Was it possible that Grace's kidnapper had decided, for whatever insane reason, to communicate with her family after all this time?

There was one way to find out.

Fetching his file on the Budd case, King dug through it until he found what he was looking for—the photostat copy of the handwritten message that "Frank Howard" had sent to the Budds on June 2, 1928, informing them that he would be delayed by a day.

Placing it beside the letter, King compared the two. He was no graphologist. But it didn't take an expert to see that the writing was exactly the same in both.

At that moment, William King could hardly have helped feeling that, after six and a half years of bitter frustration, the solution to the Budd mystery was finally —and quite literally—within his grasp.

19

·•◦◦◦◦◦◦◦◦·

"I am certain, too ... that when they got to the end of that long trail after six and one-half years ... that they were all shocked, because they found at the end of that trail an unbelievable man."

JAMES DEMPSEY

In the end, it wasn't the letter itself that led to the capture of Albert Fish. It was the envelope it came in.

Imprinted on the back flap of the envelope was a small hexagonal emblem with a circle in the center (it resembled the schematic drawing of a hex nut). On each of the inside corners of the hexagon was a single capital letter. Taken together, they spelled out the initials N.Y.P.C.B.A.

A two-line address appeared directly below the emblem. The anonymous sender had taken a pen to the top line, obscuring the street number with ink. But he had left the words below it—"New York City"—untouched. Nor had he made the slightest effort to cover up the emblem itself.

All in all, for a man with compelling reasons to cover his tracks, he had done a surprisingly careless job of it—so careless, in fact, that with the help of a magnifying glass, King could easily make out the scratched-out street address: 627 Lexington Avenue.

Grabbing his overcoat, King headed uptown, where he discovered what the letters in the hexagon stood for. The address turned out to be the headquarters of the New

York Private Chauffeur's Benevolent Association. After introducing himself to Arthur Ennis, the president of the N.Y.P.C.B.A., Detective King showed him the envelope and asked if a man called Frank Howard had ever belonged to the association. Ennis checked through his files but found no record of anyone with that name.

King then asked to examine all the personnel forms filled out by active and retired members of the organization. Ennis handed over a carton containing nearly four hundred membership forms to King, who returned to his office and began the laborious task of comparing the handwriting on the forms to that on the anonymous letter. But he was unable to come up with a match.

The following day, King went back to the headquarters and requested that Ennis call an emergency meeting of the association. It was held the following afternoon. Addressing the members, King reviewed the facts of the Budd case, described the man he was searching for, and—without going into specifics—told them about the anonymous letter that had arrived at the Budds' apartment in a N.Y.P.C.B.A. envelope. If any member knew of someone who had removed stationery from the office, King declared, it was critical that he come forward.

After the meeting, King was approached by a sheepish-looking young man, who introduced himself as Lee Sicowski and explained that he worked part-time for the organization as a janitor and errand boy. Sicowski confessed that, about six months earlier, he had stolen a few sheets of stationery and some envelopes from the office.

And what had he done with them? King asked.

Taken them back home, said Sicowski.

When King asked Sicowski where he was living, the young man gave the detective his address—a rooming house at 622 Lexington Avenue.

Here, at last, was an encouraging development. If the person who had written to the Budds was not a member of the association—and he didn't seem to be—then perhaps the envelope was one of the batch Sicowski had swiped. If so, then King knew where to look next—the rooming house on Lexington Avenue.

But when king arrived there a short while later, he could find no one who recognized his description of "Frank Howard." Nor did the register contain any signature resembling the kidnapper's handwriting. King was bitterly disappointed.

He sought out Sicowski and, once again, questioned him closely. Only then did the young man recall that, at the time he had taken the stationery, he hadn't moved to his present address. At that point, he was living in a different rooming house, located at 200 East 52nd Street. In room No. 7.

Sicowski also mentioned something else he had forgotten until that moment. He told King that he had ended up using only one or two of the letterhead envelopes.

What had happened to the others? King asked.

Sicowski shrugged. He didn't know. He had stuck them on a wooden shelf above his bed and had forgotten about them. As far as he knew, they were still there when he moved out, about five months earlier.

King immediately went to the address Sicowski had given him and spoke to the landlady, Mrs. Frieda Schneider. He showed her one of the old kidnap circulars with its detailed description of "Frank Howard."

Mrs. Schneider was taken aback. The person in the circular sounded very much like one of her boarders, a quiet old man with a gray moustache who had moved into room No. 7 just a few days after Lee Sicowski left. The old man had remained in her house for two months. In fact, he had checked out only a few days earlier—on November 11.

King asked to see the register. In his jacket pocket, he carried the unspeakable letter that had been mailed to the Budds on the very day that Mrs. Schneider's boarder had moved out. Unfolding the letter, King held it open beside the place in the register where the old man had signed in two months before.

The signature matched the handwriting in the letter exactly. King stared down at the signature. The name the old man had inscribed was "Albert H. Fish."

* * *

Stressing the urgency of the situation, King grilled Mrs. Schneider about her former tenant. The landlady had little information to offer, but she did provide one crucial fact. The old man had a son who was down in North Carolina, working for the C.C.C. (the Civilian Conservation Corps), a federal program, established as part of Roosevelt's New Deal, which put unemployed young men to work in the national parks. The old man was partly supported by this son, who mailed his twenty-five-dollar paycheck to his father every month. Mrs. Schneider knew about the checks because the old man had asked her to cash them on occasion.

Mrs. Schneider told King something else, something that made the detective very happy. Fish was expecting at least one more of these checks to arrive at Mrs. Schneider's address. Before moving out, he had asked the landlady to hold it for him. He would return for it, he had told her, in a week or so.

Beginning that very night—November 14, 1934—King set up a round-the-clock stakeout of 200 East 52nd Street. While several of King's men kept watch over the rooming house, King himself took other measures. He contacted the finance officer of the C.C.C. camp in North Carolina, who promised to alert him as soon as the next pay checks were mailed out. He arranged for New York City postal inspectors to monitor the mails for any letters directed to Albert Fish. He traveled uptown to the address Fish had given in his letter to the Budds—409 East 100th Street. He was able to learn very little from the owners of the building, a family named Costa, though the husband did recall that an elderly man had lived in the building for a few months during the summer of 1928. King also asked Arthur Ennis to hold on to any undeliverable mail returned to the association in an N.Y.P.C.B.A. envelope.

This last precaution produced an interesting result. During the third week of November, a letter, mailed in an N.Y.P.C.B.A. envelope, was returned to the association because its addressee—a Mr. Vincent Burke of the Holland Hotel in Manhattan—could not be located.

Ennis passed the envelope along to King. Inside, written in Fish's unmistakable hand, was a short note, dated November 11:

> Dear Sir,
>   I was formerly a member of the Out-Door Club, Tacoma Park, Washington, D.C. A Nudist group. Business took me away. I have travelled a lot so join up my membership in club. I am located here permanently so wish to know where you have your Nudist meetings and the hours.
>
> Hoping to be informed
I am very truly
James W. Pell

At this point, of course, there was no absolute proof that Albert Fish was the person who had kidnapped Grace Budd. But if Detective King had any lingering doubts that he was on the trail of anything but a bizarre personality, this note—written the same day that Fish had mailed his monstrous letter to the Budds and had moved from Mrs. Schneider's rooming house—served to dispel them.

In the meantime, King and his men kept up their vigil. But as the days passed with no sign of Fish—or of the check from his son—the detectives became concerned.

Finally, on December 4, a postal inspector called King to tell him that an envelope addressed to Albert H. Fish had just been intercepted at the Grand Central Annex post office. The envelope was turned over to King, who felt more confident than ever that Fish would be in his custody in a matter of days.

More time passed, however, and still the old man did not appear. Once again, King began to grow worried. Perhaps Fish had gotten wind of the stakeout. King decided to remove his men from the premises.

Then, on the afternoon of December 13, 1934, as King sat at his desk, the telephone rang. It was Frieda Schneider, calling to tell him that Albert Fish had just showed up at her rooming house, inquiring about his check.

King told the landlady to stall the old man. Then he

jumped into a squad car and sped uptown to the 52nd Street address.

Mrs. Schneider met King at the front door and ushered him into one of the furnished rooms. There, seated at a small wooden table and sipping noisily from a teacup, was a pinched and hollow-cheeked old man with a wispy moustache. He was dressed in a tweed suit-jacket and vest, shirt and tie, and shabby striped trousers that did not match the top half of his outfit. A black overcoat was draped over the back of his chair, and a soiled gray fedora lay on the table beside him.

King closed the door behind him. "Albert Fish?" he asked.

The teacup and saucer rattled slightly as the old man set them down on the table. Gazing at King with watery eyes, he rose to his feet and nodded.

As King crossed the room, the shriveled old man stuck his right thumb and forefinger into his vest pocket as though reaching for his watch. What he extracted, however, was a razor blade, which he held straight out in front of himself as King continued to approach.

King grabbed the old man's bony wrist and twisted. The razor blade went flying. Fish collapsed back into the chair.

King was not given to open displays of emotion. But standing there, staring down at the gray old man he had hunted so tirelessly for so long, he couldn't keep a note of triumph out of his voice.

"I've got you now," said William King.

PART 3

Wisteria

20

Dear and dear is their poisoned note,
The little snakes of silver throat,
In mossy skulls that nest and lie,
Ever singing, "Die, oh! die."

THOMAS LOVELL BEDDOES,
"The Phantom Wooer"

Before it was over, Albert Fish would tell his story to many people: Detective King to begin with, then King's colleagues and superiors, and eventually a whole series of psychiatrists—none of whom had heard anything like it before (and would never hear anything remotely like it again). He would even relate a version of it to the public at large in the form of a serialized newspaper autobiography.

Various details would be added and subtracted. Modifications would be made. But the confession he offered immediately after his arrest—though it certainly contained significant omissions—was essentially the story he adhered to until the end of his days.

New Yorkers first learned about the story on the following morning, December 14, 1934, when it was splashed across the front page of every paper in the city. But in the end, no one—not the police or the public or the mental health professionals who examined Fish firsthand—could ever quite believe what they were hearing. Not even after an overwhelming body of evidence corroborated Fish's story in every terrible detail.

After taking the old man into custody, King drove him down to Police Headquarters and ushered him into Room 115, the office of Captain John G. Stein, head of the Missing Persons Bureau. By now, it was around 1:50 P.M., less than two hours since King had received Frieda Schneider's phone call and hurried over to her boarding house. King and Fish were alone in the office, Stein having gone out to lunch.

King directed the old man to a high-backed wooden chair, then perched himself on a corner of Stein's desk a few feet away from the suspect. For over half a decade, Grace Budd's spectral abductor had loomed so large in King's imagination that he could hardly believe how diminutive and harmless-looking the flesh-and-blood reality had turned out to be. Fish was no more than five and a half feet tall and 130 pounds—the kind of stooped and sunken-chested old codger you'd offer to give your seat to on a crowded subway car. His decrepit appearance only made the tale he had to tell seem that much more incredible.

King showed Fish the letter that had been mailed to Mrs. Budd and asked the old man if he had written it. Without a moment's hesitation, Fish acknowledged that he had.

King then held out the letter concerning the nudist club meetings which had been sent to Vincent Burke at the Holland Hotel on 42nd Street by "James W. Pell." Had Fish written that letter, too? The old man nodded "yes."

Finally, King handed Fish the telegram that the Budds had received from "Frank Howard" six and a half years before, on June 2, 1928. Again, Fish freely admitted that he was the pseudonymous sender.

When King asked him, however, if he was the person responsible for taking Grace Budd from her home, Fish denied knowing anything about it. King's eyes narrowed and his voice grew stern. "In view of what I've just shown you," he said, "do you expect me to believe that you weren't the man who was at the Budd home?"

"I wasn't there," Fish answered. "Never saw Mrs.

Budd." King glared down at the old man, who kept his eyes fixed on the floor.

"All right," King said quietly. "I'll tell you what. I'm going to send for the manager of the Western Union Office at 104th Street and Third Avenue, where this telegraph was sent from. Then I'm going to get hold of a member of the Costa family, who owned 409 East 100th Street when you lived there in 1928. Then I'm going to send for Reuben Rosoff, the pushcart peddler you bought the little pail from—the one you carried the pot cheese in when you visited the Budds on Sunday, June 3. And then I'm going to bring down the whole Budd family and Willie Korman. I have a feeling these people will be able to identify you."

With that, King turned and headed toward the office door. Before he reached it, Fish called him back. "Don't send for those people," he said softly. "I'll tell you all about it. I'm the man you want. I took Grace Budd from her home on the third day of June and brought her to Westchester and killed her that same afternoon."

King walked back to the door and left word that he was not to be disturbed by anyone. Then, fetching a notepad and fountain pen, he sat down at Stein's desk and jotted notes, while Fish began matter-of-factly recalling that time in the summer of 1928 when his "blood thirst" (as he described it) became too ferocious to resist and he found himself driven by an overwhelming need to kill.

As it happened, Grace Budd was not Fish's intended victim at all. Not, at any rate, to begin with. Originally, Fish told King, he had meant to murder her brother, Edward.

Not that Fish felt any animosity toward Edward Budd. He hadn't even known of the young man's existence until the morning of May 27, 1928, when he had spotted Edward's classified ad in the *New York World*. It was simply that Fish felt the need for a sacrificial victim, preferably male.

Specifically, Fish hoped to lure his victim to an abandoned house in the Westchester community of

Worthington (where Fish had briefly lived a few years earlier), overpower the young man, bind him with stout cords, and then slice off his penis.

Afterward, he planned to take the train back to the city, quickly pack his bags and get out of town, leaving the trussed and mutilated boy to bleed to death on the floor of the empty cottage.

Fish had been searching for a suitable victim when his eyes fell on the "situation wanted" ad Edward had placed in the *World* in the hopes of securing a summer job in the country. After years of concocting elaborate identities for his obscene correspondence, Fish had needed no time at all to invent the fictional persona of Frank Howard, the gentleman farmer from Long Island. (When asked how he'd come up with the alias, Fish explained that "Howard" was his own middle name. He couldn't say why he'd picked "Frank." The name had just popped into his head.)

Fish went on to tell King about his first visit to the Budds. His initial glimpse of Edward had been very disappointing. The broad-shouldered young man looked like a full-grown adult—not what Fish had in mind at all. And then there was the complicating presence of Willie Korman, Edward's equally strapping friend, whom Fish had felt constrained to include in his plans.

Still, he had been determined to go through with the scheme. His blood-craving was too urgent to be denied. And he felt confident that he could handle both Eddie and Willie. As Detective King and other investigators would come to learn, the feeble-looking old man had experience in these matters. A great deal of experience.

Fish proceeded to describe his various preparations—the purchase of the enamel pail from Reuben Rosoff's pushcart, the trip to Sobel's hock shop to buy the necessary tools.

He briefly related the episode involving the two neighborhood boys, Cyril Quinn and the son of the Italian coalman. Fish explained that he had been planning to murder the Quinn boy for a while. When King asked "Why?" Fish simply shrugged. In any event, the plan hadn't worked out. Fish described how young Cyril and his friend had fled the apartment after discovering the cleaver, saw, and butcher knife stashed beneath the old man's bed.

Fish quickly sketched in the events of Sunday morning, June 2. How he had wrapped his three "implements of hell" in a piece of striped canvas tarp. How he had stopped on his way to the Budds to fill the enamel pail with pot cheese and to purchase a container of strawberries. How he had left the canvas-wrapped parcel at a newsstand on the corner of Ninth Avenue and 14th Street. How he'd joined the Budd family for a potluck lunch.

And then he described his first glimpse of little Grace.

As soon as he had seen her standing in the kitchen doorway, still dressed in the pretty outfit she had worn that morning to church, he knew that it was the girl, not her brother, that he wanted to kill. He told King how she had climbed upon his knee, and about the four bits he had given her to run out and buy candy. Before she returned, he had already thought up the imaginary birthday party at the fictitious address.

When he proposed taking Grace along, even Fish was surprised at how readily her parents consented.

Fish paused in his recitation. He asked King for some water, which the detective fetched from a cooler. The old man sipped for a moment from the glass.

Then, speaking in the same low monotone, he summoned up the events of that sweltering afternoon when he had led Grace Budd away from her home and family under the pretext of taking her to his niece's birthday party.

After bidding goodbye to Mrs. Budd and retrieving his bundle from the newsstand, Fish had led the little girl to the Ninth Avenue El and up the long stairway to the subway platform, where they boarded a train to Sedgwick Avenue in the Bronx. They switched lines at that point and traveled to the Van Cortlandt Park Station.

There, Fish, holding the little girl's hand, made his way to the ticket booth of the Putnam Division of the New York Central Railroad. Handing the man behind the window ninety cents, he purchased a round-trip ticket for himself to the Westchester community of Worthington, less than twenty miles north of the city.

For Grace Budd he purchased a one-way ticket.

Inside the train, Fish let Grace sit next to the window so that she could look out at the scenery. Lowering himself slowly onto the seat beside her, he leaned across her lap and propped the canvas-wrapped bundle against the side of the car. Then they settled back for the forty-minute ride upstate, Fish occasionally turning to Grace to tell her how much fun his niece's birthday party was going to be or reaching down to give her knee a gentle pat.

Seated beside her grizzled companion, hands folded primly in her lap, Grace stared silently through the window at the landscape rushing by. She had only been outside of the city on two occasions in her life. If she wondered now why the train seemed to be carrying her off into the green, open countryside, she never said a word. Seeing the nicely dressed couple—Fish in his dark, three-piece suit and gray fedora, and Grace in her white silk communion dress and light summer coat—another passenger would have taken them for a dapper old gentleman and his pretty little granddaughter, headed upstate for a Sunday outing.

When they disembarked at Worthington Station, Fish seemed slightly distracted. As they stepped onto the platform, Grace tugged at his sleeve. "You forgot your package," she exclaimed. Turning on her heels, she dodged back into the car. Seconds later, she reappeared with the red-and-white-striped parcel cradled in her arms. Fish took it from her without a word.

The sky had cleared, but even here, twenty miles north of the stifling city, the air seemed suffocatingly hot. As Fish led the little girl along the path that ran between the train tracks and the Saw Mill River Parkway, he asked if she felt hot. "Oh, yes," she said, sighing. At Fish's suggestion, she removed her hat and coat and handed them to the old man, who rolled the coat into a small bundle with the hat neatly folded inside.

They turned left at Mountain Road and proceeded up the steep, curving hillside for another half mile, past the house of a man named Frank Cudney. Directly across the road from Cudney's place was a farm owned by his mother, an elderly widow who was standing beside the fence that bounded her property, replacing some wooden slats that had been knocked down by her livestock. As Fish and Gracie walked past, he tipped his hat to the old "cow-woman" (as Fish described her to King) and remarked on the heat.

Then, taking Gracie by the hand, he continued up the road to his destination—an empty, two-story house known to the locals as Wisteria Cottage.

The house was set back a few dozen feet from the road, up a small slope. It was surrounded on three sides by dense woods, which served to isolate it from the neighboring houses, the nearest of which was a hundred yards away. Behind the house, the land ascended steeply. A small wooden privy stood fifty feet up the hill.

Fish led Grace up a half dozen log steps to a small grassy yard at the side of the house. The yard was blanketed with wildflowers. Fish told the child to play there while he went inside the house for a moment to fetch something. It was three in the afternoon and the lawn blazed in the sunlight. Grace had never seen such beautiful flowers. She crouched in the grass and began to pick a bouquet, humming softly to herself.

Fish walked around to the rear of the house, where patches of bare soil had been furrowed by rainwater. A large flat stone lay across one of the ruts. Laying down his canvas-wrapped bundle, Fish lifted one end of the rock and stuffed Grace's coat and hat underneath it. Then he picked up his package and headed for the side door of the house. Before he reached it, he caught sight of an empty five-gallon paint can lying in the grass. He walked over to it, lifted it by its wire handle, and carried it inside the house.

The old low-ceilinged house had been uninhabited for many years and smelled heavily of must and mildew.

The striped wallpaper in the living room was shredded and stained, and the floor was strewn with rodent droppings. Though the windows were bare, a passerby would have had trouble seeing into the house. The dirty panes blocked out everything but the daylight, which filtered into the empty rooms from every direction.

Fish climbed the staircase to the second floor of the house and entered the corner bedroom that overlooked the yard where Grace was picking flowers. Squatting underneath the window, he unrolled the canvas bundle and removed his tools one by one—the saw, the cleaver, and the double-edged knife—laying them neatly on the floor to the left of the canvas. Then he removed his clothes and dropped them in a pile a few feet away from the canvas. His legs were skinny and slightly bowed, his lumpy chest matted with tufts of white hair. Opening the window a crack, he called down to the child, asking her to come up to the house.

Carrying her bouquet of flowers, Grace walked up the porch steps and into the house. "Up here," Fish called out when he heard her enter. She began to climb the stairs. As soon as she reached the second floor landing, Fish stepped out into the hallway.

At the sight of the naked old man, the little girl began to scream. "I'll tell my mama!" she yelled. Dropping her flowers, she turned and tried to run downstairs.

With surprising speed, Fish grabbed Grace by the throat and pulled her into the empty bedroom. The little girl began to struggle wildly, kicking and scratching with her own surprising strength. Fish dug his fingers deep into her throat. He dragged her over to the canvas tarp, wrestled her to the floor, and knelt on her chest with his full weight while he continued to choke her. By then, he had become erect.

When he was sure she was dead, he lifted her head and rested it on the rim of the five-gallon paint can. Then he reached over for his double-edged knife and cut off Grace's head, taking care to catch as much blood as possible inside the empty can.

* * *

At this point, King interrupted the confession to ask if Fish had "used the girl's body" in any way. Interpreting the phrase (as King apparently intended it) to refer to rape, Fish insisted that he had not violated Grace sexually—that she had "died a virgin," as he'd stated in his letter to the Budds.

In that letter, of course, he had described putting the girl's body to a very different and even more unimaginable "use" by carrying it home and eating it. But for some reason, King did not question Fish explicitly about the matter of cannibalism. And Fish himself made no mention of it.

After a few moments, Fish said, he undressed the headless corpse and tossed the spattered clothing into an empty walk-in closet a few feet away. Getting stiffly to his feet, he shoved open the window, picked up the paint bucket, and dumped the blood out into the yard.

Returning to the body, Fish knelt beside it and, using the knife again, began to slice through the midsection, just below the navel. When he reached the spine, he switched to his cleaver. Before very long, the body lay chopped in two.

Carrying Grace's white shoes in one hand and her head in the other, Fish went downstairs, out the side door, and up the hill to the wooden outhouse. He thought about disposing of the head down the toilet hole, but the idea of dropping it into "the muss" seemed wrong to him, so he set it in a corner and covered it with some old newspapers that were lying on the floor. He did, however, stick the shoes into the hole, placing them on a small rock ledge just below the opening.

Back inside the house, he picked up the upper and lower halves of Grace's body and propped them in a corner of the room beside the closet. Then he swung open the closet door so that the body was hidden from view.

By the time he was finished, his hands were coated with blood. There was no water in the house, so he walked back outside and spent some time scrubbing himself clean with fistfuls of grass. Then he returned to the second-story bedroom and got dressed. He carefully rewrapped his tools in the canvas tarp and placed the bundle behind the closet door, next to the dismembered corpse.

It was 4:10 P.M. when he left the house and headed back down Mountain Road toward the railroad station—just slightly more than an hour since he and Grace Budd had arrived at Wisteria Cottage. Under his arm, Fish carried a small newspaper-wrapped bundle.

But this was a detail that he neglected to mention to Detective King.

King paused to refill his fountain pen, then flipped to a fresh page of his notebook. "What time was it when you arrived at your home?" he asked.

"About 6:30."

"And then what did you do?"

"I returned about four days later. I took the body and the legs out from behind the door. The legs were so stiff, they were as stiff as a board. I threw them out the window onto the lawn and carried the torso out, picking up the legs as I passed over the lawn, and went to the stone wall in back of the house. I laid the body and the legs as they would be in life behind this stone wall. I then went to the outhouse and got the head. It was all stiff, the hair was all clotted. I brought the head up and placed the head with the body just as it would be in life, the head, the torso, and the legs."

"Did you bury it?" asked King.

"No, I left it on top of the ground. Then I went back into the house, took the tools and threw them over the wall."

"Have you been there since?"

"Yes, I have been up there four or five times with my son."

"Have you seen the body?"

Fish shook his head. "No. I didn't go to see the body."

By now, it was nearly 2:45 in the afternoon. King had

been questioning Fish for nearly an hour. There was only one more question he wanted to ask. What had made the old man do it?

Fish scratched one end of his moustache and looked thoughtful. "You know," he replied after a moment. "I never could account for it."

21

~~~~~~~~~

*He that walketh upright walketh surely; but he
that perverteth his ways shall be known.*

PROVERBS 10:9

By that time, Captain Stein had returned from lunch
and was waiting outside his office, conferring with several of his men, who had heard the news of Fish's arrest. At
a few minutes before three, King emerged from the office
and, after receiving the congratulations of his colleagues,
filled them in on the details of the old man's confession.

Summoning a stenographer, Stein, King, and three
other members of the Missing Persons Bureau—
Lieutenant Scanlon, Sergeant Hammill, and Detective
Von Weisenstein—entered the captain's office, where
Fish sat fiddling with his moustache. He looked up at the
officers and smiled pleasantly.

Stein introduced himself and asked if Fish was willing
to make an official statement regarding Grace Budd's
disappearance.

"Positively," said Fish.

"Anything you say can be used against you. Do you
realize that?" said Stein.

"Yes."

Then, while the stenographer—Detective Thomas F.
Murphy of the Main Office Division—wrote out a
short-hand transcription, Stein commenced his interrogation. The time was 3:15 P.M.

Stein began by eliciting some basic information—
Fish's age, place of birth, current address, and occupa-

tion. In response to the last question, Fish identified himself as a "painter" (an answer which, as the Fish case entered the folklore of crime, underwent significant distortions, until the old housepainter was transformed, in certain accounts, into "a failed cubist artist").

Fish explained that he had been married since 1898, though he and his wife had not lived together for many years. He was the father of six children, ranging in age from twenty-one to thirty-five, and was particularly close to his two married daughters, Mrs. Anna Collins and Mrs. Gertrude DeMarco, both housewives in Astoria, Queens. Neither woman was well-to-do—indeed their families were both on Home Relief. Still, Fish was always welcome in their households and, from time to time during the past several years, had lived with each. The rest of the time, he had resided in various boarding houses, sometimes renting a room by himself, at other times, sharing it with one or another of his sons.

Stein then turned to the details of the crime itself. Coolly and concisely, Fish repeated the story he had told Detective King only a short while before, beginning with his discovery of Edward Budd's classified ad in the *World* and concluding with his disposal of the dismembered sections of Grace Budd's corpse behind the stone wall bounding Wisteria Cottage.

"After the child was killed," Stein asked, "did you tell anyone about this occurrence?"

Fish shook his head. "Not a living soul. My own children had no idea. They read about the case in the paper like everyone else."

At that point, Stein opened the file on the Budd case and removed the anonymous letter Fish had mailed to Mrs. Budd. Stein, wanting a sample of Fish's handwriting, asked him to sign his full name on the back of the letter, and the old man complied without hesitation.

"What was your purpose in writing this letter?" Stein wanted to know.

The old man shrugged his rounded shoulders. "I don't know. Just reading some books on things such as that. I just had a mania for writing."

"In substance, do you remember what you wrote in that letter?"

"That there was a famine in China and that human bodies had been consumed for food purposes," Fish answer matter-of-factly. There was a satchel in his room, he explained, containing various newspaper clippings that he liked to save. One of them dealt with some "fellows who used human bodies for food after the war was over." If the police went up to his room, they would find that clipping in the satchel.

Captain Stein whispered something to one of his men, who immediately stepped out of the office to dispatch a couple of detectives to Fish's current address, 55 East 128th Street. Then Stein turned back to Fish.

Showing him the N.Y.P.C.B.A. envelope that the Budd letter had been mailed in, Stein asked Fish where he had obtained it. The old man replied that he had found a "dozen or more" of them on a shelf in his room at Frieda Schneider's boarding house. "I had some paper but just run short of envelopes," Fish explained. "I wouldn't have known there was any there, only I was sitting in a chair one night and there was a roach on the wall, and I got up on the chair to kill the roach and saw the envelopes."

At 3:45 A.M., a half-hour after it began, the interrogation was over. Captain Stein, like the others, was struck by Fish's complete lack of emotion. Judging strictly by his tone, anyone would have thought that he had done nothing worse than bring Gracie home late from the party instead of leading her to a ghastly death in the silence of Old Wisteria.

Perhaps the most sobering detail of all, however—at least from the police's point of view—was the one about the roach. For six years, Grace Budd's abductor had been the object of one of the most intensive manhunts in New York City history. The full resources of the Missing Persons Bureau had been applied to the pursuit. Detective King alone had devoted countless hours to the case. Ultimately, of course, Fish had been apprehended. But as it turned out, his capture had as much to do with pure chance as with the skill and dedication of the police.

In a very real sense, a cockroach had led to the capture of Albert Fish.

22

~~~~~~~~~~~~~~~~~~~~~~~

That skull had a tongue in it, and could sing once.

SHAKESPEARE, *Hamlet*

It was nearly five P.M. when a pair of squad cars pulled away from police headquarters and headed north in the thickening darkness toward Westchester County. In addition to the driver, the lead car carried two members of the Missing Persons Bureau, Sergeants Thomas J. Hammill and Hugh Sheridan. Bureau Chief John Stein occupied the front passenger seat of the second car. Behind him, flanked by Detective King and Deputy Chief Inspector John Ryan, sat Albert Fish.

It took over an hour for the cars to reach White Plains, where they switched positions at a stoplight on Central Avenue. Then, with Fish providing directions, they proceeded to the Saw Mill River Road, following it until they reached the village of Irvington in the Westchester town of Greenburgh.

Turning right at Mountain Road, they ascended the steep, winding hillside and pulled up at Frank Cudney's house, a few hundred yards east of Wisteria Cottage. While the others waited in the cars, King went up to the front door, knocked, and after identifying himself to the owner, disappeared inside. A few moments later, King emerged again accompanied by Cudney, who walked around to the side of his house where he fetched a shovel and pick from his tool shed. Meanwhile, Sergeant Hammill had unlocked the trunk of his car and removed an electric emergency lamp—a portable device resembling an automobile headlight attached to a large battery.

With Hammill's beam lighting the way in the blackness of the country night, the party of men, Cudney included, marched up the road to Wisteria Cottage.

"Over here," said Fish, leading the others up the little rise toward the yard. Then, while Hammill trained his light on the frozen ground, Fish pointed out the grim landmarks of his crime.

Here was the place where he had left Gracie picking wildflowers. Here was the spot where he had found the old five-gallon paint can. Back there, he said pointing, was the tumbledown outhouse where he had stashed the girl's shoes and (until he had returned to move it to a different location) concealed her blood-drenched head beneath some old newspapers.

It was nearing seven by now, fully dark and very cold. The old man's breath frosted as he spoke, and in the dead silence of the remote, rural neighborhood, his voice—as whispery as the rustle of dry leaves—carried clearly.

Fish led the men along the wraparound porch to the front entrance, then up the stairs to the second-story bedroom, where the actual atrocity had taken place. There, he continued with his grim guided tour, moving around the room as he re-created the murder in all its details.

He pointed to the spot where he had unwrapped his bundle and neatly laid out his cleaver, saw, and knife. He stood beside the window, just as he had six years earlier when he had called out to Gracie, telling her to come upstairs. He assumed the position he had taken behind the bedroom door as he waited, naked, for the little girl to reach the landing. He indicated the dark corner where he had stowed her butchered body before deciding to dispose of it outside.

The house was without electricity, and as Fish moved about the abandoned room, reenacting the crime, Hammill kept his emergency beam fixed on him like a theatrical spotlight. In the bright yellow glare, the little man's shadow loomed behind him, sliding along the decaying walls.

It took only a few minutes for Fish to complete the macabre performance. Then it was time to go back outside. Time to show the police the final resting place of Grace Budd's dismembered—and crudely reassembled—corpse.

Fish led the others up the hill behind the house, where an old stone wall, about three feet high, marked off the eastern boundary line of the property. In the darkness, Fish couldn't say precisely where he'd deposited the remains, though he indicated a general area that seemed about the right distance from the house.

Carrying the pick and shovel supplied by Frank Cudney, King and Stein stepped over the wall along with Sergeant Hammill, who kept his light directed downward while his colleagues began turning over the top layer of soil with their tools.

A few minutes later, Stein scraped up a faded piece of fabric. Examining it in the light, he saw that it was an old scrap of canvas, badly weatherworn. Even so, it was easy to tell that at one point it had been striped.

Fish, meanwhile, had been making his way back down along the wall, squinting in the darkness for any recognizable landmarks. King, Stein and Hammill were still inspecting the tattered piece of fabric, when Fish's voice came drifting up to them. "Come down further," he was calling. "You're too far uphill."

The three men walked downhill about fifty feet, where they found Fish and the others standing by a big tree stump.

"This looks like the place," Fish said. "I recall the stump."

Once again, Hammill turned the beam on the ground while Stein and King scraped at the surface of the rocky soil. And once again, it took only a few minutes before the diggers came upon something. This time, it was King who turned it up—a smooth, rounded object which he recognized at once. Stooping, he lifted it gently out of the earth and raised it to the light.

It was a human skull, minus the jawbone. Its condition made it clear, even to an untrained eye, that it had been lying out in the woods for a long time. And its size made it equally clear that it was the skull of a young child.

Without a word, King passed it over to Stein, who examined it for a moment before showing it to the others. Then he knelt and replaced it precisely where it had been found.

The tiny circle of men remained silent as the diggers returned to their work.

Back in the city, the press had gotten wind of a major break in the Budd case. By 7:30 P.M., a crowd of reporters had assembled at police headquarters and were clamoring for more information. Finally, sometime around 8:00, Police Commissioner Lewis J. Valentine appeared to confirm that a suspect in the Budd case had, indeed, been arrested and had made a full confession to the police. He then passed out copies of a typed transcript of Fish's statement to Captain Stein. Immediately, the reporters began shouting out questions. Had the Budds been notified? Had they identified the suspect? Where was the prisoner now?

Valentine had just begun to answer the barrage of questions when a sergeant stepped up to notify him that word had just come down from Westchester County. Fish's story had been confirmed. Grace Budd's head had been found in the woods behind Wisteria Cottage.

By now, Stein and King had uncovered enough bones, including the missing jaw, to satisfy themselves that they had located the corpus delecti. It was time to notify the local authorities.

Sergeant Sheridan was dispatched to Frank Cudney's house to place the necessary calls. In the meantime, Stein and Hammill agreed that Fish should be returned to Manhattan and booked. Hammill would stay behind with Sheridan to advise and assist the Greenburgh police.

The old man—who had stood by impassively during the exhumation of the Budd girl's remains—was handcuffed to Detective King and led back to the squad car, with Stein and Inspector Ryan following close behind. The four men resumed their former positions, Stein up front beside the driver, Fish in the rear sandwiched between Ryan and King.

A moment later, the car had disappeared down the dark, winding steepness of Mountain Road, carrying the benign-looking child-butcher back to the city.

By the time Greenburgh Police Chief Phillip J. McQuillan arrived at Wisteria Cottage around 8:40 P.M. a handful of his men were already on the scene, along with Westchester District Attorney Frank H. Coyne. By nine, a dozen more had arrived, bringing the total up to twenty. Under McQuillan's supervision, the Greenburgh officers began scouring the woods behind the house, their search illuminated by flares, oil lamps, and electric torches.

Drawn by the strange lights and uncustomary noises, a small crowd of curiosity-seekers began to gather on the front lawn of Wisteria. Within an hour, their number had swelled to more than a hundred as news of the grisly discovery of the little girl's skeleton spread through the tightly knit community. By then, several carloads of reporters from the New York City dailies had also found their way to the scene.

Hammill, Coyne, and McQuillan were conferring near the spot where Grace's skull had been found when a car carrying New York City Police photographer Joseph Prefer pulled up in front of the property. Following Hammill's instructions, Prefer (who had been summoned from Manhattan by a phone call from Sergeant Sheridan) began taking flashbulb shots of the crime scene and evidence. He had just finished photographing the eroded skull lying in the dirt beside the stone wall when another car arrived, this one driven by Dr. Amos O. Squire, the Westchester County Medical Examiner.

Squire was quickly ushered over to the exhumation site. Kneeling, he inspected the skull in the flickering light of an oil lantern, paying particular attention to the condition of the teeth and the size and shape of the cranium. Examining the other bones that were scattered around, some of them still half-sunk into the soil, he recognized them instantly as the remains of a child—vertebrae, shoulder blades, ribs, finger bones, and the lower jaw, which was split in two.

Squire jotted some notes in a pad he removed from his coat pocket. When he was finished, all of the exposed bones, the skull included, were piled into a grocery carton that Frank Cudney had fetched from his house. Taking the box, Hammill returned to his car along with Sergeant Sheridan.

Then, while the Greenburgh police set up barricades around the murder site, the two investigators returned to their car and headed back to Manhattan. On the car seat between them, the weatherworn bones—the meager remains of the child they had sought for so long—rattled softly in their cardboard container.

23

"None of us are saints."

ALBERT FISH

It had taken about an hour for the car carrying King, Stein, Ryan and Fish to arrive back at police headquarters. To avoid the reporters clustered around the front entrance, the officers hustled Fish through a side door and up to Stein's office. It was after 9:00 by now—still just the beginning of what already had been a long, grueling night—and Stein and his men were feeling wrung out and cold to the bone. Besides everything else, none of them had eaten a bite since early afternoon.

While one of his men fetched coffee and sandwiches from an all-night restaurant across the street, Stein put in a call to the D.A.'s office. By the time Assistant District Attorney P. Francis Marro showed up, around twenty minutes later, the three officers and their prisoner had polished off their suppers.

It took another half-hour for Marro's stenographer, Detective Thomas Luddy, to make it downtown to headquarters. Stein and King spent that time filling in Marro on the facts of the case, on Fish's earlier confessions, and on the grisly discoveries they had made up in Westchester, which had confirmed every detail of the old man's story.

Then, at exactly 10:00 P.M., Marro turned to his interrogation of Fish. The questioning lasted about forty minutes. Once again, Fish was the soul of cooperation,

Grace Budd.
(Bettmann Archives)

Thousands of these circulars were distributed throughout the United States and Canada in the weeks following Grace Budd's abduction. (*New York Daily News*)

DETECTIVE DIVISION
CIRCULAR No. 6
JUNE 11, 1928

POLICE DEPARTMENT
CITY OF NEW YORK

BE SURE TO FILE
THIS CIRCULAR
FOR REFERENCE

Police Authorities are Requested to Post this Circular for the Information of Police Officers and File a Copy of It for Future Reference

ARREST FOR KIDNAPPING

FRANK HOWARD, Age, 58 years; height, 5 feet 7 inches; weight, 135 pounds; blue eyes; light complexion; mixed gray hair; small gray mustache which may be removed; teeth in poor condition three protruding upper teeth; slightly bow-legged; white; wore blue suit, black shoes, and soft black felt hat; large diamond ring; is a smooth talker and when last seen had considerable money on him.

This man called at the residence of Mr. and Mrs. Budd, 406 West 15th Street, New York City, on May 28, 1928, to make inquiries about Edward Budd, their 18 year old boy, who had advertised in the New York World for a position as a farm hand. Howard left the home of the Budds and came back the following Sunday, June 3, and while there saw Grace Budd, 10 year old daughter, and took her to attend a birthday party on West 137th Street, and neither of them has been seen since.

DESCRIPTION OF KIDNAPPED GIRL:

GRACE BUDD, Age, 10 years; height, 4 feet; weight, 60 pounds; large blue eyes; dark brown hair, bobbed straight; sallow complexion; anaemic; born in United States; white; residence, 406 West 15th Street, New York City. Wore light gray coat, gray fur on collar, cuffs, and down the front; white silk dress and socks; white pumps; gray silk hat with blue ribbon streamer from back; white pearl beads about neck; pink rose on lapel of coat; carried a brown pocketbook.

The photograph appearing on this circular does not answer the description of this girl, as to her clothing.

If arrested, immediately notify Detective Division, Police Headquarters, New York City, by telephone or telegraph, and an officer will be sent with necessary papers to cause his return to this jurisdiction.

JOSEPH A. WARREN,
Police Commissioner.

Telephone Spring 3100

GRACE BUDD

Delia Budd poses for news photographers with a portrait of her missing daughter. (*New York Daily News*)

Charles Edward Pope (left) under arrest. (Bettmann Archives)

The *Daily Mirror* "fleet photograph" that led, indirectly, to the capture of Albert Fish. The arrow points to sixteen-year-old Florence Swinney, mistakenly identified as the grown-up Grace Budd. (Bettmann Archives)

Albert Fish being booked, early Friday morning, December 14, 1934. Detective King is on the left. (Bettmann Archives)

Albert Fish and his nemesis, Detective William King.
(*New York Daily News*)

Night view of Wisteria Cottage.

Grace Budd's skull lies in the dirt behind the stone boundary wall above Wisteria Cottage.

Searchers comb the hillside behind Wisteria Cottage for Fish's "implements of hell." (*New York Daily News*)

Mug shot of Albert Fish taken in 1903 after his arrest for grand larceny. Fish was thirty-three at the time. (*New York Daily News*)

Medical Examiner Amos Squire (in hat and coat) examines one of the human bones found at Wisteria Cottage. (*New York Daily News*)

Albert and Delia Budd await the start of Fish's trial. (AP/Wide World Photos)

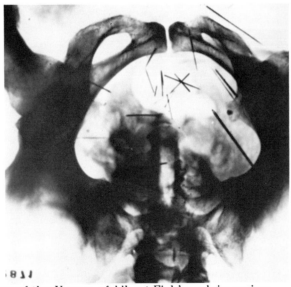

One of the X-rays of Albert Fish's pelvic region which revealed a total of twenty-nine needles shoved up inside his body. (*New York Daily News*)

Albert Fish at his trial. (AP/Wide World Photos)

patiently rehashing every detail of the crime and even adding a few particulars. He described how much blood Grace's hair had soaked up when he'd cut off her head, and how hard it had been to chop through her spine because his cleaver was dull. "I had to do a lot of work," he explained.

When Marro asked Fish why he'd done such a dreadful thing, Fish repeated that he had no explanation other than that "a sort of blood thirst" had come over him. Once that terrible need had subsided, he was overwhelmed with remorse. "I would have given my life within a half-hour after I done it to restore it to her," he swore.

"Did you commit any rape on her?" Marro asked.

"Never entered my head," Fish insisted.

Marro returned to the question of the old man's motivation. "What made you kill her, choke her and kill her?"

This time, Fish's answer was slightly more involved. He began by explaining that he'd been reading "a lot of cases of children being kidnapped." Abruptly, however, the old man began to talk about something entirely different. "I had a brother who served five years in the United States Navy," he said. "And he used to relate to me when I was quite small—he was the oldest of my mother's seven children. Walter H. Fish his name is. He had been to China when there was a famine, when they were using human flesh for food. He used to tell us a lot of these things and that got into my head." Fish paused, then added, "I was in Bellevue twice for mental observation and Kings County."

Apparently, Marro was satisfied by this explanation. In any event, he abruptly dropped the question of Fish's motivation and moved on to a few other matters. The interrogation lasted only a few minutes longer. Captain Stein put the final question to Fish. "Will you tell us how you feel now, how your conscience feels?"

Fish glanced around the room at his captors. "Much better," he said, smiling pleasantly.

Fish had now been questioned three times since his arrest earlier that day for a total of over two hours. Each of his interrogators had asked him dozens of questions about the smallest details of the crime, from the price of the train ticket he had purchased for Grace to the exact size of the paint can he had placed under her neck to catch her blood in.

Remarkably, however, not one of them had asked Fish directly about the single most appalling claim in his letter to the Budds. Though the old man had admitted at several points to a morbid fascination with cannibalism, he had never been asked to confirm or deny his assertion that he had performed that very atrocity on the flesh of Grace Budd.

Perhaps the claim simply seemed too insane to credit. Whatever the case, no one—not King, not Stein, not Marro—had ever asked Fish whether it was true, as he had written, that he had taken parts of the girl's body back to his rooms, cooked them in the oven, and consumed them over a span of nine days.

And on that subject, Fish himself volunteered no information.

Shortly after midnight, the Budds were awakened by a loud knock on their apartment door. Pulling on his bathrobe, Mr. Budd hurried to the door, opened it a crack, and peered out into the dimly lit hallway. There stood a young man, notepad in hand, who identified himself as a reporter from the *New York Herald Tribune*. He was wondering if the Budds had heard the news.

"What news?" replied Mr. Budd.

"They've arrested the man who kidnapped your daughter. He's confessed to the crime." By then, the rest of the family had gathered around the doorway. Mr. Budd invited the reporter inside. Removing his hat, the young man stepped into the apartment and—in response to the question that the missing girl's parents were almost too afraid to ask—broke the bad news.

Within half an hour, the Budds' cramped apartment was crowded with reporters and photographers. Mrs. Budd, massive in a shapeless housedress, sat torpidly at her kitchen table, sipping tea and doing her best to sound the way the mother of a murdered child should. But after six and a half years, her sorrow had turned to dull acceptance. At the request of the cameramen, she stared mournfully at a framed portrait of Grace and dabbed at her eyes with a handkerchief. But her eyes remained dry.

Even her outrage seemed strangely perfunctory. When a reporter showed her an old police photograph of Fish, she glanced at it briefly before saying mechanically, "That dirty bum. I wish I had him here so I could get my hands on him."

Meanwhile, in the living room, her spindly, soft-spoken husband leaned forward in a fake-leather arm-chair and described the day of Grace's abduction again and again, as though it were a story that he couldn't quite get himself to believe. He, too, displayed no strong emotions, though he seemed less like a person who had passed beyond grief than one who had been stunned into a permanent state of bewilderment by it.

While the reporters scribbled and the flashbulbs popped, he kept repeating the same words. "It seemed all right to let her go," he said in a voice only slightly louder than a whisper. "He seemed like such a decent man."

Sometime around 1:00 A.M., Detective King showed up to drive Mr. Budd and Edward (by now a powerfully built young man of twenty-four) down to police head-quarters to identify the suspect. On their way back downtown, King stopped to pick up Willie Korman. King wanted Edward's friend there as an additional eyewitness.

Mrs. Budd, who had proven herself unreliable at providing a positive identification, was left behind with her youngest daughter Beatrice, now eleven years old.

At headquarters, King and the others—accompanied by the throng of reporters who had followed them there from the Budds' place—proceeded upstairs to the Missing Persons Bureau. There, before the closed door of Captain Stein's office, King took Edward by the arm. "Go in there, Eddie. See if you can find the man that took your sister."

Eddie opened the door and stepped inside the room. As many as a score of police officers were milling around (including Sergeants Hammill and Sheridan, who had arrived from Westchester with their cartonful of evidence shortly after midnight). A few of the officers were standing beside a desk, examining the contents of a small leather satchel, which—as far as Eddie could see—seemed to be stuffed with old magazine and newspaper clippings.

Spotting the young man, several of the officers moved away from a desk they were blocking from Edward's view. There, sitting in a straight-backed chair behind the desk, was a hollow-cheeked old man with a drooping gray moustache and melancholy eyes. Edward's own eyes blazed.

"It's him!" he cried. Shoving past several of the police officers, he lunged at the old man, shouting, "You old bastard! Dirty son of a bitch!"

Fish gazed up impassively while several of the officers grabbed Edward by the arms and wrestled him out of the room.

A few moments later, Grace Budd's father entered the room.

He stood in the doorway for a moment, glancing around. Then he walked straight over to the old man and stood before him.

The hat in his hands trembled slightly, and his Adam's apple bobbed in his throat. Fish looked up at him expressionlessly.

"Don't you know me?" Albert Budd finally asked in a quivering voice.

"Yes," Fish said mildly. "You're Mr. Budd."

"And you're the man who came to my home as a guest and took my little girl away," said Mr. Budd. His voice broke and, for the first time that evening, his eyes filled with tears. He put a hand over his eyes and began to cry silently. Detective King, who had followed him into the office, placed an arm around his shoulder and led him from the room.

By that time, Fish's police record had been dug out of the files. As it turned out, he had been in trouble with the law before. His record went all the way back to 1903, when he'd spent sixteen months in Sing Sing on a grand larceny charge. That the old reprobate had a long criminal history came as no surprise to his captors. What did surprise and dismay them was the discovery that Fish had been arrested no less than six times since the Budd abduction on charges ranging from petty larceny to vagrancy to sending obscene literature through the mail.

Three of those arrests had occurred within twelve weeks of the kidnapping. The first, for trying to pass a bad $250 check, had taken place only six weeks after Fish had taken Grace Budd from her home. And in each case, the charges against Fish had been dismissed.

King could only shake his head in wonderment. He'd spent six and a half years tracking a shadowy criminal all across America. And in the meantime, the man he was hunting had been in the hands of the New York City police no less than half a dozen times. And then simply let go.

Fish was booked and placed in the detention pen at police headquarters to await his arraignment on kidnapping and murder charges, scheduled for the next afternoon at the Jefferson Market Court. By this time, the events of the day seemed to have gotten to the old man. Though he hadn't slept in twenty-four hours, he kept circling his cell, tapping his forehead with his fingertips and mumbling incoherently. At around 4:30 A.M., a sandwich was passed through the bars of his cell, but Fish seemed not to notice it and left it untouched.

In the meantime, the newsmen covering the case had managed to track down several members of Fish's family, including his thirty-five-year-old son, Albert Jr., who had shared an apartment with his father the previous summer until the old man's behavior had grown intolerably bizarre.

At daybreak, the younger Albert, who was living in Astoria, Queens, was awakened by a bunch of reporters who informed him of his father's arrest. The son's response was striking. "The old skunk," he said bitterly. "I knew something like this would happen sooner or later."

When the reporters pressed him to elaborate, he explained that, during the months he and his father lived together, the old man had shown signs of extremely disturbed behavior. Often he would wake up in the middle of the night "screaming terribly." At other times "he would take off his clothes and whip himself." "Once," the younger Fish went on, "a woman said he had taken her little girl into an empty apartment and removed his clothes." Albert Jr. made a disgusted gesture with his hand. "I want nothing to do with him, and I won't do anything to help him."

While the reporters scribbled frantically, the younger Fish thought for a moment, then asked, "Say, what was the name of the girl he murdered?"

Several voices answered at the same time. "Budd. Grace Budd."

Albert Fish, Jr., gaped. "My God," he exclaimed, shaking his head. "My God. That's the name he used to scream out in his sleep."

24

With these words the wicked Wolf leaped upon
Little Red Riding Hood and gobbled her up.

CHARLES PERRAULT,
"Little Red Riding Hood"

Early Friday morning, December 14, Sergeant Jerome Hogan of the Greenburgh Police Department, along with fellow officers Theodore Newman and William Moore, set out for Wisteria Cottage, the trunk of their squad car loaded with shovels and picks. By the time they pulled up at the house at around 8:30 A.M., a large crowd of townspeople, mostly male, had already assembled.

There were schoolboys in beanies, teens in woolen caps, middle-aged men wearing topcoats and fedoras. Some were gathered in clusters, shoulders hunched against the cold. Others roamed the property in search of clues and souvenirs. A group of newsmen, some from local papers, others from the big-city dailies, were milling about, notebooks and cameras at the ready.

Tools in hand, Hogan, Moore and Newman strode uphill about a hundred feet north of the house and began digging behind the stone wall. Within a short time, they were joined by Sergeants Hammill and Sheridan of the Missing Persons Bureau, who had just driven up from Manhattan. Dr. Amos Squire, the Westchester County medical examiner, arrived a little after 9:00. By then, Hogan and the others had already turned up a substantial pile of bones.

Squire inspected each of them carefully, taking measurements and making notes. By 9:30, the diggers had uncovered eleven vertebrae, plus assorted bones from the pelvis, thighs, lower legs, upper arms, and hands.

The size and state of the bones left no doubt in Squire's mind that they were the remains of a prepubescent. And it was equally clear to him that the child had been the victim of a savage act of violence. One of the lumbar vertebrae—a piece of the lower spine—was scored with a deep groove, as though it had been hacked with a sharp implement.

Sergeant Hogan was dispatched to a nearby bungalow belonging to a woman named Thornton. A short while later, he returned with a wooden picnic basket. Squire carefully laid the bones in the basket, then handed it to Officer Moore, who carried it by the handle while the rest of the men continued their search.

Standing there in the woods, holding the picnic basket packed with the little girl's bones, the grim-faced policeman made a weirdly incongruous sight. A child coming upon the scene might well have imagined that he was witnessing the recovery of Little Red Riding Hood's remains after the Big Bad Wolf had finished with her.

And after all, he wouldn't have been so far from the truth.

While the digging continued in Westchester, Albert Fish was being grilled once again, this time under the hot glare of klieg lights.

Shortly after 9:00 A.M., the withered old man—looking even more haggard and shabby than usual after his long, sleepless night—was taken from the detention pen to the lineup room and led onto the brightly lit platform. The room was packed with police and other law enforcement officials, including Captain McQuillan of the Greenburgh Police Department and Westchester District Attorney Frank Coyne, who had driven down to Manhattan together first thing that morning. Also jamming the room were a mob of reporters and even a scattering of celebrities who had risen early so as not to miss the show.

Among the notables in the audience were Dr. Allan

Roy Dafoe—the simple country doctor who had been catapulted to international fame as the caretaker of Canada's Dionne quintuplets—and Mrs. Alfred E. Smith, wife of the former New York governor. Their presence was a sign of the sensational interest that Fish had already begun to generate less than twenty-four hours after his arrest. Before long, as the full extent of the old man's monstrosity was revealed in the press, his notoriety would spread nationwide.

This time Captain Thomas Dugan of the Homicide Division did the questioning. "Why did you take the Budd girl away and murder her?" he began by asking.

Blinking his watery blue eyes under the blazing lights, Fish stood on his tiptoes and spoke into the microphone. "I don't know," he said. "It just occurred to me." Even amplified, his voice was so soft that the audience had to strain to hear his answer.

"Why did you kill her?" Dugan repeated.

"I didn't intend to kill her. I intended to take her brother, Edward."

"Did you have any trouble with the Budd family?" The crowded room was hushed. In the brief pauses between Dugan's questions, the scratch of the reporters' pens was clearly audible.

"I never had any trouble with the Budd family, nor did I ever hear of the Budd family before this."

After having Fish run through the details of the kidnapping, Dugan asked him if he'd ever had "anything to do with any other children."

"I never had anything to do with another child," said Fish without hesitation.

Dugan asked him once again why he had killed Grace Budd. Fish gave a small, almost imperceptible shrug. "The temptation just came over me. That's all I can say. I can't account for it. I don't understand it."

The interrogation went on for another few minutes, then Detective King escorted Fish off the little stage and hurried him out of the room.

As the spectators headed for the exit, the newsmen swarmed around the luminaries, asking for their responses. They were particularly interested in Dr. Dafoe's professional opinion of the mousy-looking little killer. Dafoe thought for a moment, then pronounced Fish "a study." He declined to offer any further diagnosis, explaining that psychology was outside his domain.

Fish was led directly from the lineup to Captain Stein's office, where, at 9:45 A.M., he made his fifth and final confession. His interrogators on this occassion were Captain McQuillan and District Attorney Coyne. A stenographer named Monroe Block transcribed the statement.

For the most part, Fish added nothing new to the story he had been telling since his capture. He did reveal that his familiarity with Westchester County, and specifically with the area around Irvington, dated back to 1917, when he had been hired to do a painting job for the Second Presbyterian Church in Tarrytown. Though he was strictly a journeyman painter, not an artist, he had been permitted to paint some angels on the church ceiling. The memory of that accomplishment seemed to fill Fish with pride.

Indeed, it had already become clear to the investigators that, incredible as it seemed, religion occupied an important place in the old man's life. Coyne in particular appeared deeply troubled by the disparity between Fish's beliefs and the monstrous criminality of his behavior. He kept pressing Fish on the matter of contrition. Didn't the old man realize that what he had done to the Budd girl was "against the Commandments?"

"Yes, sir," said Fish.

"What are the exact words?"

"Don't kill."

Coyne corrected him. "Thou shalt not kill."

"Yes, sir," Fish agreed. "That's it."

"Do you know the others?" Coyne asked.

"Yes, sir. Thou shall not commit adultery or steal."

"So you knew you sinned when you did it?"

"Yes," said Fish earnestly. "I did." Fish's expressions of remorse were palpably unconvincing. But his tone of voice—flatly indifferent when he spoke of Grace Budd —took on a solemn, even reverential, quality whenever he referred to Scripture.

"And yet you went there prepared to kill?" Coyne continued.

"Yes, sir. I was prepared."

"You had intentions of doing it on the boy?"

"Yes, sir."

"But when you could not get the boy, you took the girl?"

"Yes, sir," Fish replied. Then he said something surprising. "I thought it was a boy for the moment."

This was a striking—even startling—response. But for some reason, neither Coyne nor any of the other investigators seemed to think it worth pursuing. No one asked the bizarre old man to explain what he meant.

Instead, Coyne asked if Fish had "derived a sex pleasure from that?"

Fish was emphatic in his denial. "No, sir. No, sir. No sex at all. I did not outrage her."

It was another jarring remark. Apparently, from Albert Fish's point of view, luring the little girl to an abandoned house in the country, choking her to death, and then dismembering her body with a carving knife and cleaver did not constitute an outrage.

About the dismemberment itself, Coyne pressed Fish for specific details. "Did you have to keep hacking away to get the head off?" he asked at one point.

"Yes."

"Did much blood fall?"

"Yes."

"After you got the head off, what did you do?"

"I cut her through the navel." Fish reached out and pointed to Coyne's belly, just above his belt.

"You noticed the intestines?"

"Yes. It looked like one thing wrapped around another."

The interrogation was over by 10:30 A.M. Emerging from the office, Coyne and the other investigators were besieged by reporters, who pelted them with questions.

In spite of Fish's insistence that he had not raped the little girl, Coyne declared that "this is a sex case, clear and simple. The authorities are working on the theory that this man has committed many sex crimes, although he denies sex was a motive in the killing of the Budd girl."

The reporters then turned to Captain Stein. For the first time, he divulged the details of Fish's murderous designs on the Quinn boy and his friend. One reporter asked if there was any news from Wisteria. In fact, there was. Only minutes before, just as the interrogation was drawing to a close, Stein had received a phone call from Sergeant Hammill, informing him of the morning's developments. Dozens of human bones had already been found. The searchers were well on the way to recovering the complete skeleton of the little girl.

Whether any of the bones belonged to other victims as well was a question that no one was yet prepared to answer.

Even as Stein was conferring with the press, more discoveries were being made at Wisteria.

Shortly before eleven, Sergeant Hogan was lifting a bone from the ground when he noticed a small bead embedded in the soil. Digging it out with his fingers, he uncovered sixteen more. They were imitation pearls. Their position made it clear that they had once been strung together into a necklace. Grace Budd had been wearing just such a necklace on the morning of her disappearance.

Shortly afterward, police officers searching through the woods behind Wisteria Cottage came upon several pairs of shoes. At first, the discovery seemed to confirm the growing suspicion that Fish had used the isolated house as a murder farm. Only after a neighbor came forward and identified the shoes as discarded trash did investigators learn that, for many years, the property had served as a local dump.

By that time, however, the ramshackle outhouse had been torn down and the fetid pit beneath it excavated by Officer Newman. There, half-buried in the muck, lay two moldering shoes, exactly matching the description of the ones worn by Grace on the day of her murder.

As noon approached, the hunt for more evidence moved into the house itself. Searching the upstairs bedroom where Grace had been strangled and butchered, Dr. Gilbert Dalldorf, chief toxicologist at nearby Grasslands Hospital, discovered a large splotch of brown on the floorboards and a spray of suspicious brown clots on the wall nearby. While Dalldorf scraped a sample of the clotted matter into a test tube, officers ripped up a section of the discolored floor. Later that afternoon, the boards were shipped off to Dalldorf's lab for analysis.

Meanwhile, two levels below, a second party of police officers was busily tearing up the basement floor. Earlier, Dr. Amos Squire had ordered a single board removed at random, on the theory that—as he explained to reporters—"a man such as Fish would be apt to commit more murders." And what better place to stash the bodies than underneath the basement floor? Sure enough, when the floorboard was pried up and a flashlight beamed into the darkness, Squire saw a bone.

Armed with crowbars and picks, the officers immediately set about ripping up the rest of the floor. No one could say, of course, how many corpses might be down there. But Squire was convinced that more human remains would be found. It seemed too coincidental that—as he told reporters—he would "casually lift one floorboard and find a bone."

"We will take no chances," Dr. Squire declared. "In view of Fish's confession, there is no telling what else he has done of a criminal nature to which he has not confessed. That he wanted to kill others is evident in the fact that he intended to slay Edward Budd, the child's brother, and changed his mind only when he saw the little girl."

The possibility of Fish's involvement in other crimes was being explored back in Manhattan, too. Right after his questioning by McQuillan and Coyne, Fish had been taken to the Jefferson Market Court and arraigned before Magistrate Adolph Stern, who ordered him held without bail. Since Grace Budd had been kidnapped in Manhattan and murdered in Westchester, the question of where —and for which crime—Fish would be tried remained temporarily unresolved.

As soon as Fish stepped out of the courtroom, he was mobbed by reporters and cameramen. Handcuffed to Detective King, the old man obligingly posed for pictures, while the newsmen bombarded him with questions about other unsolved child-snatchings. "Well boys," the old man said mildly. "You might as well accuse me of all of them. You can't do me any more damage."

It wasn't much of an answer, and the newspapermen kept at him, calling out the names of the missing. One name in particular kept coming up again and again—that of Billy Gaffney, the four-year-old boy who had vanished from his Brooklyn tenement the year before Grace Budd's abduction.

After a few minutes, King cut the impromptu press conference short and led Fish back to headquarters. Meanwhile, attorneys from the Manhattan D.A.'s office were conferring with their counterparts from Westchester about the jurisdiction issue. Shortly before noon, Assistant D.A. James Neary met with reporters to announce the decision.

Fish would be moved to the Tombs and held there until a murder indictment was returned against him—probably on the following Tuesday, December 18, when the Westchester Grand Jury was expected to reconvene. At that point, Fish would be surrendered to Westchester authorities. Neary expected that Fish would probably go on trial sometime around the first of the year, though the date might be delayed by the mental examinations which the old man would clearly have to undergo.

Several reporters wanted to know if Fish had ever been seen by psychiatrists before. Neary confirmed that the old man had spent several brief periods under observation following previous arrests. On each of those occasions, Neary explained, Fish had been judged sane—perverted but sane.

By then, Fish was back in his cell in the detention pen, awaiting transfer to the Tombs. Shortly before noon, a Nassau County police inspector named Harold King (no relation to Fish's nemesis) arrived to question the prisoner about a pair of sensational, unsolved murder cases on Long Island.

The first was the kidnapping and killing of a sixteen-year-old high school girl named Mary O'Connell, whose bludgeoned body had been discovered in a lonely stretch of woods near her Far Rockaway home in February, 1932. The second was the murder of a man named Benjamin B. Collings, who had been slain onboard his yacht on Long Island Sound in 1931. King interviewed Fish for nearly an hour, but all he got from the old man was a string of increasingly sullen denials.

After Inspector King's departure, Captain Stein and a few of his men spent some time hammering away at Fish about the disappearance of Billy Gaffney. Fish, sitting hunched on a wooden stool, simply shook his head and protested his innocence. But the investigators were unconvinced. They had, in fact, begun to suspect that Fish was responsible not only for the Gaffney crime but also for another, older atrocity as well—a case which still rankled in the memory of the New York City police, since it had been committed against one of their own. This was the 1926 murder of eight-year-old Francis McDonnell, the Staten Island patrolman's son who had been savagely attacked and strangled in the woods near his home.

By 4:15 P.M., the woods around Wisteria Cottage were growing dark. Most of Grace Budd's skeleton had been located by then, and the searchers had turned their attention to the recovery of the tools Fish had used to dismember the little girl's corpse.

A man named Robert Walton, one of the dozens of locals who had spent the day tramping around the property, found the first of Fish's "implements of hell" —the curve-handled compass saw, its tapered blade corroded with rust. Shortly afterward, another Greenburgh man, a trucker named Jerry Reale, showed up at Wisteria with an interesting story. About two years earlier, while strolling through the woods behind the abandoned house, he had come upon an old cleaver with a rotted wooden handle. Deciding that the tool was beyond salvaging, he had pitched it into the underbrush. Reale pointed to the place where he had tossed it. Sure enough, as soon as the police began searching the area, they came upon the rusty remains of the cleaver.

That left only one more tool to find. But in spite of the number and diligence of the searchers, no one could turn up the butcher knife. Finally, Captain McQuillan, who had arrived from Manhattan earlier in the afternoon, decided to try burning off the underbrush. A fire was lit and immediately began burning out of control. By the time the Greenburgh Fire Department arrived and extinguished the blaze, it was too dark to continue the search.

McQuillan took charge of the evidence. After posting some of his men around the property for the night, he returned to Greenburgh police headquarters with the two rusted tools and the picnic basket full of bones.

Sergeant Hogan was sent around the corner to Butler's grocery for a larger container. A short while later, he came back carrying a shipping carton imprinted with the name of a popular brand of canned beans. McQuillan carefully transferred the little girl's remains into the grocery carton and locked the evidence in his closet.

The picnic basket was shaken clean of bone chips, pebbles, and dirt and returned to Mrs. Thornton, with the thanks of the Greenburgh police.

Suppertime was approaching, but back in Manhattan, Detective King hadn't relaxed his exertions. Specifically, he was searching for a piece of evidence that would help identify the skeletal remains found at Wisteria as Grace Budd's. At around 6:30 P.M., he found it.

Digging through the records of the dental clinic at New York Hospital, where Grace had been treated the year before her disappearance, he came upon the little girl's records. The chart indicated the position of several teeth which had been filled during her visit to the dispensary. At a glance, King could see that the fillings matched the ones in the skull that Captain Stein had brought back from Wisteria.

By that time, reporters covering the case already recognized that King was the true hero of the story, the indefatigable manhunter who had refused to rest until the Budd criminal had been tracked down and brought to justice. At a news conference to announce the discovery of the dental chart, Commissioner Valentine was asked if King could expect any official recognition for his work on the case.

The commissioner confirmed that King could look forward to a promotion from second- to first-grade detective. The higher rank would mean a pay hike of $800 per year, bringing King's annual salary up to $4,000.

King had one final task to perform that day. He was one of the officers who accompanied Fish when the old man was transferred to the Tombs.

Arriving at the prison shortly before midnight, Fish was stripped of his necktie, belt, and shoelaces. A round-the-clock guard was posted outside his cell to make sure that he did not inflict any harm on himself. The police, of course, were thinking about suicide. At that point, no one knew anything about the other far more extravagant, if less fatal, forms of self-abuse that were among the old man's dearest pleasures.

25

~~~~~~~~~~~~~~~~

*"Budd Murder Mystery Solved . . .
Justice Always Wins!"*

Page One, *New York Daily Mirror,*
Dec. 16, 1934

From the moment it broke on December 14, the Fish
story kept New York City spellbound with horror. By
Friday afternoon, the news of the arrest was splashed
across the front page of every paper in town, and for the
following two weeks, the dailies covered each new development in lavish detail.

The *Mirror* and *Daily News* in particular served up a
nonstop feast of juicy revelations, seasoned with the
tabloids' own special blend of prurience and moral
indignation. The *Mirror* did an especially loving job of
dishing out lurid tidbits for its readers' delectation and
never hesitated to spice up the facts when the truth
wasn't zesty enough for its sensationalistic standards.
Fish's statement that he had strangled Grace Budd
slowly, for example, was transformed into the even more
horrific but completely fictitious admission that "It must
have taken me fully an hour to strangle her once I got my
hands on her throat."

The *Mirror* scribes were particularly inventive in coming up with lurid labels for the decrepit old killer. In the
course of a single story, Fish was described as the "Ogre
of Murder Lodge," the "Vampire Man," the "Orgiastic
Fiend," the "Modern Bluebeard," the "Aged Thrill-
Killer," and the "Werewolf of Wisteria." The articles

themselves were written in an equally inflammatory style: "Out of the slime of the sadistic butchery of Grace Budd by the benign-looking Albert Howard Fish," began a typical piece, "there emerged last night the hint of an even greater horror. A horror of multiple killings. Revealing a new type of Jack the Ripper . . . in the guise of a kindly old gentleman."

Compared to the visual aids which accompanied the stories, however, the writing was a model of cool objectivity. On Saturday, December 15, for example, the *Mirror* ran an artist's graphic rendition of the Budd murder. Headlined "HOW THE THRILL VULTURE POUNCED ON HIS COWERING PREY," the drawing was a step-by-step reconstruction of the killing, culminating in a close-up of the little girl's strangulation. In a bow to the public's sensibilities, Fish was shown fully clothed. The *Mirror*, after all, was a family newspaper.

On another day, the paper printed a sequence of photographs that traced the route Fish and Grace had taken on their trip to Wisteria. Each photograph was accompanied by a breathless caption that did its best to summon up the titillating horrors of that day. "What were you doing on Sunday, May 28, 1928?" began the caption under the first picture in the series, a shot of the Budd's old apartment building on West 15th Street. "On that day, Albert Fish was killing little Grace Budd!" The other landmarks in the series were the "el" at 14th Street ("Perhaps you used the station that day, rubbed shoulders with them . . ."), the Sedgwick Avenue Station ("Perhaps you were on that very train. Were you? The horrible ogre sat beside the little girl, planning his horrible crime"), Worthington Station ("Fish left his bundle on the train. She went after it, carrying her own death weapons!"), and, of course, Wisteria Cottage ("The old man went inside, leaving the little girl out of doors picking flowers. When he called her, she went trustfully to him, and he killed her").

The *Mirror* also tried to take as much credit as it could for Fish's capture. In a sidebar headlined "FIRST AGAIN!" it quoted Walter Winchell's fortuitous prediction of November 2. It also reprinted the June 4 fleet photograph of the two sailors and their dates, claiming (with some justification) that the picture had ultimately led to Fish's arrest.

The *Daily News*, though less melodramatic than its competitor, also tricked out the truth for the sake of added color. It was the *News*, for example, which first promulgated the fiction that Fish—whose creative aptitude consisted of an ability to slap several coats of paint on an apartment wall—had been known in his younger days as "a pleasant, affable artist struggling to support his wife and five children. Cubism was an enthusiasm of his at the time and he often asked friends to admire the products of his queer artistic fetish." Clearly, as far as the *News* was concerned, a taste for cubism was itself a symptom of incipient madness and a possible precursor of child-murder.

Though the *News* avoided the horror-movie metaphors favored by the *Mirror*, it lost no time in suggesting that Fish was very probably a mass murderer of historic dimensions, who had slain untold victims in the deserted precincts of "Old Wisteria House." The paper was also the first to disclose the cannibalistic content of Fish's letter to the Budds. The old man, reported the *News*, had been driven to kidnap the little girl by a sudden "yearning for the thrill of eating human flesh and drinking human blood," a desire which had come over him "as a result of reading of cannibalistic practices in the Orient."

In one instance, however, the *News* did demonstrate an unusual degree of self-restraint. Though the paper was the first to draw a connection between Fish and the illustrious family he claimed to be part of, it never made specific mention of the old man's namesake—U.S. Congressman Hamilton Fish. Instead, the paper simply asserted that Fish was "descended of Revolutionary stock."

Like the *Mirror*, the *News* tried to find parallels for Fish among the "most bestial" criminals in history. The *Mirror* came up with Bluebeard and Jack the Ripper. But the association made by Jack Alexander of the *News* was much more interesting—and, as it turned out, apt. Ranking Fish with "the worst human monsters of modern times," Alexander could think of only one comparable case: that of the German psychopath Fritz Haarmann, the notorious "Vampire of Hanover."

Born to a working-class couple in 1879, Haarmann was a sullen and slow-witted child whose favorite pastime was dressing up as a girl. At seventeen, he was committed to the Hildesheim asylum after being arrested for child-molesting. The examining doctor declared him "incurably feeble-minded." Six months later, he escaped to Switzerland and gradually made his way back to Hanover.

For a while, he attempted to lead a more settled life, working with his father in a cigar factory, getting engaged to a young woman he had impregnated. This period of relative normalcy didn't last. Haarmann's ill-tempered father detested his son. And Haarmann's baby was stillborn. Haarmann deserted his fiancé and ran off to join the Jäger regiment in Alsace. His commanding officer declared him a "born soldier."

Back in Hanover in 1903, Haarmann launched into a life of petty crime. Throughout his early twenties, he was in and out of jail for various offenses, ranging from pocket-picking to burglary. He spent World War I locked up in prison.

Released in 1918, he returned to Hanover and joined a postwar smuggling ring that trafficked in black-market meat, among other commodities. Haarmann also functioned as a police stool pigeon, a sideline which afforded him protection for his illicit activities. In 1919, however, after being caught by police *in flagrante delicto* with a young boy, Haarmann was shipped off to prison again.

After his release nine months later, Haarmann commenced his career of unparalleled depravity. Living in Hanover's seamy Old Quarter, he fell under the sexual thrall of a handsome male prostitute and petty thief named Hans Grans. Together, the two systematically set about preying on the young male refugees that were flooding into the war-ravaged city. Though Haarmann was ultimately charged with twenty-seven murders, it seems likely that he was responsible for at least fifty. The method he employed to kill his victims was always the same.

After luring a hungry boy to his rooms, Haarmann would feed him a meal, then overpower him (often with Grans's assistance) and fall upon his throat, chewing through the flesh until he had nearly separated the head from the body. Generally, he would experience a sexual climax while battening on the boy.

Afterward, Haarmann and Gans would butcher the body and dispose of the flesh by peddling it as steak at the Schieber Market, across from the Hanover railway station. During the five years that he engaged in these atrocities, Haarmann himself subsisted largely on the meat of his victims. The victim's clothes would also be sold and the inedible portions of his body dumped in the Leine canal.

Gradually, Haarmann fell under suspicion. A woman who had purchased one of his black market "steaks" became convinced that it was human flesh and turned it over to the authorities. After inspecting it closely, a police analyst declared that it was pork. But as the number of missing boys mounted, the police suspected Haarmann and began to investigate. In May 1924, several skulls were found on the banks of the canal. Several weeks later, some boys playing near the spot stumbled upon a whole sackful of human bones. Two detectives from Berlin were called in on the case. Searching Haarmann's rooms, they discovered bundles of boys' clothing. The young son of Haarmann's landlady was wearing a coat that belonged to one of the missing boys.

In the end, Haarmann confessed. He was tried at the Hanover Assizes in early December, 1924, found guilty, and condemned to death. Gans received a life sentence that was later commuted to twelve years. At Haarmann's trial, one of his neighbors, an elderly lady, testified that he had once given her some bones and suggested she make soup with them. She did as he proposed, but dumped out the soup without tasting it because the bones looked "too white." Her suspicions saved her from unwitting cannibalism.

While awaiting execution, the forty-six-year-old Haarmann produced a written confession in which he recounted, with undisguised relish, the details of his killings and the pleasure he derived from committing them. At his own request, he was beheaded with a sword in the city marketplace. After the decapitation, his brain was removed from his skull and shipped to Goettingen University for study.

Comparing Fish to Haarmann, the *Daily News* pronounced that, of the two "lust slayers," Fish was the more "baffling" case. Haarmann, after all, had come from a disadvantaged background, whereas Fish was (supposedly) descended from an old and distinguished American family. Moreover, Haarmann was not only an epileptic but also a homosexual—a trait which, the *News* implied, went a long way toward explaining his penchant for mass murder and cannibalism. Fish, on the other hand, was "the father of six children and the grandfather of many more."

Nevertheless, according to the reporter for the *News,* the "mousy soft-spoken" Fish and "the postwar German werewolf" were two of a kind. And in fact there *was* a connection between Haarmann and Fish, more of a connection than the *News* reporter could have possibly known about, since no one was aware of it at the time besides a handful of investigators from the Missing Persons Bureau.

Fish was an inveterate clipper of newspaper and magazine articles dealing with subjects that excited his diseased imagination. Searching his rooms immediately after his arrest, detectives had discovered a large cache of these clippings, some stored in an old leather satchel, others squirreled away in various hiding places around the apartment—under his mattress, on cupboard shelves, beneath the rugs. Carrying this bizarre collection back to headquarters, the investigators had made a careful examination of it and had catalogued each of the items.

There was a newspaper clipping about the marriage of two nudist couples in Chicago and another, datelined

Hamden, Connecticut, about the arrest of several nude sunbathers on a disorderly conduct charge. There was a story about the forced sterilization of 325 people in Berlin. Another article from Europe, datelined Lille, France, dealt with a scientific operation that had transformed a woman into a man. One small packet of articles, all of them reports of various kidnappings, was held together by fourteen sewing needles threaded through the paper.

And then there was another, much larger sheath of clippings, carefully scissored from various newspapers and neatly bound together with a piece of twine. When investigators undid the string and began reading these articles, they discovered that Fish had cut out and saved every news story he could find containing details of Fritz Haarmann's enormities.

26

I must not dwell upon the fearful repast which immediately ensued. . . . Let it suffice to say that, having in some measure appeased the raging thirst which consumed us by the blood of the victim, and having by common consent taken off the hands, feet, and head, throwing them together with the entrails into the sea, we devoured the rest of the body, piecemeal. . . .

EDGAR ALLAN POE, *The Narrative of Arthur Gordon Pym of Nantucket*

For the next few days, investigators in both New York City and Westchester continued to probe a possibility which the tabloids were already trumpeting as established fact—that Albert Fish, the "Ogre of Old Wisteria," had murdered untold victims in the "charnel chambers" of the abandoned house and buried their remains around the premises.

By the time the first carloads of Greenburgh police arrived at Wisteria Cottage early Saturday morning, the property was already aswarm with sightseers, eager for a close-up glimpse of the notorious Westchester "death lodge." Before very long, traffic along Mountain Road and the nearby Sawmill River Parkway had become so snarled that a special squad of officers was dispatched from White Plains to keep the cars moving and prevent everyone except neighborhood residents from parking near the crime scene.

Meanwhile, under Dr. Squire's supervision, Sergeant

Hogan and several of his fellow officers spent the morning tearing up the rest of the basement floor and digging in the hard-packed earth underneath. By lunchtime, they had managed to exhume an additional thirty bones, ranging in size from one to eight inches. Suspecting that more might be hidden behind the cellar's big log-burning fireplace, the officers began dismantling it brick by brick. Outside, another group of officers worked steadily at pumping out a pair of wells, each eight feet deep, under the theory that they were a perfect place for Fish to dispose of corpses.

Interviewed by reporters late in the morning, Dr. Squire admitted that he could not be sure whether the remains found in the cellar came from humans or animals. If the bones did turn out to be human, they would represent incontestable proof that Fish had slain other victims besides Grace Budd, since the little girl's entire skeleton had already been recovered. The morning's finds, Squire explained, would be shipped off immediately to professors of comparative anatomy at Columbia University for classification.

The *Mirror,* however, deemed it unnecessary to wait for an expert opinion before announcing, on the front page of its weekend edition, that evidence of "new ogre deaths" had been unearthed in the "haunted charnel house" in Westchester. The thirty bones "dug out of two shallow graves" in the cellar "represented an almost complete pelvic frame, hip joint, three shattered shin bones, innumerable sections of vertebrae, and a miscellaneous assortment of other sections of human anatomy"—clear-cut proof, the *Mirror* proclaimed, that the "wizened housepainter" had used Wisteria Cottage as a site for "weird torture rites" and "cannibalistic orgies."

Squire's expressions of uncertainty underwent a significant alteration in the tabloid, which neglected to mention the possibility that the bones might have come from animals. The only question in the medical examiner's mind, according to the *Mirror,* was "whether the skeletons were those of men, women, or children."

The photographs accompanying the story were every bit as sensationalistic as the text. One shot, of several investigators examining a length of cord dangling limply from a ceiling pipe in the basement, was headlined, "DID HANGING FIGURE IN FISH'S PLAN?"

Another, more unsettling picture showed the skeletal remains of a young child, half-buried in weeds. This was a police photograph of an unidentified victim, four to six years old, whose corpse had been discovered the previous summer in Darien, Connecticut. A laborer working in an overgrown field about a thousand feet from the Boston Post Road, not far from a bus stop, had stumbled upon the bones.

The child's head, which was lying a few feet away from the rest of the body, appeared to have been severed with a sharp instrument. No clothing had been recovered at the scene. The remains had been submitted to specialists at the Yale University medical lab, who had been able to determine the approximate age of the victim but not the sex.

The caption explained that Fish had become the prime suspect in this case, too. The headline above the photograph conveyed the same information in a far shriller and more characteristic form: "WAS THIS ANOTHER WERE-WOLF VICTIM?"

Two Darien officials—Henry J. Case, chairman of the police board, and Detective Amos Anderson—were hoping to answer that question when they drove down to Manhattan on Saturday afternoon to interview Fish in the Tombs. But the old man, who could be either forthcoming with authorities or sulkily uncooperative, depending on his mood, simply shook his head in response to their inquiries. After a frustrating hour, Case and Anderson turned the interrogation over to Detective King and Captain Stein, who finally managed to pry some information out of Fish.

Back in police headquarters later that day, King informed reporters that, though Fish stoutly denied his guilt, he had admitted to being in Darien the previous spring. He had only gone there, however, to "visit friends." All he knew about the dead child, the old man insisted, was what he had read in the papers.

By Saturday afternoon, reporters delving into Fish's past had managed to locate his estranged wife, Anna, the mother of his six children. Living in Astoria, Queens, with a man named John Straube—by whom she'd had three more children—the pleasant-faced, gray-haired woman heard the news about Fish as though she'd been expecting it for years. Nothing that her former husband did would surprise her—she was prepared to believe anything about the old man. Had Fish ever behaved strangely while they were married, the reporters wanted to know? Mrs. Straube thought for a while before answering. "He used to beat himself with a whip," she replied, then refused to say more.

Before the day was out, another of Fish's wives would turn up—a sixty-four-year-old housemaid from Waterloo, Iowa, named Estelle Wilcox, who had been married to Fish for two months in early 1930. They had met through a matrimonial agency and had lived together for only one week when Fish began placing classified ads in the local newspaper, offering work to young girls. "I knew he didn't have any work for them, but I didn't know what to think," Mrs. Wilcox told newsmen, her voice beginning to break. "I think he was crazy." She started to weep, her tears called up partly by the memories of her brief, awful life with Fish and partly by the unwelcome publicity that her relationship with him had suddenly brought on her. Fish had disappeared after a few weeks, Estelle explained, and she'd never heard from him again, nor had she made the slightest effort to locate him. "I was glad he was gone," she said through her tears. "I don't care what happens to him."

Meanwhile, in an effort to establish conclusively that the skeleton found at Wisteria Cottage was Grace Budd's, detectives from the Missing Persons Bureau, King included, continued their search for the dentist who had filled three of the girl's teeth at the dispensary in 1927. In the view of the authorities, this individual was a key to establishing the corpus delecti, since he could positively identify the dental work in the skull. But, though Captain Stein made a public appeal to all the dentists in the city, no one had yet come forward by the end of Saturday.

The Greenburgh police were back on the job first thing Sunday morning, continuing their search for more human remains and for the still-missing butcher knife. By late morning, the two wells had been drained and excavated. Five additional bones of indeterminate origin had been dug out of the muck. With typical moderation, the *Mirror* lost no time in announcing the discovery of another "ogre bone pile," dredged from the wells behind "the charnel house where Fish dissected the still-quivering body of the hapless Budd child." According to the paper, the new finds consisted of four human ribs and a woman's kneecap that had "apparently been hacked in two by an axe or a cleaver." "WOMAN'S BONES IN MURDER WELL!" blared the headline. "HOW MANY DID FISH KILL?"

As reporters pursued their own excavations, digging deeper into Fish's past, new and increasingly bizarre revelations came to light. Fish's twenty-one-year-old son, John—whose monthly paychecks from the C.C.C. camp in North Carolina had helped lead to his father's capture—described the elder Fish as a "firebug" who derived unnatural gratification from the sights, sounds, and smells of burning houses. "The screams of endangered humans, the shrieking of sirens, and the clanging of bells were said to awaken 'sex impulses' in Fish's twisted brain," reported one newsman. According to John Fish, the old man had to be forcibly restrained on several occasions from setting fire to tenements. Fire Marshal Thomas P. Brophy announced that he would order an immediate search of his records for any unsolved arson cases that might be connected to Fish.

Even more disquieting were the disclosures of a woman named Helen Karlson, who presented herself at police headquarters on Sunday morning with a most interesting story. Mrs. Karlson, a widow, owned a house on 56th Street in Brooklyn, where she lived alone with her two sons. In 1927, she had rented the upstairs rooms of her house to an elderly man and his two sons, whom she knew at first only by their last name—Fish.

In the beginning, the elderly gentleman seemed the soul of kindness. He was particularly attentive to Mrs. Karlson's youngest son, who was seven at the time. "He was always buying him candy and urging me to let him take the boy to the movies," she explained. Mrs. Karlson didn't regard Fish as a danger. On the contrary, "he appeared to be such a harmless old man." Even so, she was reluctant to let her son go off with a relative stranger, particularly since—like so many Brooklyn mothers— she had been deeply unnerved by the Gaffney abduction, a crime which had occurred only a short time before.

Her boarders had been living in the house for almost a month when Mrs. Karlson awoke one morning to find that an envelope had been shoved under her bedroom door. Inside was a handwritten letter of unspeakable vileness. It was signed "Albert." Mrs. Karlson was dumbfounded. She destroyed the letter instantly and didn't speak a word about it to anyone. But after receiving two more such missives, each filthier than the first, she confronted the old man and demanded that he leave.

"He became very angry and abusive," she told the police. "He shook his fist at me and shouted that he would put a curse on me for life."

It was a great relief to Mrs. Karlson when the old man and his sons packed up and left. As soon as they were gone, she went upstairs to clean their rooms. On the floor of the old man's room she discovered the nasty thing that she still couldn't bring herself to discuss without blushing. "A little mess" was the way she described it to the police. And in the attic directly above his room, she found something even more disconcerting—a crudely made wooden paddle, two feet long and studded with nails. It was wrapped inside one of Mrs. Karlson's linen tablecloths. Both the cloth and the paddle were clotted with old blood.

Mrs. Karlson let out a deep breath as she concluded

her story. "It makes me shudder when I think what might have happened to my own son."

Mrs. Karlson's son wasn't the only child to have had a close call with Fish. Indeed, as the weekend progressed, the city seemed to be filled with youngsters who had "narrowly escaped Fish's fiendish clutch" (as the *Mirror* put it).

Mr. and Mrs. Alonzo La Furde, who lived in a house near Wisteria Cottage, trembled with "after-fear" as they told news reporters how, only two months earlier, Fish had tried to lure away their curly-haired little daughter, Marion, by promising to show her "funny pictures" and giving her "huge handfuls of candy and peanuts."

Another young girl who got her name in the news by recalling an encounter with Fish was an eleven-year-old named Mary Little. Seeing Fish's picture in the papers, she suddenly recognized him as the "horrible old man" who had accosted her in 1928, when she was five years old.

"I was playing by the candy store while Mummie stood by the baby carriage," she explained to reporters. "He came up and took hold of my hand. I was frightened because he was such a bent old man. He asked me if I was alone, and I told him no, my mother was over there. Then he looked at her, and I pulled my hand away and ran back to Mummie."

At that point in her recitation, Mrs. Little interrupted with her own recollections of that moment. "Mary kept staring at him, and I asked her what was the matter. Then I noticed him. All hunched up with his hands buried in his pockets, he was. He looked at us and started laughing. It was a horrible, cackling sound."

Little Mary let out a deep sigh. "Oh, what he did to that poor little girl," she said. "If only he had taken the boys. They were bigger and could have fought him. Poor little Gracie."

Marion La Furde and Mary Little were only two of many children who would recall encounters with the hunched, gray-haired "boogey man" in the days to come.

Some of these memories were clearly the product of overheated imaginations, the kinds of fantasies commonly generated by highly publicized crimes. But others were authentic.

One youngster who, by the old man's own admission, had narrowly escaped death was Cyril Quinn, the adolescent boy whom Fish had intended to butcher as a warm-up for the Budd murder. On Sunday, the police announced their plans to bring Quinn down to the Tombs to identify Fish. Another witness scheduled to confront Fish that day was an unnamed nine-year-old girl who had been attacked by an old man near her home on Amsterdam Avenue two years earlier. At the time of the incident, Fish was working as the superintendent of two apartment buildings close to the little girl's home.

Fish was also visited that day by various law enforcement officials, seeking to connect him to virtually every unsolved child murder in the Northeast. Among his interrogators were the Long Island police inspector Harold King, who still seemed convinced of Fish's involvement in the slaying of the fifteen-year-old girl from Massapequa, Mary Ellen O'Connor, and Lieutenant Amos Anderson of Connecticut, who had not given up on his efforts to link Fish to the skeleton of the unknown child discovered in Darien.

Investigators from the Manhattan Missing Persons Bureau also spent time grilling Fish again about the Gaffney case. This time, they had more success. Though Fish continued to maintain his innocence, he did reveal an intriguing fact, which Detective King announced to reporters at a news conference late in the day.

At the time of the Gaffney boy's disappearance, in February, 1927, King said, Fish had been employed as a housepainter by the Brooklyn real estate firm of Wood, Harmon & Co. and was working at a location only a few miles away from the Gaffneys' apartment building on the day the child vanished.

In his free moments, when he wasn't pacing about his cell or being questioned by lawmen, Fish pursued one of the few compulsive activities still permitted him—

writing letters. In the weeks ahead, he would spew out a constant flow of them—to his children, to his lawyers, to prison officials and others.

The first of these letters was to Detective King. Fish seemed to have developed a strange regard for his captor, or perhaps he simply perceived a streak of compassion in King upon which he hoped to play. Whatever the case, when King came to visit him in his cell late Sunday afternoon, Fish passed him an envelope.

King waited until he was back in his office to open it. Inside was a four-page handwritten letter. Seated at his desk, King—a two-pack-a-day smoker—lit a cigarette and began to read. Like many of Fish's letters, this one was a crazy scramble of biographical facts, bizarre self-revelations, and shameless appeals for sympathy:

Dear Mr. King

In 1906 or 7 I lived at 519 Main st, Bridgeport Conn with my wife and 2 childrn. Albert now 35 and Anna 33. They took part in a play at Palis Theatre called Little Orphan Annie. From there we moved to Springfield Mass where I done some painting for Rev Charles F. Slattery rector of Christ P.E. Church. In April or May of 1933 my son Henry drove me in his Car to New Haven, Conn to see a widow who had an ad in Friendship Magazine for a husband. When we got there she had gone to town. . . . During these 4 years I wrote to about 20 widows who claimed to have money but it was all hot air. . . . I write as habit—Just cant seem to stop. A few months after I done that deed I shoved 5 needles into my belly—legs—hip. At times I suffer awful pains. An Ex Ray will show them. Three weeks ago I spilled Alcohol on my behind and then lit a match. I can hardly sit still now. You know as well as I that if I had not written that letter to Mrs. Budd, I would not be in Jail. Had I not lead you to the spot no bones would have been found and I could only be tried for kidnapping. So again I say it was fate, due me for my wrong. Now my dear Mr. King I am going to ask you In Gods Name do this for my poor childrens sake. For my self I ask no mercy. Write to Hon Wm. F. Brunner ask him to get in touch with Hon Hamilton Fish. See if you cant have me tried in N.Y. City on the *kidnapping charge.*

When 5 yrs old I was placed by my mother in St Johns Orphanage Washington D.C. There I learned to lie—beg—steal and saw a lot of things a child of 7 should not see. . . . I hear they are going to take me out to Westchester next week. Suppose I *deny* the killing. I have *signed* no statement *as yet.* You tell me. I only want to live *long enough* to see my poor children at work and out of want. *Misery leads to Crime.* I saw so many boys whipped it took root in my head. I have many hundreds of times whipped and *tortured* myself as marks on my behind will show. . . . the Blessing of Almighty God on you.

> I am
> Albert H. Fish

King read the letter over several times. Clearly, Fish, for all his professed indifference to his own fate, was not eager for a murder trial. He even clung to the desperate and delusional hope that Congressman Hamilton Fish might intercede on his behalf, presumably out of family loyalty. But the parts of the letter that struck King most forcibly were the confessions of self-torture. Could it possibly be true that the old man poured alcohol onto his backside and lit it? And shoved five needles into his own body?

King, of course, was well aware of the fourteen sewing needles that had been threaded through the packet of clippings in the old man's leather satchel. And he knew about something else, too, something which the press hadn't yet gotten wind of.

In searching through Fish's rooms, the police had come upon a leatherbound volume lying on a shelf. Riffling through it, they had found a page with ten more needles stuck into it.

The book was Edgar Allan Poe's *The Narrative of*

DERANGED

Arthur Gordon Pym—a story about a boy who stows away on a whaling ship that is seized by savage mutineers. Eventually, the hero, along with three other survivors, finds himself adrift on the ocean without water or food. In desperation, the four men agree to draw straws. The one who picks the shortest is sacrificed by the others—stabbed in the back, butchered, and devoured in a frenzied blood-feast.

27

"This man is undoubtedly an abnormal individual."

DR. THOMAS S. CUSACK,
consulting psychiatrist to the U.S. Army

The old man hooked his fingers through the wire mesh separating him from the crowd of reporters and pressed his haggard face close to the screen. "I wouldn't lie," he said softly. "My conscience is clear now and I want to keep it that way. I did kill Grace Budd, God help me. I did it on an impulse that I can't understand. But don't you believe those other stories they're telling about me."

It was midmorning on Monday, December 17, and in the visitors' room of the Tombs, enclosed within a coarse chicken-wire screen, Albert Fish was pouring forth a detailed but highly selective autobiography for the benefit of the New York City press.

"I was born May 19, 1870, in Washington, D.C.," he said, speaking slowly enough for the newsmen to copy down his remarks. "We lived on B Street, N.E., between Second and Third. My father was Captain Randall Fish, 32nd-degree Mason, and he is buried in the Grand Lodge grounds of the Congressional cemetery. He was a Potomac River boat captain, running from Washington to Marshall Hall, Virginia. His father and grandfather came from Maine, and they were old English stock.

"My father dropped dead October 15, 1875, in the old Pennsylvania Station where President Garfield was shot, and I was placed in St. John's Orphanage in Washington." The old man paused and let out a theatrical sigh. "I was there till I was nearly nine, and that's where I got started wrong. We were unmercifully whipped. I saw boys doing many things they should not have done.

"I sang in the choir from 1880 to 1884—soprano, at St. John's. In 1894, I came to New York. I was a good painter—interiors or anything.

"I got an apartment and brought my mother up from Washington. We lived at No. 76 West 101st Street, and that's where I met my first wife. After our six children were born, she left me. She took all the furniture and didn't even leave a mattress for the children to sleep on." As he spoke of his children, the old man's watery blue eyes grew noticeably wetter. Extracting a yellowed handkerchief from his pants pocket, he wiped away his tears, then blew his nose loudly.

"I'm worried about my children," he continued after a moment, still sniffling back tears. "You'd think they'd come to visit their old dad in jail, but they haven't. Maybe they haven't got the car fare." He nodded at the reporter from the *Daily News.* "Do you think you could fix it up so they can get Christmas baskets?" he pleaded. "I'll give you their addresses if you want."

Bowed and teary-eyed behind his wire enclosure, Fish might have moved an onlooker to genuine pity—assuming that the onlooker knew nothing at all about the monstrous old man or the nature of his crimes.

"Tell us about the killing," one of the newsmen called out.

Fish lifted a bony hand to his forehead and rubbed. "I've gone through it so many times," he murmured. But the reporters were insistent. They wanted to hear the story from the killer's own lips. And the old man seemed reluctant to disappoint them.

Fish had told the story so often by now that it had begun to sound as formulaic as a fairy tale. He started by describing, once again, how he had led Grace Budd "by her trusting little hand" to the musty old house in Westchester under the pretext of taking her to his niece's birthday party. "I let her play in the yard for a while and then I called her upstairs. I guess it was about four o'clock in the afternoon. I did it then. It was a terrible thing to do. She was such a nice little girl. As soon as I had killed her I would have given my life to have her standing there beside me again.

"But it was too late by then. After I had cut her into three pieces and hid her clothes in a closet, I got away as fast as I could. I went home and took a bath and tried to sleep. But I couldn't. I went up to the zoo in Central Park and wandered around. I slept there in the park for two nights. I couldn't eat. All I could drink was coffee. It stimulated me.

"It wasn't until I went back to Wisteria and put her out behind the wall that I could sleep again.

"They've asked me about a lot of other crimes. I told Detective King and the others that I don't know anything about them. I can't tell what I don't know. I can't lie.

"My conscience is clear," he repeated.

The little man then launched into a self-pitying account of the evil influences that had warped his life. He spoke about his older brother, who had returned home from the navy full of "dirty stories" that had instilled "overpowering urges" in the younger man, urges that had ultimately driven him to commit his awful crime against Grace Budd.

For someone who kept insisting that life meant nothing to him any longer, Fish displayed a remarkable interest in the outcome of his case. "I'm ready to die for my crime," he declared solemnly—then he immediately added, "But do you think I might get charged with second-degree?" On several other occasions during the interview, he interrupted his narrative to ask worriedly, "Do you think they'll give me the chair?"

As Fish rambled on, it became increasingly clear to the reporters that he was doing everything possible to mitigate the monstrous image of himself presented in the press. "Remember, I didn't attack her," he declared during his account of the killing. He reminded them that if it hadn't been for his willingness to lead police to the crime scene, "they wouldn't have had any proof—they wouldn't have found the skull and bones if I hadn't showed them."

He insisted once again that he had slain no one except Grace Budd. "I don't know anything about those other bones they say they've found," he exclaimed. "And cannibalism!" He screwed his face into an expression of exaggerated disgust. "The very thought sickens me."

Fish did admit that, in his imaginings, he had murdered many times. "These lustful thoughts have frequently come over me," he said. "I could see myself killing people. But I never did it, only that once.

"I don't know—I guess I must be crazy," he announced. "Yes, I must be insane. I'm almost sure I am." As he spoke, Albert Fish peered through the spaces in the wire-mesh screen to make sure that the reporters were getting down every word.

As the devious old man clearly knew, the question of his sanity would be the key to his fate. Fish had yet to be assigned a lawyer, but anyone could see that insanity was the only possible defense. Anticipating this tactic, Westchester D.A. Frank Coyne announced on Monday afternoon that his office had engaged two psychiatrists or "alienists," as they were commonly called in those days, of its own—Dr. Charles Lambert of Scarsdale, New York, and Dr. James Vavasour of Amityville, Long Island—to examine Fish in the Tombs. The *Mirror*, meanwhile, sought out the opinions of a separate pair of psychiatrists which it published in an article headlined, "FISH VICIOUS MORON, TWO EXPERTS AGREE."

Actually, "vicious moron" was the paper's own diagnosis. The language of the specialists was considerably more circumspect. Indeed, the pronouncement of Dr. Thomas S. Cusack, a consulting psychiatrist to the U.S. Army during World War I, managed to sidestep any meaning at all.

Cusack did go out on a limb and declare that Fish was "undoubtedly an abnormal individual." On the vital question of responsibility—whether the old man could be held accountable for his crimes on the basis of his ability to distinguish right from wrong—the doctor was less willing to commit himself. "He is one case where it seems he knows the nature and quality of his act," the doctor opined, then added, "But does he really know it in the true sense of the word?" Nevertheless there was no doubt in the doctor's mind that "This is rather an unusual crime, especially at his age. He is a case for intensified neuro-psychiatric survey and study. It is," the doctor concluded sagely, "a crime of an unusual nature."

The second expert interviewed by the *Mirror,* Dr. Nathaniel Ross of Bellevue Hospital, was one of the psychiatrists who had examined Fish during the old man's brief commitment in 1930. Unlike Cusack, Ross spoke from firsthand knowledge of Fish, but his diagnosis was equally vague. The old man was a "pathological case," he observed. Ross seemed less interested in analyzing Fish than in justifying Bellevue's decision to set him free: "Such pathological tendencies as Albert Fish showed are, unfortunately, under the law, not in themselves evidence of insanity," he explained. "We were compelled to consider him legally sane and return him to the courts.

"It seems a shame that the community, from a purely enlightened scientific point of view, does not provide some form of prolonged or permanent confinement for such incurably abnormal types." Clearly, Ross feared that Bellevue's psychiatric staff might be blamed for its failure to perceive the full and terrifying extent of Fish's "abnormality." And Ross would turn out to be right.

It would be several more months before psychiatric examiners began to understand just how appalling, indeed unbelievable, a phenomenon Fish truly was. In the meantime, scattered details of his past perversities continued to surface.

Another of Fish's obscene communications turned up when a well-dressed Brooklyn woman appeared at Police Headquarters with a handwritten letter she had received after placing a "Room to Let" ad in the papers. Signed "A.H. Fish," the letter was yet another variation on one of the old man's favorite sadomasochistic themes, the spanking and sexual humiliation of teenage boys:

DERANGED

Dear Madam

I am a widower with 3 boys, 13-15-19 I wish to board out until the two youngest are thru school. I want good plain food clean beds, sew mend darn and do their laundry. I prefer *a widow,* who has a girl old enough to aid her. Henry and John have caused me a lot of trouble by not going to school. . . . Their principle Miss Bruce said to me, if they were her boys, she would spank both of them soundly 3 times a day for a month and give John a dose of the Cat-o-nine-tails at bed time. She blames him most so do I. I have no time to do this and besides I think whipping children is *a woman's job.* I want a good motherly woman, who can and will assume full charge of the 3 boys. Make them obey you and when they dont take down their pants and *spank them good.* Dont hesitate to strip them to the skin and *use the Cat-o-nine-tails on them,* when *you* think they need it. Robert is feeble minded due to a fall. Tho going on 20, well built and strong he is much easier to spank or switch than Henry. He kicks like an army mule when being spanked. I want a woman who will whip any one of the 3 or all 3 at once if they need it. Our own doctor says if Bobby *is not* spanked and switched when he gets cranky he is apt to lose his reason entirely. So *he* must be spanked as well. He is now in Phila Pa in charge of a Colored woman I have known 25 years. She has a daughter 17 and between them he is getting *plenty* of the paddle and Cat-o-nine-tails. Henry and John are in Upper Darby Pa in charge of two Maiden Sisters, both ex School Teachers. They conduct a boarding school for boys and girls up to 17 yrs. Both are very strict and any *boy* or *girl* who misbehaves is spanked in front of the entire class. John is a big boy for his age and it shames him to have his pants taken down and be spanked in front of a lot of girls. I want a place where *all 3* can be together. . . . I am willing to pay you $35.00 a week for the 3 boys, $15.00 a week extra when I am there. But if you take them you must *assure me you will Use the paddle* and *Cat-o-nine-tails freely on all 3 boys.* I want a woman who will *not be embarrassed* in stripping Bobby any more than Henry and John. So if you are interested tell me how to reach your place by car.

The letter had been mailed November 21, just ten days after the Budds had received their own, even more insane communication from Albert Fish.

The same Monday Fish was interviewed in the Tombs, the Budds themselves were in court to appear before the New York County Grand Jury, which was expected to return a quick indictment against Fish for abduction. Though Fish was to be tried first in Westchester on a charge of murder one, the Manhattan D.A.'s office had decided to seek the kidnapping indictment as a backup against the remote possibility of his acquittal.

Only two family members testified before the Grand Jury—Mrs. Budd and her son Edward, who were called upon to recount the circumstances of the kidnapping. Detective King also appeared as a witness, describing his long, frustrating manhunt and the sequence of events that began with the Budds' receipt of Fish's letter and culminated one month later in the old man's arrest.

One legal question needed to be resolved before the jurors could return an indictment. The statute of limitations on kidnapping cases was fixed at five years, and more than six had elapsed since the Budd abduction. According to a provision in Section 143 of the Code of Criminal Procedure, however, the statute did not apply if the defendant had moved out of state or lived under an assumed name after commiting the crime. Assistant D.A. Albert Unger was able to show that, in the years since the Budd kidnapping, Fish had lived briefly in New Jersey (where he had been arrested twice for passing bad checks) and had also used a variety of aliases, including Robert Hayden and James Pell.

Satisfied by Unger's argument, the Grand Jury promptly moved to indict Fish for abduction. Within the hour, Westchester D.A. Frank Coyne called a press conference in White Plains to announce that evidence to support a first-degree murder charge against Fish would be presented to the Westchester Grand Jury on Thursday. Thirteen witnesses would testify, including the Budd family, Detective King, and members of the Greenburgh police force.

With only three days left before the Grand Jury assembled in Westchester, the police redoubled their efforts to track down the dentist who had treated Grace Budd and could identify the fillings in her skull. Dozens of dentists were called down to police headquarters for questioning, and a circular containing a diagram and description of the work performed on Grace's teeth was printed up for distribution to clinics and dispensaries throughout the city. By Tuesday afternoon, however, the police had still not managed to locate their man.

The hunt for more evidence at Wisteria Cottage had also proved fruitless. For all their doggedness, the police had failed to turn up the missing butcher knife, even with the aid of a special electromagnetic device supplied by the Westchester Lighting Company. Their search for Grace's hat and coat, which the old man claimed he had rolled up and stuck under a stone, was also unavailing. And since the discovery of the skeletal fragments in the muddy beds of the two cisterns, no additional bones had come to light.

A few more discolored beads from Grace's necklace were the only new finds of any significance. Without the testimony of the unknown dentist, the string of fake pearls would, in the view of the Westchester D.A., constitute a key piece of evidence when the Grand Jury met on Thursday.

Another, of course, would be the child's skeleton itself.

On Tuesday afternoon, the pieces of that skeleton—along with the other bones recovered from the premises of the Wisteria "murder lodge"—were in the laboratory of Dr. Dudley J. Morton, Associate Professor of Anatomy at the College of Physicians and Surgeons, Columbia University.

Earlier in the day, Captain McQuillan had removed the boxes of bones from his office closet and driven them down to Yonkers Police Headquarters. There, he was joined by Medical Examiner Squire, who transferred the evidence to a large, black leather satchel, making sure to keep the child's skeleton separate from the thirty-odd bones that had been found in the basement and at the bottom of the two wells. McQuillan and Squire then took the satchel of bones to the medical school at 168th Street and Broadway, arriving around noon.

They were met in the lobby by Sergeant Hammill of the Missing Persons Bureau, who was carrying a leather satchel of his own. Inside were the weatherworn skull and other skeletal fragments which Hammill and his colleagues had unearthed on the night of December 13, when Albert Fish had first led them to the spot behind the mossy stone wall where he had left the little girl's butchered corpse to molder.

The officers delivered the bags to Doctor Morton, who at once began the task of piecing the bones together and comparing them to the skeleton of a twelve-year-old child in the college museum. Two hours later, the examination was over. Judging by their size and texture, Morton concluded that the bones found behind the stone wall constituted the nearly complete skeleton of a child who had not yet reached puberty.

The bones removed from the cellar and cisterns— identified by the *Daily Mirror* as "hacked sections of human anatomy"—were, in fact, the remains of an indeterminate number of four-footed animals, including at least one dog, a pig, and a cow.

Though Morton's findings supported Fish's claim that Wisteria Cottage was not the "ogre's lair" portrayed in the tabloids, police remained convinced that Grace Budd was not the only child Fish had slain. Indeed, even as the little girl's bones lay spread out on the anatomist's lab table, investigators were checking into the old man's possible involvement in five more child killings. These were the molestation and murder of four Brooklyn girls ranging in age from five to seven—Barbara Wiles, Sadie

Burroughs, Florence McDonnell, and Helen Sterler—plus the 1927 killing of eleven-year-old Yetta Abramowitz of the Bronx, who had been lured to a tenement rooftop by an elderly stranger, where she was raped, strangled, and savaged with a knife.

For the murder of the six-year-old Sterler girl, a man named Lloyd Price—described in the papers as a "Negro vagrant"—had been arrested, tried, and sentenced to die in the electric chair. Price had recanted his confession, insisting that it had been beaten out of him by his interrogators. His final words before the switch was pulled at Sing Sing were "By the Grace of God, I am innocent."

Now the police had begun to think that Price might have been telling the truth after all.

Investigators in Brooklyn, meanwhile, were making progress in their efforts to link Fish to the Gaffney disappearance. On Wednesday, December 19, they got the break they were hoping for.

Disabled by a stroke, fifty-seven-year-old Joseph Meehan was retired now, but for many years he had worked as a motorman on the BMT trolley line in Brooklyn. On the evening of February 11, 1927, it was Meehan, along with conductor Anthony Barone, who had been struck by the strange-looking pair huddled in the back of his car—a jittery old man trying to hush an underclothed little boy, who cried continuously for his mother from the moment he was led onto the trolley until the moment he was dragged off into the night.

Only later had Meehan and Barone realized that they had been eyewitnesses to the abduction of little Billy Gaffney.

Like millions of his fellow New Yorkers, Meehan had been transfixed by the unfolding horrors of the Fish story, and on December 18, his eye had been caught by a special feature in that day's edition of the *Mirror*. Running along the bottom of page two was a series of close-up photos, five in all, showing the face of the hollow-cheeked "thrill murderer" from various angles. "REMEMBER THIS FACE?" the headline asked.

The text accompanying the pictures urged readers to recall whether they had ever seen Fish "in real life. *If so—when—where—under what circumstances?* You may be in a position to aid police in solving a number of mysterious disappearances. . . . If you can add to what is already known about Fish's movements, communicate instantly with the City Editor of the *Daily Mirror,* MUrray Hill 2-1000, or call personally at the *Mirror* office, No. 235 E. 45th Street."

Studying the photos, Meehan realized with a shock that he did, in fact, remember that face. It belonged to the wizened old man he had observed that long-ago night on his trolley car. Meehan waited until the next morning, Wednesday the 19th, before taking action. Then he made his way to the nearest telephone and dialed the number of the *Daily Mirror.*

Later that day, Lieutenant Elmer Joseph, who had been in charge of the Gaffney investigation seven years before (when he was still a sergeant), arrived at Meehan's apartment. After questioning the former motorman for over an hour, Joseph was convinced that the case had finally been cracked. Arrangements were made to transport the semi-invalid Meehan to the Tombs the following day. In the meantime, several police officers set about tracking down Anthony Barone, whose testimony at the time of the Gaffney disappearance had been, along with Meehan's, the only solid lead in the case.

Shortly before noon on Thursday, December 20, Lieutenant Joseph, along with Detectives James Dwyer and Jeremiah Murphy of the Fifth Avenue police station in Brooklyn, picked up Meehan at his apartment and drove him to the Tombs, where he was scheduled to view Fish in a lineup. Barone, who had been located and interviewed at his home the previous evening, arrived at the prison shortly afterward.

The two former co-workers were ushered into the lineup room. Under the harsh glare of the klieg lights, nine men—five of them aged and gray, the rest somewhat younger—shuffled onto the platform. Barone and Meehan studied them carefully. Though Barone thought he recognized Fish, he couldn't positively identify him as the man he had seen with the little boy on his streetcar seven years before. But Meehan had no doubt. He pointed his cane at Fish and exclaimed, "That's the man!"

"Are you sure?" asked Lieutenant Joseph.

Meehan nodded emphatically. "I'm positive. I would remember him anywhere. He looks the same now as he did then. The only difference is that he was wearing an overcoat when I saw him with the boy."

Within twenty-four hours, the story would be carried in every newspaper in the city. The "boogey man" who had spirited four-year-old Billy Gaffney away from his Brooklyn tenement seven years earlier, setting off one of the most intensive manhunts in New York City history, had been identified as Albert Fish.

Even as Meehan was making the identification, the Westchester Grand Jury was in the process of indicting Fish for the murder of Grace Budd.

The proceedings lasted less than two hours. During that time, the jurors heard the testimony of thirteen witnesses, including Albert, Delia and Edward Budd, Captains Stein and McQuillan, Detective King, Sergeant Hammill, several Greenburgh police officers, and Medical Examiner Squire. Dr. Morton's findings were offered as evidence, along with Grace's dental chart and the small, sad pile of imitation pearls, which Mrs. Budd identified as the remains of her daughter's favorite necklace. Both Mrs. Budd and her husband broke down at the sight of the yellowed, weatherworn beads.

The jurors needed little time to complete their deliberations. Shortly after two P.M., they returned an indictment accusing Albert H. Fish of murder in the first degree for the slaying, "with malice aforethought," of Grace Budd.

The shock of Meehan's bombshell was still reverberating when the Fish investigation took another dramatic turn, the second in as many days.

Early Friday morning, Fish—dressed in the same, shabby, mismatching suit he had worn when he was captured—was arraigned in Homicide Court before Magistrate Benjamin E. Greenspan. The proceedings were over quickly. Surrounded by detectives, Fish stood silently, eyes downcast, while Frederick W. Ruscoe, Chief Deputy Sheriff of Westchester County, stepped forward and handed Magistrate Greenspan a bench warrant. After commending Detective King for his outstanding work on the case, Magistrate Greenspan formally surrendered the prisoner to the Westchester authorities.

Fish was to be transferred to the county jail in Eastview to await trial for the Budd murder. Instead of taking him directly to the car that would drive him up to Westchester, however, detectives led him into the courthouse detention pen. Then, they brought in a man who walked straight over to Fish, took a long look at his gaunt, stubbled face and declared without hesitation, "That's him."

This latest accuser was Hans Kiel. Ten years earlier he had owned a farm in Port Richmond, Staten Island. In February, 1924, Kiel's daughter Beatrice, then eight years old, had been approached by a gray-moustached stranger, who offered her a nickel if she would accompany him into the woods and show him where to find "wild rhubarb." Kiel's wife, Alice, had appeared at that moment, and the old man had hurried away. That night, however, Kiel had discovered the grizzled stranger sleeping in his barn. He had roused him awake and driven him off his property.

Three days later, eight-year-old Francis McDonnell was brutally assaulted and strangled to death in the woods adjoining Kiel's property by a gray-moustached stranger who precisely matched the description of the vagrant Kiel had chased from his barn. Kiel had never forgotten the face of the gray-moustached stranger. And so he had gone straight to the police when he'd seen it again just a few days before, looking out at him from the pages of his Sunday newspaper.

Following Kiel's identification, Fish was questioned for two hours by Assistant District Attorney Edward T. Kelly of Richmond County. At first, Fish denied having ever laid eyes on Kiel. Finally, he admitted that he had, in fact, been doing a painting job on Staten Island at the time of the McDonnell boy's murder and vaguely recalled seeing Kiel a few times on the ferry. But he firmly maintained that he was innocent of Francis McDonnell's murder.

The authorities remained as firmly convinced that he was lying. Kelly announced that Kiel's wife and daughter would be driven to Eastview to view Fish sometime during the next week. If they, too, identified him as the man lurking on their property a few days before the McDonnell crime, Kelly would seek an indictment against Fish for murder.

Mrs. McDonnell's ten-year-old prayer appeared to have been answered. It looked as though the "Gray Man" had been found at last.

During the next week, Fish was interrogated several times in his second-tier cell in Eastview. Just a few hours after his arrival, he was visited by the two psychiatrists hired by the DA's office—Doctors Vavasour and Lambert—who examined him for slightly more than three hours.

Several Connecticut detectives traveled to the jail to question Fish again about the decapitated child found in Darien. And Harold King, the Nassau County police inspector investigating the 1932 murder of fifteen-year-old Mary O'Connor, paid several calls.

Inspector King had learned about Fish's obscenity arrest in the summer of 1931, when the old man was employed as a dishwasher in the Steeplechase Hotel in Far Rockaway. As it happened, the O'Connors lived only a short distance from the Steeplechase, and Mary—who had befriended one of the guests, a teenage girl on vacation with her parents—was known to have visited the hotel a number of times during that summer.

King had also discovered that, early in 1932, at around the time of the O'Connor girl's murder, Fish had been painting a house in Massapequa, less than half a mile from the lonely stretch of woods where the girl's bludgeoned body had been dumped.

Fish, however, steadfastly continued to deny any knowledge of either the Connecticut or Long Island crime.

While police on Staten Island searched for other eyewitnesses who could link Fish to little Francis McDonnell, a Brooklyn man named Benjamin Eiseman came forward with a story that investigators found extremely interesting, since it placed Fish on Staten Island at the approximate time of the McDonnell murder. Eiseman's experience also bore striking parallels to some of the particulars of the Budd case.

The twenty-six-year-old Brooklyn man (who, like Meehan and Kiel, had recognized Fish's picture in the newspapers) told police that in July, 1924, when he was sixteen, he had been sitting on a bench in Battery Park, watching the incoming ocean liners when a gaunt, gray-moustached man sat down beside him and struck up a conversation. Discovering that Eiseman had worked as a painter's helper, the friendly old man—who described himself as a housepainter and handyman—told the boy of a job he was doing on Staten Island and asked if he would like to work as his assistant. Eiseman, recently arrived from Russia and unemployed, readily agreed, and the pair set out together on the ferry.

Arriving at St. George, Staten Island, they boarded a train and rode for half an hour. The old man then led the boy to a deserted shack. "Wait here while I get my tools," he said, then disappeared inside the house.

Eiseman was standing outside when another man—"an elderly Negro," in Eiseman's words—suddenly appeared. "Listen, son, you better get out of here," the man said. "A lot of kids have gone in there and didn't never come out." Alarmed by the stranger's warning, Eiseman turned and fled back to the ferry.

The penniless boy prevailed on the conductor to let him ride back to Manhattan for free. Back home, he spilled out the story to his mother, Mrs. Rose Eiseman, who immediately contacted the Clinton Street police station. Several detectives were dispatched to the Eisemans' Henry Street apartment. According to Eiseman, the detectives offered him one dollar if he would return to Battery Park the next day and act as a decoy. But the teenager, deeply shaken by his experience, refused.

Now, having seen Fish's face in the papers, Eiseman was absolutely certain that the old man was the same one who had lured him to the isolated shack ten years before. "I would never forget that face," he declared. He would never forget the man's strange, coarse whisper, either. Indeed, said Eiseman, if the police brought him to Eastview and positioned him so that he could hear Fish speak without seeing him, he would be able to identify the old man from the sound of his voice alone.

On Sunday, December 23, while Brooklyn police were checking their records to substantiate Eiseman's story, four more witnesses were brought to the Westchester County penitentiary to view Fish. For the first time since Fish had been arrested, he refused not only to speak to his visitors but also to so much as look at them.

The four witnesses were the wife and three daughters of Hans Kiel, the Staten Island farmer who had identified Fish as the suspicious stranger he had chased off his farm a few days before the McDonnell murder.

Informed of the women's arrival, Fish announced that he would not allow himself to be seen by them. The McDonnells were led to the corridor directly outside his cell. Seeing them approach, Fish covered his face with a newspaper. The women withdrew, but returned about ten minutes later. This time, Fish knelt on his cot and buried his face in the blankets.

Once again, the four women pretended to depart, only to tiptoe back in another ten minutes. Fish was caught off guard. Though he hastily lowered his head between his knees, eighteen-year-old Beatrice was able to get a glimpse of his face.

It was all she needed. Fish, she declared, was the old man who had approached her ten years before and offered her five cents to accompany him into the woods —the same woods in which Francis McDonnell's brutalized corpse had been discovered four days later.

* * *

DERANGED

Christmas Eve, 1934, was the first day since Fish's transfer to Eastview that no one came to interview, interrogate, examine, or inspect him. He passed the day quietly, gazing through the bars of his cell at the Christmas tree that had been set up in the corridor. Late in the afternoon, he asked to see an Episcopal minister.

The next day, he joined the other inmates for a special chicken dinner, then received a visit from Reverend Reginald Mallett, rector of the Grace Church in White Plains. The two men prayed together. Afterward, Fish asked the minister to send him a pen so that he could write some letters. Informed of the old man's request, prison officials told Reverend Mallet that a pencil would be safer. By then, they had reason to be leery of the uses to which Fish might put a pointed metal object.

On Thursday, December 27, Benjamin Eiseman's story was verified when police at the Clinton Street station, searching through their records from 1924, located their files on his case.

That afternoon, Thomas J. Walsh, District Attorney of Richmond County, announced that Eiseman's story, plus the testimony of Hans and Beatrice Kiel and several other Staten Island residents, had persuaded him to seek an indictment against Albert Fish for the murder of Francis McDonnell.

28

~~~~~~~~~~~~~

"These X-rays are unique in the history of medical science."

FREDERIC WERTHAM

Charles Lambert and James Vavasour, the two alienists engaged by the Westchester District Attorney to evaluate Fish's sanity, had spent three hours and ten minutes examining him in his cell on the evening of December 21. According to their subsequent testimony, the old man spoke freely and frankly about the darkest secrets of his life—secrets that would, when they were divulged during Fish's trial, make even hardened lawmen realize how little they had known about the limits of human depravity.

Among his other astonishing admissions, Fish revealed—as he had in his December 16 letter to Detective King—that, as an act of contrition for killing Grace Budd, he had purchased a pack of sewing needles, and, using a thimble, had shoved five of them up behind his testicles, so deeply that they had remained permanently embedded inside his body.

Though the claim seemed impossible to credit, authorities already had enough evidence of Fish's manifold degeneracies to take it seriously. It was also true that the old man walked with an odd, bowlegged gait and seated himself very gingerly, as though suffering from some sort of discomfort between his legs. And so, on December 28, a week after his transfer from the Tombs to the Westchester County jail at Eastview, prison officials decided to check the old man's story.

Fish was driven to Grasslands Hospital, where he was X-rayed by the chief roentgenologist, Dr. Roy D. Duckworth. When the X-rays were developed, Duckworth clipped them to a shadow box and examined them closely. They were like nothing he had ever seen before. Or would ever see again.

The X-rays were of Fish's pelvic region. Scattered throughout the area of the old man's groin and lower abdomen were a number of sharp, thin objects—long, black splinters that appeared to be floating in the bright tissue around and between his hip bones. The objects varied in length. A few were fragmented, though most were intact. It was obvious that they were needles, not only from their size and shape but also from their eye-holes, which were clearly visible in many cases.

Duckworth saw at once that the needles could not possibly have been swallowed. Their location—around the rectum and bladder, just below the tip of the spine, and in the muscles of the groin—made it clear that they had been inserted into the old man's body from below, evidently through his perineum, the flesh between his anus and scrotum.

Duckworth's response to the X-rays was the same as that of everyone who saw them in the days and weeks to come: he wouldn't have believed it if he hadn't seen it. The old man had been telling the truth after all.

Or at least part of it. As it turned out, Fish hadn't been entirely forthcoming. He had told both Detective King and the two alienists that he had punished himself by pushing five needles into his body. But Duckworth did several counts of the black objects and came up with the same figure each time.

Lodged inside the old man's lower body were twenty-seven needles.

That same day, December 28, all of the city's newspapers reported on the results of the alienists' psychological examination of Fish. Vavasour and Lambert had submitted their findings to Westchester's new District Attorney, Walter Ferris, who had announced them at a press conference the previous afternoon.

According to the two psychiatrists, although the old man suffered from some "limited abnormalities," there was no question in their minds that Albert Howard Fish was legally sane.

PART 4

Bloodlust

29

~~~~~~~~~~

*"I trust in Almighty God and have no fear as to
what the outcome will be. He has the Power to
Save."*

ALBERT FISH

Albert Fish's murder trial would take place in early
March, 1935, and when it did, its daily parade of horrific
disclosures would make Fish a front-page fixture all over
again. In the meantime, the Fish case was overshadowed
by an even more sensational event—the trial of the
accused Lindbergh baby killer, Bruno Richard Hauptmann, a courtroom extravaganza that dominated the
headlines for six solid weeks, from January 2, when jury
selection began, until Hauptmann's conviction on February 13.

Like the rest of his countrymen, Fish followed the
press accounts of the Hauptmann melodrama with keen
interest. Reading newspapers, in fact, was one of his
principal daily pastimes, as it had been throughout his
adult life. He continued to search their pages for items of
interest, though he could no longer indulge in two of his
favorite activities—clipping articles about sex crimes
and answering classified ads from landladies and professional masseuses in the hope of establishing an obscene
correspondence.

This is not to say that Fish was forced to give up his
cherished letter-writing entirely. On the contrary, he was
supplied with stationery and stamps and was permitted
to write as many letters as he pleased, provided that he

used the blunt-pointed pencil furnished by the warden. His correspondence was also restricted to family members and officials involved in his case.

During the weeks leading up to his trial, a steady stream of letters flowed from Fish's cell. The bulk of them were addressed to his children—or at least to five of them. His namesake, Albert Jr., who had publicly denounced his "old skunk" of a father, had become anathema to Fish. Indeed, the perfidy of his oldest son—whose name, from that point forward, he refused ever to mention again, either in speech or in writing—was a recurring theme in Fish's letters to his other offspring.

In a letter dated January 17, for example, Fish wrote to his married daughter (and favorite child), Gertrude: "What A does I don't care, he is no son of mine . . . Now dear Gertie if you never do anything else for me, I want you to do this. Don't you ever call him your brother again. Never allow him inside your home. Teach your little ones to despise him."

Fish urged his other children, Henry, Annie, John, and Gene, to extend the same treatment to their brother. "Slam the door in his face," he wrote to Annie.

The old man was equally vicious toward his first wife, Anna. In classic paranoid fashion, Fish blamed everyone but himself for his problems and traced the source of his troubles to the day in 1917 when his wife had run off with their boarder, a man named John Straube. (The fact that Fish's life, from early adolescence onward, had been one long nightmare of sexual criminality and that he'd done a stretch in Sing Sing from 1903 to 1905 were only two of the many realities that the old man had trouble hanging on to.) "All I hope for," he wrote to Gertrude, "all I want to live for, is to be able to go in court that I may tell what a bitch of a mother all of you had, the kind of wife I had." In the same vein, he wrote to Annie: "Tell old Peg Leg, your bitch of a mother, that the day I go into court and take the stand will be a sorry one for her."

Fish's estranged wife (whom he'd never bothered to divorce) wasn't the only family member he blamed for his woes. From Fish's demented point of view, his current predicament was chiefly the fault of his twenty-four-year-old son, John. If the boy hadn't joined the Civilian Conservation Corps, Fish (so he maintained) would never have ended up in hot water. It was only because the old man had gone to Frieda Schneider's rooming house to fetch the monthly paycheck from his son that he had been captured. As he wrote to John in a letter dated January 8: "I don't blame you, my son, for my trouble but if you had not joined the C.C.C., I would not be in here. I waited for the check until Dec. 13. When I went to 200 E 52, I got caught."

The fact that Fish had been arrested because he had committed an unspeakable deed against a child—and then written an incriminating letter without bothering to obliterate the return address—seems never to have crossed his deeply disordered mind. Fish's prison correspondence clearly revealed the true stripe of his contrition. For all his public professions of remorse, the only thing he confessed to feeling bad about, in the relative privacy of his letters, was having gotten caught. "It was that damn check that tripped me up," he wrote his son, Gene.

John took exception to the old man's accusation and complained about it to his sister, Gertrude, who mildly reprimanded her father for assigning any blame at all to John. Fish wrote back, "I don't blame poor John for *what* I done. I only said if he had not joined the C.C.C. then there would have been no checks to go after."

Fish's resentment over John's participation in the Civilian Conservation Corps, however, did not prevent him from maintaining a lively interest in the young man's paychecks. Indeed, for a person facing the prospect of the electric chair, he displayed a striking concern with financial matters, worrying obsessively over the whereabouts of John's monthly salary. "I don't know where the money is going to," he wrote to Gene on January 24. "All I got since John joined the C.C.C. was $18.00 from October. There is $25.00 due me from Nov—$25.00 from Dec and on Feb 1 there will be $25.00 from Jan.

There is $75.00 *tied up somewhere.*" Fish fretted over these matters in virtually all of the letters he sent to his children during the weeks of his imprisonment.

To a certain extent, Fish's money cares reflected his concern for the well-being of his children, particularly his two daughters. In several letters, he promised to distribute the bulk of John's C.C.C. money to Gertrude and Annie, whose families were subsisting on Home Relief. And he urged Annie not to "spend your 5 cents coming up here to see me. Not that I don't want to see you." (Detective King, who visited Annie's flat shortly after Fish's arrest, was so appalled by her poverty that he ended up leaving her a few dollars to buy food.)

Improbable as it seemed, given the kind of creature he was, Fish had been a genuinely devoted if intensely bizarre father, who had, as he put it in one of his letters to Warden Casey, "done every honest thing a man could do in order to provide for my family." According to his own testimony, which was confirmed by his children, he had "acted as both father and mother to them" after his wife had run off with her lover. He had worked steadily to support them and had never struck or beaten them when they had misbehaved. His daughters in particular treated him with affection and respect, dismissing his habits—self-flagellation, strolling around the house naked while declaring he was Christ—as more-or-less harmless eccentricities.

At least one of Fish's daughters knew about the needles. In a letter written to Gertrude shortly after he was taken to Grasslands, Fish wrote: "You remember the needles I suffered with when you were living at 529 Franklin St. They took an ex-ray of me in the Hospital up there. I am full of them." The language in this passage is revealing. Apparently, Fish's oldest daughter was so accustomed to his aberrations that she could no longer distinguish them from normalcy. In her eyes, her poor old father "suffered with" the problem of self-inserted sewing needles, the way other parents suffer from bad hearts or arthritis.

Fish did appear capable of experiencing and expressing the normal sentiments of parenthood. He seemed genuinely concerned that thirty-one-year-old Gertrude, who had been treated for a coronary problem at Bellevue, not subject herself to unnecessary strain. "Now Gertie dear don't you come up here to see me," he wrote to her on January 17. "I am afraid of your heart and besides I really believe I would go all to pieces when I saw you." He reminded her to enroll her children in Sunday school and reminisced warmly about "Christmas night 1933," when he had stayed with her family and they had "all sat near the radio in the front room and listened to the music. We heard choir boys singing in England, Germany and all over."

In fact, Fish sounded like any other parent when he scolded John gently for his sloppy penmanship. "Your writing is very hard to read," he complained. "It is all I can do to make out some of it. Take your time, write in ink, and as plain as you can. Dont jumble your letters so close together."

Fish's warmest feelings were reserved for his eleven-year-old granddaughter, Gloria, Gertrude's oldest child, whom he claimed "to idolize." Writing to Fish on January 28, Gertrude enclosed a little note from Gloria. Fish's reply to his granddaughter showed him at his most human:

My Dear little Gloria

Your poor old grand pa got your sweet note you sent in Mamas letter. I am so glad to hear you still love me and always will. You know as a baby and at all times, I loved you. . . . There have been times when I was at Mamas that I was cross and cranky. But I had *much* on my mind. Since this has happened, Mama can tell you what that was. I am so happy to know that you . . . are doing so well at school. *Stick to it* and learn all you can. Some day before long now, you will be able to go to work and help poor Mama & Papa. They have struggled hard for each of you, as I have also struggled hard for each of them, in the years that have passed. I am well. Trust in God and have no fear as to what the result will be. You know I love each of you dearly and always will. Pray every night for your poor old grand pa—Write soon again.

Anyone reading this note might have momentarily forgotten that the little old man who composed it was the confessed butcher of a young girl roughly his granddaughter's age. And that this same individual, who could sound so human and who could claim, with apparent sincerity, that he "loved children and was always softhearted" had spent the better part of his lifetime performing unimaginable cruelties on them.

But Fish couldn't keep his true nature concealed for very long even from his young relatives. A few weeks after writing to his granddaughter, he sent a letter to his teenage stepdaughter Mary Nichols, the child of one of the three widows he had married between 1930 and 1931 (bigamously, since he was still legally wed to his first wife, Anna). With its chaotic mixture of paternal tenderness and pornographic fantasy, this document is far more characteristic of Fish's extravagantly perverse psychology than his sentimental note to little Gloria:

Dearest Sweetest Mary—Daddys Step Kiddie

I got your dear loving sweet letter. I would have answered you long before this. But between ex rays, doctors and my lawyer I have been busy. Then you know I am 65 and my eyes are not so good as they were when you saw me last. . . . So my sweet little big girlie will be 18 on the 28th. I wish I could be there, you know what you would get from your daddy. I would wait until you were in bed, then give you 18 good hard smacks on your bare behind. . . . Now Mary dear, I will get a check from the U.S. Government in a few days. As soon as it comes I will send you $20.00. I am not able to get you a watch, but you can get one that you like. I hope dear Mama who I loved and *still love* and all of you are well. You speak of being at the big games. Here in N.Y. City there is nearly always some kind of a game going on.

In the Public Schools and all of the Y.M.C.A.s they have large swimming pools. If a man or boy wants to use this pool he must take all his clothes off and go in bare naked. There is one of the largest pools in the U.S. in the West Side Y.M.C.A. 8th Ave & 57 St. The water varies from 3 to 8 ft deep. Sometimes there are over *200 men and boys, all of them naked.* Any boy or man can go in and see them for 25¢. Now you know well sweet honey bunch that most all *girls like to see a boy naked.* Especially the *big boys.* Do you know, my dear Mary, what the girls do to get in and *see the show?* Many of them have boyish bobs. They dress up in their brothers clothes, put on a cap, then go to the Y. Quite often a boy will come out of the water and stand so close to a girl dressed in boys clothes, she can and does touch his naked body. Many of the men and boys know the girls are there and see them naked, but they dont care. . . . Be careful all of you my sweet kiddies. Dont go out doors in the snow unless you have on rubbers. Now listen my little miss, dont you keep me waiting so long for another of your sweet dear letters. If you do some day I shall come out there again and give you another sound spanking—you know *where!*

For a man who continued to insist that he had "nothing to live for" and was "better off dead" (as he wrote to Warden Casey on January 15), Fish showed remarkable concern for his personal welfare and devoted considerable energy during his first few weeks at Eastview to securing the services of the best defense lawyer he could find.

For a short while, Fish was represented by a lawyer named Carl Heyser of Port Jefferson, Long Island. Heyser was related by marriage to a young woman named Alice Woods, a childhood friend of Fish's daughters, Gertrude and Annie. It was through their old acquaintance that the Fish children were put in touch with Heyser, who volunteered to take the old man's case.

Heyser's first step was to enter a plea of not guilty by reason of insanity when Fish appeared before Justice

William Bleakley in Supreme Court on Monday, January 7. Heyser asked the court to appoint an insanity commission to examine Fish, a request which Justice Bleakley took under advisement. Two days later, he denied the request, explaining that the two alienists retained by the District Attorney's office had already declared Fish legally sane. Fish would have the opportunity to offer evidence of his insanity at his trial.

Even before Justice Bleakley issued his decision, however, Fish had grown unhappy with Heyser, largely because the old man believed that he would be better served by a local attorney, someone known and respected in the courtrooms of Westchester. The name he heard mentioned most often by his fellow inmates at Eastview was James Dempsey.

Born in Peekskill, New York, in 1901, Dempsey, the son of a prominent Westchester attorney, had graduated from Colgate University at nineteen and earned his law degree at twenty-three from New York University Law School. He spent three years as Assistant District Attorney of Westchester, and between 1932 and 1933 also served as Mayor of Peekskill. When the elder Dempsey died in 1933, James quit public office to take control of his father's extensive practice.

Impressed by Dempsey's reputation, Fish immediately launched an epistolary campaign to get rid of Heyser. He fired off letter after letter to the Port Jefferson lawyer, informing him that his services were no longer required. At the same time, he petitioned both Justice Bleakley and D.A. Ferris to assign his case to Dempsey.

Finally, on February 6, the old man got his wish when Heyser withdrew and Dempsey was appointed as his replacement. Fish was jubilant. "I am very glad that [Heyser] dropped out," he wrote to his son Gene that afternoon, "for now I have a real lawyer. I heard of him when I got here. He was over 3 years Assistant Dist. Attorney in White Plains and everybody here knows him well." In letter after letter, he described Dempsey in the most glowing terms—as a "high-grade man," "one of the best," "a great lawyer" who "knows every trick there is." "Heyser is not in the same class with him," he wrote to

Gertie. "He is only a country lawyer and would have been very little use to me."

With Dempsey now in charge of his case, Fish seemed filled with new confidence. "I have a good ground to stand on and with a lawyer like Mr. Dempsey I still have hopes," he wrote to John. "He has been up here to see me *nearly every day* this week. He was here last night and is coming again tonight. Just before he went he said to me cheer up Pop. *Things are shaping up fine.*"

Confident in the skills of his new lawyer, Fish settled back to await his trial, scheduled to begin in early March. He whiled away the time with his newspapers and letters and also with his Bible, which he read devotedly every day, dwelling on those passages that were most meaningful to him. Fish knew various Scriptural passages by heart. One of his favorites, which he could cite from memory, was Isaiah 36:12: "But Rab-shákeh said, 'Hath not my master sent me to thy master and to thee to speak these words? *hath he* not *sent me* to the men that sit upon the wall, that they may eat their own dung, and drink their own piss with you?'"

As the days passed, however, the old man found it increasingly hard to concentrate on his Bible studies. He was distracted by a constant disturbance emanating from the adjoining cell, whose inhabitant was a young man named Lawrence Clinton Stone.

Whereas Fish liked to believe that he stemmed from "Revolutionary stock," Stone truly was the descendant of an old and distinguished American family that had settled in Litchfield County, Connecticut, in the early seventeenth century. Stone, however—a burly, somewhat feeble-minded twenty-four-year-old, who had done several terms in reformatories during his teens—had been estranged from most of his family for years.

On Sunday afternoon, October 14, 1934, Stone was loitering on East Third Street in Mount Vernon, New York, where he had once been employed as a worker on a street-widening project. Across from where he stood, a five-year-old girl named Nancy Jean Costigan was happily playing with a small rubber ball on the terrace of the

Pelhutchinson Apartments, one of the most exclusive apartment buildings in Mount Vernon. Nancy Jean's parents, Mr. and Mrs. Richard Costigan of Forest Hills, New York, were upstairs visiting friends.

At around five P.M., the building hallman, Carl Hutchinson, decided to go down to the basement to adjust the oil-burning furnace. Walking around to the basement entrance, which opened onto a side street called Warwick Avenue, Hutchinson was surprised to discover that the door was locked. He returned to the lobby and rode the elevator down to the basement, a dimly lit labyrinth of corridors, storage rooms, and locker space.

As he proceeded toward the steep metal staircase that descended into the sub-basement where the furnace was located, he noticed an erratic trail of red splotches that led from the Warwick Avenue entranceway across the basement floor, through the Ping-Pong room and toward the sub-basement.

Later, Nancy Jean's little rubber ball would be found in the Ping-Pong room, where it had rolled into a corner.

As soon as Hutchinson stepped inside the sub-basement, he saw a puddle of blood on the cement floor directly beneath the white hot firebox of the furnace. He turned and ran to call the police. As he rushed for the stairway, he thought he glimpsed the shadowy figure of a thickset young man crouched in a dark corner of the basement.

A short time later, Detective Frank Springer arrived. The two men returned to the sub-basement. Springer opened the furnace door. Inside were the charred remains of a young child.

Springer immediately telephoned police headquarters, and a patrol wagon, carrying two more detectives and a patrolman, was dispatched to the scene. As the wagon neared the apartment house, however, it collided with an automobile. The three police officers were slightly injured. It took only a few minutes for an ambulance to arrive from Mount Vernon Hospital. As the attendants were seeing to the injured officers, a powerfully built young man in blood-spattered clothing stumbled up to the ambulance and clambered inside, insisting that he was badly hurt. He was driven to the hospital along with the officers. When physicians examined him, however, they discovered that he had sustained no injuries at all. At that point, the doctors couldn't say where all the blood on his clothing had come from. But it certainly wasn't his own.

The young man—Lawrence Clinton Stone—was taken to police headquarters for questioning. That night, he confessed to the murder of Nancy Jean Costigan, though the story he stuck to at first was that the little girl's death had been accidental. According to Stone, he had taken the child down into the basement to play catch with her. At one point, he had carelessly tossed the small rubber ball too hard and hit her on the brow. The child "toppled to the floor," struck her head on the cement, and began bleeding from her mouth. Stone took her limp body into his arms, began carrying her upstairs and then—believing that she was dead—panicked and decided to dispose of her body in the furnace.

Eventually, Stone admitted that he had deliberately strangled the child. Investigators later ascertained that Stone had sexually assaulted the girl before he killed her, and that she had probably still been alive when he threw her into the furnace.

Shut away in Eastview until his trial began, Stone passed his days pacing around his cell and cursing incessantly. Several months later, Fish had arrived and was placed in the adjoining cell. His delicate sensibilities offended by his neighbor's profane ravings, Fish wrote a letter of complaint to Warden Casey, requesting that Stone be moved to a different cell. "The cell I am in now is nice and light but I can't stand Stone. I can't read my Bible with a mad man raving—cursing—snarling. Can't you put him down at the other end in #1?"

Fish's plea was ignored and Stone remained where he was. The old man was compelled to pursue his religious activities as best he could. It was hard for him, though, to practice his singular form of worship under the constraining circumstances of prison life.

Every Sunday morning, for example, a Mass was held for the Catholic prisoners. During one of these occasions, several weeks before the start of Fish's trial, the ceremony was in progress when a guard heard strange grunting noises coming from the old man's cell. The guard walked over to investigate. There stood Fish, pants pulled down around his ankles, masturbating furiously to the rhythm of the prayers. Hastily unlocking the cell door, the guard stepped inside and forced him to stop.

At the time, Albert Fish was just three months shy of his sixty-fifth birthday.

30

But the thing which in eminent instances signalizes so exceptional a nature is this: Though the man's even temper and discreet bearing would seem to intimate a mind peculiarly subject to the law of reason, not the less in heart he would seem to riot in complete exemption from that law. . . . That is to say: Toward the accomplishment of an aim which in wantonness of atrocity would seem to partake of the insane, he will direct a cool judgment sagacious and sound. These men are madmen, and of the most dangerous sort. . . .

HERMAN MELVILLE, *Billy Budd*

With Fish's trial date set for March 12, James Dempsey had to move fast, and one of his first steps was to secure the services of two psychiatrists of his own. The men he engaged were an impressive pair. Smith Ely Jelliffe was one of the country's most distinguished neurologists. A tireless champion of Freud's revolutionary ideas, Jelliffe was a pioneering figure in the history of American psychoanalysis (though Freud himself had a somewhat disparaging view of him, as he did of the United States in general). Jelliffe had already served as a psychiatric expert in a number of sensational cases, including the trial of millionaire playboy Harry K. Thaw. (In June, 1906, Thaw shot and killed architect Stanford White on the roof of Madison Square Garden, a building that White himself had designed. Thaw committed the crime after discovering that his wife, former showgirl

Evelyn Nesbit, had been White's mistress. He was declared criminally insane and institutionalized for nine years.)

The second psychiatrist Dempsey retained was Dr. Frederic Wertham. Born in Nuremberg in 1895, Wertham was educated in Germany, London, and Vienna (where he had a brief but memorable encounter with Freud). Emigrating to the United States in 1922, he joined the Phipps Psychiatric Clinic at Johns Hopkins, authored a standard textbook on neuropathology called *The Brain as an Organ,* and began a long and at times controversial career that would make him one of the best-known psychiatrists of his day.

Among Wertham's proudest achievements was the establishment of the LaFargue Clinic in Harlem. Created with the support of such prominent figures as Ralph Ellison, Richard Wright, and Paul Robeson, the clinic offered psychological counseling to the disadvantaged for the nominal fee of twenty-five-cents per visit.

A few years after the clinic was established, in the early 1950s, Wertham gained widespread renown (and undying notoriety in certain circles) for spearheading a national campaign against comic books, which he saw as a major cause of juvenile delinquency. His bestselling 1954 diatribe, *Seduction of the Innocent,* led to a Congressional investigation of the comic-book industry and the creation of the Comics Code Authority, a strict self-regulatory agency that remains in force to this day.

Comic-book devotees still regard Wertham as a sort of boogey man and lump him together with more recent, right-wing proponents of media censorship. In fact, Wertham was a political liberal and humanitarian, whose anticomics crusade was only one manifestation of a lifelong obsession with the social roots of violence.

At the time that Dempsey approached him, in mid-February, 1934, Wertham had been senior psychiatrist at Bellevue for two years, as well as the director of the psychiatric clinic for the Court of General Sessions, a pioneering program which provided a complete psychiatric evaluation of every convicted felon in New York City.

Of all the psychiatrists who interviewed Fish in the weeks leading up to the trial, Wertham came to know the old man best, partly because they spent the most time in each other's company—more than twelve hours in all during Wertham's three visits to Eastview (Vavasour and Lambert together had traveled to the prison only once and examined Fish for a total of three hours). Moreover, though Fish seemed indifferent to Wertham at first ("Some *Doctor* came . . . last night and asked about 1,000,000 questions," he sneered in a letter to Anna on February 14), he warmed up to the psychiatrist when he realized that Wertham had a sincere, scientific interest in understanding the workings of Fish's baroque psychology.

As Wertham later wrote in a published reminiscence of the case, Fish began to show "a certain desire to make himself understood and even to try to understand himself." The old man conceded that he might be suffering from some psychological problems. "I do not think I am altogether right," he declared at one point in their conversation.

"Do you mean to say that you are insane?" Wertham asked.

"Not exactly," answered Fish. "I compare myself a great deal to Harry Thaw in his ways and actions and desires. I don't understand it myself. It is up to you to find out what is wrong with me."

Accepting Fish's challenge, Wertham probed into every aspect of the old man's sordid past, grotesque fantasy life, and appalling sexual history. So many of Fish's assertions seemed incredible that, in an effort to verify them, Wertham spent hours checking the old man's medical and psychiatric records, interviewing his family members, and studying criminological literature for comparable cases.

In the end, Wertham was forced to conclude that there *were* no comparable cases. Fish's life had been one "of unparalleled perversity," Wertham later wrote. "There was no known perversion that he did not practice and practice frequently." Wertham determined that all these depravities had been fueled by a single, monstrous need—an unappeasable lust for pain. "I always had a desire to inflict pain on others and to have others inflict pain on me," Fish told Wertham. "I always seemed to enjoy everything that hurt. The desire to inflict pain, that is all that is uppermost."

Wertham was the first to learn another significant fact from Fish, too—a piece of information that the doctor promptly transmitted to James Dempsey, who saw it as a key to the insanity defense he was preparing. Fish told Wertham that, after decapitating Grace Budd, he had tried drinking her blood from the five-gallon paint can he had shoved under her neck. The warm blood had made him choke, however, and he had stopped drinking after three or four swallows.

Then he had taken his double-edged knife and sliced about four pounds of flesh from her breast, buttocks, and abdomen. He also took her ears and nose. He had wrapped the body parts in a piece of old newspaper and carried them back to his rooms. Simply holding the package on his lap as he rode the train back to New York put him in a state of such acute excitation that, before he had traveled very far, he experienced a spontaneous ejaculation.

Back in his rooms, Fish had cut the child's flesh into smaller chunks and used them to make a stew, with carrots, onions and strips of bacon. He had consumed the stew over a period of nine days, drawing out his pleasure for as long as he could. Later, Fish would tell Dempsey that the child's flesh had tasted like veal, though he had found her ears and nose too gristly to eat.

During all that time, he had remained in a state of absolute sexual arousal. He had masturbated constantly. At night he would lie in the darkness, savoring the lingering taste of the meat, and masturbate himself to sleep.

The next morning he would awaken, hungry for more.

31

Perverseness is one of the primitive impulses of
the human heart.

EDGAR ALLAN POE, "The Black Cat"

When Fish wanted to smoke, he handed a cigarette
to a guard, who lit it and then passed it back through the
bars of the old man's cell. On Monday, February 25,
however—the day after Wertham's last visit took place
—Fish kept badgering the guards for matches. He
wanted to light his own cigarettes, he said.

Eventually, one of the guards grew suspicious,
searched Fish's cell, and discovered a box of absorbent
cotton and a bottle of alcohol. No one knew how the old
man had gotten hold of these items (apparently one of his
children had smuggled them into the jail). But there was
no doubt about the use to which he had intended to put
them. Fish had already told both Wertham and Detective
King that, in addition to shoving needles inside his body,
he liked to soak pieces of cotton in alcohol, cram them up
his rectum, and set fire to them.

He had also told Wertham that, on a number of
occasions, he had tortured children in the same manner.
Sometimes, he had found it necessary to gag them,
though he preferred to leave their mouths unobstructed
since part of his pleasure came from hearing their
screams.

As the trial date drew nearer, Fish spent more and
more time kneeling on the hard floor of his cell, begging

God to save him from the chair. He also appealed to more proximate authorities. On Tuesday, March 5, James Dempsey conveyed a unique proposition to Westchester District Attorney Walter A. Ferris. Fish was willing to turn himself over to science as a "human guinea pig" in exchange for a life sentence. "Humanity will profit more by a study of my brain and body than by sending me to the electric chair," he explained.

Unsurprisingly, the D.A. did not leap at this opportunity. The law would not permit such a bargain, Ferris told newsmen. And even if it did, he would never consider striking a deal with the old man. "As long as Fish is alive," the District Attorney declared, "he will be a menace."

Five days later, on the eve of his trial, Fish extracted a three-inch chicken bone from the bowl of soup he was served at lunch and sharpened it to a needle point on the concrete floor of his cell. After removing his shirt, he began ripping at the flesh of his chest and abdomen with the improvised weapon. Hearing his moans, Warden Casey hurried over to Fish's cell and summoned a guard who unlocked the door, rushed inside, and wrestled the bone away from the old man, who had managed to inflict only minor flesh wounds on himself.

That evening, the newspapers reported that Fish had been thwarted in a suicide attempt. But people like Dr. Wertham and James Dempsey, who were closely acquainted by now with the workings of the old man's freakish psychology, knew that he hadn't been trying to kill himself. He had simply been enjoying an act of autoeroticism—an ecstatic release after his long, enforced abstinence from pain.

With Bruno Richard Hauptmann sentenced and sequestered on death row, the trial of Albert Howard Fish for the murder of Grace Budd became the biggest courtroom drama in town when it opened at the Westchester County Supreme Court Building in White Plains on Monday, March 11, 1935. More than three hundred people, most of them women, jammed the hallway outside the courtroom doors, pressing for admission. A dozen deputy sheriffs were posted at the entrance to keep the crowd orderly.

Spectators were admitted by ones and twos until the benches were full. No standees were allowed, which caused a good deal of grumbling among the scores of curiosity seekers who didn't manage to get seats. But Justice Frederick P. Close was determined to avoid the circus atmosphere that had prevailed at the Hauptmann trial. "I intend to conduct a quiet, orderly trial," he announced.

At the front of the courtroom, the big press table was packed with representatives from newspapers throughout the metropolitan region. For weeks, the city's tabloids, basing their information on leaks from various officials involved in the case, had offered previews of coming attractions, hinting at the horror-show sensations the trial held in store. "From the witness stand," wrote a reporter for the *Daily Mirror,* "Fish will recite the story of his life, admitting atrocities not surpassed by even that story of terror and bloodlust, *Dracula.* He will make his hair-raising confessions to save his own, miserable life." By opening day, New Yorkers were primed for the most lurid revelations—tales of sexual depravity, cannibalism, human sacrifice and ritual torture.

They were not disappointed.

At around ten A.M. Fish, dressed in a shabby gray coat, dark dusty trousers, rumpled blue shirt, and badly knotted striped tie, shuffled into the courtroom on the arms of two deputy sheriffs. His head was bowed and his face hidden behind the fingers of one bony hand. As he was led to the defense table, where James Dempsey sat waiting with his assistant, Frank J. Mahoney, a dozen news photographers leapt to their feet and began shooting pictures. Even with his eyes covered, Fish winced at the exploding bulbs, and the cameramen were promptly banished from the courtroom by Justice Close.

The first day's business, the impaneling of the jury, proceeded smoothly. By 5:30 in the afternoon, seventy talesman had been examined by Dempsey and his opponent, Elbert F. Gallagher, Chief Assistant District Attorney, who (along with another Assistant D.A. named Thomas Scoble) was in charge of the prosecution.

Many of the talesmen were dismissed for personal reasons—family illness or jobs they couldn't neglect. The first person questioned, a Peekskill laborer named William A. Waite, was unwilling to serve unless he could go home every night. His wife couldn't tend the furnace by herself, he explained. Waite was promptly excused. Other talesmen were dismissed because they had already decided that Fish was guilty or insane.

In questioning the potential jurors, Dempsey gave a strong indication of the strategy he planned to follow during the trial itself. Each of the talesman was asked whether he, a family member, or any acquaintance had ever been treated at Bellevue Hospital. It was clear that Dempsey intended to attack the competence of the Bellevue psychiatrists who had examined Fish in 1930 and declared him sane. Dempsey's references to Bellevue were so contemptuous that, at one point, Gallagher bitterly objected to his "snide remarks."

"Oh, you'll hear plenty about Bellevue before this trial is finished," Dempsey snorted in reply.

During a later, angry exchange with Gallagher, Dempsey revealed another part of his defense plan. He intended to establish that Fish was suffering from lead colic, an occupational disease of housepainters, which was believed to cause dementia.

The defense lawyer also warned of the "gruesome details" that jurors would be exposed to, including "obscene testimony" about cannibalism. "Would the fact that there is evidence that Fish, like yourself the father of six children, killed a little girl and ate her body so shock you that you could not weigh the evidence?" he demanded of one of the talesmen, an elderly farmer. The old man blanched visibly, admitted that it might, and was excused.

"This trial will be sordid, to put it mildly," Dempsey emphasized to each prospective juror. "Will that affect you and if you find, after hearing the evidence, that the defendant is insane, will you agree to send him to Matteawan Asylum for the criminally insane?"

Gallagher—a large, imposing man who would later become a State Supreme Court Justice—required less time with each talesman. The gist of his examination could be summed up in two questions: First, "If you find that Fish knew the difference between right and wrong, will you vote him guilty?" And second, "Have you any prejudice against the death penalty?"

The first juror accepted—and automatically made foreman—was John Partelow of Mount Pleasant, New York, a forty-eight-year-old carpenter and father of three children. By the end of the day, eight more jurors had been selected. Except for one, all of them, like Partelow, were middle-aged family men. Among them, they had eighteen children. The only bachelor in the group, a steamship agent from Yonkers named Gilbert Nee, was engaged to be married after Lent.

Throughout the day's proceedings, Fish—"the benign-looking Bluebeard," as the tabloids had taken to calling him—sat slumped in his chair at the defense table, right elbow resting on the arm of his chair, head propped in his hand, eyes closed. He displayed no interest at all in the proceedings. Indeed, he showed few signs of life, though he did stiffen slightly at Gallagher's first mention of the death penalty.

For the rest of his trial, Fish would maintain the same indifferent pose. To one observer, Arthur James Pegler of the *Daily Mirror,* he resembled "a corpse insecurely propped in a chair." To others he appeared to be dozing.

Much of the time, he was.

32

~~~~~~~~~~~~~~

*"Sometimes I myself am not sure what is real
and what is not, what I've really done and what
are things I want to do and thought about doing
so long that it got to be as if I had done them, so
that I remember them just as clearly as the real
things."*

ALBERT FISH

On the morning of Tuesday, March 12, the *Daily
News* published the first of a five-part serialization
of Albert Fish's life story. The series was supposedly
written by Fish himself, though its spirited style and
dramatic structure were clearly the work of a professional.

For the most part, this ostensible autobiography was
simply a titillating, though highly bowdlerized, account
of Fish's adult life, with particular, prurient emphasis
placed on his wife's infidelity and Fish's own geriatric
sexual escapades. "The thing that started me on the real
big things I have done in the last fifteen years was the
trouble I had in 1917 with my wife and that man John
Straube," the author proclaimed in a typical passage.
"Marriage is not all that it is cracked up to be, but it
certainly serves one purpose. So long as the man and
woman keep the bargain, they will both stay out of other
trouble. It is a good safety valve. As long as Anna stuck to
me, and the children kept coming one after the other
until there were six, I might have had my outside fancies
but would keep my end of the bargain.

"But when I found out about Straube, my eyes were opened to the fact that no bargains hold and that only fools know any restraints. That freed me. It threw off my chains. I had a right after that to any fun I could find or grab."

Most of "KILLER FISH'S OWN STORY" (as it was advertised on page one) operated on the same crudely suggestive level. None of it was nearly as shocking as the disclosures that would be made at Fish's trial in the coming days.

There was one brief passage, however, which did succeed in capturing the intensely bizarre quality of Fish's imagination, and that was the very start of the series, which recounted a story that Fish had told more than once. It was presumably a childhood recollection, though it may well have been a dream. In either case, it was revealing:

I am a man of passion, [the passage began]. You don't know what that means unless you are my kind. At the orphanage where they put me just before Garfield was assassinated, there were some older boys that caught a horse in a sloping field.

They got the horse up against a fence down at the bottom of the field and tied him up. An old horse. They put kerosene on his tail and lit it and cut the rope. Away went that old horse, busting through fences to get away from the fire. But the fire went with him.

That horse, that's me. That's the man of passion. The fire chases you and catches you and then it's in your blood. And after that, it's the fire that has control, not the man. Blame the fire of passion for what Albert H. Fish has done.

It is impossible to say whether this episode was memory or fantasy. Perhaps even Fish could no longer tell. But given his particular method of torturing himself with alcohol-soaked cotton, there is no doubt that the story had symbolic meaning for him, that on some level he did indeed associate himself with the nightmarish image of the fiery-tailed horse—a creature propelled through the world by the searing ecstasies of pain.

The selection of the three remaining jurors and one alternate occupied the morning of the trial's second day. The court recessed for lunch at ten minutes before one and reconvened an hour later. Shortly after two P.M., prosecutor Gallagher cleared his throat and rose from his chair at the front of the hushed, crowded courtroom to present his opening statement.

After a few preliminary remarks to the jury, Gallagher proceeded to lay out the state's case against Fish. Speaking in a somber, modulated voice, Gallagher sketched out the details of the crime as though reciting a story he'd read in a pulp horror magazine—*Weird Tales* or *Eerie Mysteries*. His speech held the audience spellbound. The only person in the courtroom who seemed completely uninterested was Fish, who sat drowsing in his chair, head resting in one hand, fingers visoring his eyes.

"In 1928, the People will prove, there lived in the city of New York the Budd family," Gallagher intoned. "They lived at 406 West 15th Street. They lived in a small apartment in the rear of the apartment house. There was the father Albert, the mother Delia, there was Grace, there was Edward, and several other members of the family.

"Edward Budd was looking for a job. And so he made application to the *New York World* to have them put an ad in their newspaper. That ad appeared on Sunday, May 27, 1928, under the classified ad section, situations wanted, and it read as follows in substance: 'Youth 18 wishes position in country. Signed, Edward A. Budd, 406 West 15th Street.'

"The following day or so there appeared this defendant at the Budd home. In the latter part of the afternoon there came a knock on the door. Mrs. Budd opened it, and this defendant was there. He said his name was Frank Howard, that he had seen the ad in the *New York World,* that he had come to see Edward about the job he had advertised for. He said he had a farm located down in Farmingdale, Long Island, a truck farm, and wanted to know if Edward could work on it. So Edward agreed to go down on the farm.

"This defendant said, 'I will come for you on Saturday.' That was on June 2, 1928."

After explaining how "Howard" had failed to show up at the appointed time and describing the telegram he had sent to the Budds, Gallagher went on to recount the events of that fateful Sunday morning when Fish first laid eyes on little Grace.

"She was a young girl at that time, approximately ten years and nine months of age. She had been to church that morning. She came in. She sat in this defendant's lap, he stroked her head, and he allowed her to play with the money he had. While she was sitting there, he said to the Budd parents that his sister was giving a birthday party for her children, up at 135th Street in the city of New York, and he thought it would be nice if Grace would go along with him. He said he loved children, he would return early that night, they need not worry, it would be all right. They hesitated to let her go, but finally consented.

"So she left home, that little flat, on Sunday afternoon shortly after the noon hour with this defendant." Here Gallagher paused for effect.

"The afternoon passed, the night went by, and she did not come back."

At this point, Dempsey cut in impatiently. "If your honor please, I am going to object to the dramatics on the part of the district attorney. He is supposed to outline what he intends to prove, sir. I submit that he has gone beyond that."

Justice Close concurred. "I think you are going into the evidence in too much detail, Mr. District Attorney," he said to Gallagher.

Gallagher nodded toward the bench. "I will slide over it as quickly as possible."

The prosecutor then sketched out the events of the ensuing years: Detective King's untiring manhunt, the dead-end clues and fruitless leads, the misidentified suspects, the tragicomical episode involving Charles Edward Pope. And then, on the eleventh day of November, 1934, the Budd's receipt of Fish's vile, taunting letter.

After summarizing—and somewhat expurgating—the contents of the letter (Gallagher substituted the phrase "I did not have connection with her" for Fish's "I did not fuck her"), the prosecutor quickly reviewed the events leading up to the old man's arrest, the discovery of the skeletal remains at Wisteria Cottage, and Fish's various confessions of the crime. Far from "sliding over" the murder itself, Gallagher described it in vivid detail.

"He said that he knew what he was doing," the prosecutor stressed. "He said that he knew it was wrong to kill, and that after he had done so he felt guilty. He knew it was a Commandment that 'Thou shalt not kill.' That is what he says."

Gallagher's voice rose as he moved toward his conclusion. "Now in this case, there is a presumption of sanity. The proof, briefly, will be that this defendant is legally sane and that he knows the difference between right and wrong and the nature and quality of his acts, that he is not defective mentally, that he had a wonderful memory for a man of his age, that he has complete orientation as to his immediate surroundings, that there is no mental deterioration, but that he is sexually abnormal, that he is known medically as a sex pervert or a sex psychopath, that his acts were abnormal, but that when he took this girl from her home on the third day of June, 1928, and in doing that act and in procuring the tools with which he killed her, bringing her up here to Westchester County, and taking her into this empty house surrounded by woods in the back of it, he knew it was wrong to do that, and that he is legally sane and should answer for his acts.

"That," concluded Gallagher, "is a brief résumé of what the People will prove in this case."

Right from the start, it was clear that James Dempsey's success in defending Fish would depend largely on his ability to remove the old man from the ranks of Gothic monsters, where the tabloids had relegated him, and present him in psychiatric as opposed to supernatural terms—as a human being in the grip of a raging psychosis. Appealing for understanding and open-mindedness in the face of undisputed horror, Dempsey studiously avoided theatrics in his opening remarks.

He began by pointing out the prime "consideration from the standpoint of the defense . . . namely, whether or not the man was sane."

"We do not have to prove that he is insane," Dempsey stressed. Rather, it was up to the "the State to prove that he is sane." Nevertheless, Dempsey declared, the defense would offer "proof, overwhelming proof, to demonstrate conclusively, beyond any doubt, that that man was insane in 1928 and is insane today."

Whereas Gallagher's statement was essentially a dramatic account of the Budd killing, Dempsey barely mentioned the crime at all, concentrating instead on Fish's bizarre life history. After summarizing the old man's brutalized childhood, Dempsey described his "progressive state of mental depreciation," detailing the tortures Fish had inflicted on himself with needles and nail-studded paddles and his compulsive habit of sending "unspeakable letters through the mail to people that he had never seen."

Making good on his promise to cast blame on the Bellevue psychiatrists who had diagnosed Fish as harmless, he lost no time in attacking them for having "turned this man out on the street" in 1931. "In that year that Bellevue turned him out as not being a criminal he married three other women outside of his own wife without ever getting a divorce, three different marriages in that year after Bellevue let him go. At the end of that year he was again apprehended for sending obscene letters through the mail. Bellevue has a lot to account for here, I submit," Dempsey charged.

By way of humanizing Fish as well as underscoring his erratic nature, Dempsey went on to describe the old man's paradoxical devotion to his children. "In spite of all these brutal, criminal and vicious proclivities, there is this other side of the defendant. He has been a very fine father. He never once in his life laid a hand on one of his children. He says grace at every meal in his house. In 1917, when the youngest one of his six children was three years of age, his wife left him. And from that time down until shortly before the Grace Budd murder in 1928 he was a mother and father to those children.

"We will show you, gentlemen, that in addition to the complex sex side of the man's makeup, which is something that is almost incomprehensible, he has this other side. It is nature's compensation."

Dempsey concluded by repeating the point he had made at the beginning of his statement: "And so I frankly say to you I have only scratched the surface. The defense is going to raise the question as to whether, in June, 1928, Albert Fish was sane. We will have lay witnesses and we will have very competent and learned medical witnesses to address that point, although I repeat as I close my brief remarks that it is incumbent upon the Prosecution to show that this murder where this little girl, they say, was killed and cut up and eaten was committed by a sane man."

Apart from a single gripping incident, the rest of the afternoon proceeded uneventfully. Delia Budd, looking more massive than ever, took the stand first. Dressed in black, with a gilt necklace quivering on her bosom as she spoke, Mrs. Budd recalled the events of June 3, 1928, and—when asked by Gallagher whether she saw "in the courtroom the man who came to your place" on that date—pointed calmly at Fish. "There he is, sitting at the end of the table."

"You mean the man with the hand up to his face?" asked Justice Close.

"Yes, that's him," Mrs. Budd said flatly.

Her face remained fixed in a look of absolute impassivity as Dempsey cross-examined her about the earlier suspects she had identified with equal certainty. "On the witness stand on a number of occasions," he asked, "you identified Charles A. Pope as Frank Howard, didn't you?"

"Yes, well I made a mistake."

"Now altogether, how many different people have you identified as Frank Howard?"

"Only Mr. Pope."

"Didn't you identify the head of the Missing Persons Bureau?"

"Not as I remember of," said Mrs. Budd.

"Don't you remember a lineup one day down at the police station when you picked out one of the New York detectives and said he was Frank Howard?"

"No. I don't remember."

"Don't you remember, Mrs. Budd, identifying a man by the name of Albert E. Corthell?"

"No."

"You didn't identify him?"

"No."

When Dempsey continued to press her on the matter, Mrs. Budd simply gazed away from him and refused to reply.

By then, however, Dempsey had made his point. "May I ask you one more question, Mrs. Budd, before you leave? You objected to your daughter going with Frank Howard, did you?"

"No," Mrs. Budd replied, her voice, like her face, betraying not the slightest trace of emotion. "We trusted the old man. We thought he was all right."

"Who was the one that consented, your husband or yourself?"

"We both consented."

Edward Budd was next on the stand. After recounting his version of the circumstances that had led to his little sister's abduction, he pointed out Fish as the gray-haired deceiver who had shown up at his door six years earlier in the guise of a benefactor. Willie Korman, also called as a witness, seconded Edward's story. The testimony of the two young men was brief and to the point, almost perfunctory.

The one truly dramatic moment of the day occurred during Albert Budd's testimony. In contrast to his wife and oldest son, Mr. Budd was visibly distraught during his time on the stand and spoke with a tremulous voice as he conjured up that long-ago day when the soft-spoken old man, who seemed so generous and kind, had come into his home as a guest and taken his child away.

"He asked me would I give my permission, consent, me and Mrs. Budd, to let the child go and attend that party, and that he would take very good care of her, and he would return her no later than nine o'clock."

Speaking in gentle tones, Gallagher asked, "What did you say to that?"

"Well, I judged his appearance and his personality and everything about him—"

At this point, Dempsey cut in. "I move to strike that out as not responsive."

Justice Close leaned toward the witness. "What did you say? Did you consent?"

Budd gave a deep, ragged sigh. "I gave my consent. Yes."

A few moments later, it was time for Albert Budd to identify Fish. "How is your eyesight?" asked the prosecutor.

"Well, my eyesight is not very good. I can't see very far because I have one glass eye and the other has a cataract in it. I can't see very far away, just about as far as you are there. I can't see back of that so good."

"I ask you to step down from the stand and see if you can locate the defendant in this court," said Gallagher.

As Arthur James Pegler wrote in that evening's edition of the *Mirror,* "a pin could have been heard to fall in the courtroom" as Albert Budd rose from his seat and moved gropingly toward the defense table. Stopping beside Fish's chair, Budd bent over the old man, who peered up through the cracks between his fingers.

Suddenly, Budd snapped erect. "This is Frank Howard," he rasped. "That is the man that took my child away. This man right here." His right hand jerked toward Fish, who shrank back in his seat—the single sign of life he had shown all afternoon. Whether the overwrought father was simply pointing at the old man or getting ready to strike him no one could say. But Deputy Sheriff John Toucher took a quick step forward and interposed himself between Fish and the trembling witness.

By then, however, Albert Budd had turned away. Shoulders slumped, he covered his face with both hands and began to sob loudly as Gallagher led him by an elbow back to the witness stand.

Once Budd was seated, Gallagher fetched a glass of water from the prosecutor's table. As he carried it over to Budd, James Dempsey half-rose to his feet, saying, "I will consent to have a few minutes' rest here, and excuse Mr. Budd."

Gallagher held out the glass, but Albert Budd, his face wet with tears, shook his head and whispered, "Just a minute. I can't drink the water for a minute." A few silent moments passed as he struggled for control. The only sounds in the courtroom were his spasmodic breaths and the scratching of pens as reporters rapidly transcribed the details of the heartbreaking scene.

Finally, Budd accepted the water from Gallagher, emptied the glass, and, after wiping his eyes with a handkerchief, turned his face in the direction of the defense table.

"That sight," he said bitterly. "That is enough to make anybody shiver."

William King was the last witness called to the stand that afternoon. Under direct examination by Gallagher, he described precisely how he had traced Fish to his former address—Frieda Schneider's rooming house at 200 East 52nd Street—and arrested him there on the afternoon December 13, 1934.

Afterward, Dempsey tried to force King to admit that Fish's confession had been beaten out of him with a rubber hose, but the detective placidly denied that any coercion had been used on the old man.

At that point—a few minutes before five P.M.—Justice Close recessed the court for the day, informing the jury members that they would be put up at the Roger Smith Hotel and admonishing them not to "discuss this case among yourselves, express any opinion about it, or permit anyone to speak to you about it. You will be permitted to have newspapers, but all references to this trial will be clipped from them before the papers are given to you."

King was back on the stand first thing the next morning, Wednesday, March 14, and remained there for most of the day. He began by reciting the confession Fish had made immediately after his arrest—a far more graphic account of the crime than the one Gallagher had given during his opening statement. The detective then described in equally vivid detail the initial trip to Wisteria Cottage, when Fish had re-created the killing and led King and his fellow officers to the spot behind the stone wall where the child's skull lay half-buried in dead leaves and dirt.

This third day of the trial had its dramatic high point, too, and it occurred precisely at this juncture, when— over the loud protests of Defense Counsel Dempsey— two bailiffs carried a grocery carton full of human bones to the front of the courtroom.

"If your Honor please," shouted Dempsey. "I submit that there is enough gruesome evidence in this case without putting any skeleton in evidence."

Justice Close was unimpressed by the objection. "He has to establish the corpus delecti."

"I submit that doesn't have to be done by putting bones in evidence."

"Objection overruled," declared the judge.

"Exception," Dempsey said angrily. "May I note on the record that the defense objects to putting in evidence any bones or any skulls upon the ground that they are of little probative value here in this case, sir, and upon the further ground that the introduction of that evidence would be highly prejudicial to this defendant, and it would undoubtedly tend to arouse and inflame the minds of the men on the jury. I submit it is only offered for that purpose."

"Objection overruled."

"Exception," said Dempsey. "I further state that I don't recall a murder case in this county where they have ever put in evidence any bones."

"This county has not any different rules than any other county," Justice Close replied.

"I would like to see the authority as the right of the district attorney to put the bones in evidence," Dempsey continued.

"I will assume the responsibility," Justice Close said calmly.

At that point, Dempsey called for a mistrial, a motion which Justice Close promptly denied.

With that, Gallagher reached into the cardboard carton, lifted out Grace Budd's skull, and held it aloft for a moment before handing it to Detective King. At the sight of the small, weather-stained skull, the spectators gasped audibly. One well-dressed matron began crying noisily and had to be led from the room.

Once again, Dempsey offered strenuous objection, insisting that "I am entitled to the declaration of a mistrial by the very exhibition of this skull before the jury." Once again, Justice Close denied the motion.

Dempsey's cross-examination of King, which began shortly after the controversy over the bones, occupied the remainder of the morning session and continued after the lunch recess. For a significant part of that time, Dempsey zeroed in on an issue that was clearly central to his insanity defense—the question of cannibalism. It was obvious that the lawyer wanted to establish beyond any reasonable doubt that Fish had indeed cut off and consumed portions of the little girl's body—an atrocity that no sane human being could possibly have performed.

Dempsey began by asking King about the anecdote that Fish had related in his letter to the Budds: the story about the famine in China which had driven the starving populace to cannibalize young children.

"Did you have a talk with Mr. Fish about that reference in that particular letter, sir?" Dempsey asked Detective King.

"Yes, sir."

"And what did he tell you about that?"

"He said that he had a brother who was in the Navy.

That when he was a young boy this brother would come home on his leaves of absence and recite these tales to him of famines in the Far East and various things he had witnessed as the result of these famines."

"In other words," Dempsey continued, "he said to you, substantially, that he had heard that children in China were sold for food?"

"Yes, his brother told him."

"Did he tell you, sir, that ever since 1894 or so when he heard about this human flesh in China that that had been on his mind?"

"No, sir."

"Did he tell you, sir, that he wanted to eat human flesh and it had been an obsession with him for years and years?"

"No, sir."

"Did he tell you that he had talked about it any number of times, sir?"

King admitted that Fish had.

"Did he tell you it was a frequent subject of his conversation?"

"Yes, sir."

"Did he tell you that he had read other books with respect to cannibalism and other things?"

"He said he had read books on this."

At this point, Dempsey seemed to shift gears. He abruptly dropped the subject of cannibalism and began questioning King about the rest of the letter—Fish's detailed descriptions of his visit to the Budds' apartment, his first glimpse of little Grace, the lie he had invented to lure her from her home, their trip to Westchester, her awful death at his hands in the silence of Old Wisteria. Dempsey proceeded methodically through each of these points, asking King whether or not they had all been "corroborated by other evidence."

King acknowledged that they had.

By this time, Dempsey's strategy had become clear. If every one of Fish's statements in the letter had been substantiated, wasn't it reasonable to assume that he had also been telling the truth, hard as it was to believe, about making Grace's "meat" into a stew?

King, however, refused to give ground. Unflappable as ever, he continued to maintain that, to the best of his knowledge, Fish had not committed cannibalism on the dead child's body.

"Didn't you ask him why it was that he took the head of this little girl, upon which there is no flesh, and put it outside and retained the torso and the limbs, upon which there would possibly be edible flesh, if you can conceive of such a thing?"

"I didn't ask him that question in just that way. I did ask him, 'Wasn't it a fact that you used this body?' And he said, 'No, I did not.'"

"In other words, he denied having any relations with it?"

"Any relations at all."

"But weren't you interested in the course of your investigation to find out why, after this little girl was dead and after her body was dismembered, why the head was put outside in the privy, and why the fleshy parts of the body were kept in the house?" Dempsey pressed.

King stared levelly at Dempsey. "I did ask the defendant, 'Why did you do that?' And he said, 'I don't know.'"

Dempsey allowed a note of impatience to enter his voice. "Didn't he tell you, sir, that the reason why he put the pail under the girl's head when he cut off the little girl's head was to get the blood?"

"Yes."

"Didn't he say that after he caught the blood, he took some swallows of it, and he didn't like it?"

"No, he didn't. He said he threw the pail out of the window onto the lawn. He made no mention of having used the blood himself."

Dempsey tried a different tack, asking King if he had interviewed any of Fish's children following the old man's arrest.

Yes he had, King answered. Four of them.

"Did you find out from any of his children about any unusual tendencies of this defendant with respect to the meat that he ate?"

Immediately, prosecutor Gallagher objected to the

question "as incompetent, irrelevant, and immaterial." His objection was sustained by Justice Close.

Dempsey rephrased the question. "Did you find out that he liked to eat raw meat," he asked King.

Gallagher again made objection, which was sustained by the court, and Dempsey, after protesting the ruling, moved on to other matters.

Following Detective King's testimony, his colleague, Sergeant Thomas Hammill, was called to the stand to corroborate King's account of Fish's arrest and the expedition to Wisteria Cottage. The rest of the afternoon was given over to a miscellany of witnesses, including Frieda Schneider, Fish's former landlady, who gave her own version of the stakeout of her premises; Joseph Prefer, the police photographer who had taken the first pictures of the crime scene; and several staff members of the dental clinic in New York City where Grace Budd had been treated in 1927.

At 5:30 P.M., court was recessed for the day. As Dempsey was departing, several reporters approached him to ask how Fish felt about the possibility of dying in the chair.

"He is indifferent," Dempsey said, then immediately amended the statement. Though it was true that Fish often seemed unconcerned about his fate, Dempsey had recently received a note from the old man in which he had expressed a desire to live because, as Fish had written and as Dempsey now repeated with a poker face, "God still has work for me to do."

The fourth day of Fish's trial—Thursday, May 14— began with the testimony of two more dentists as the state continued its efforts to establish the corpus delecti. After describing their examination of the victim's jawbone and teeth, Doctors Harry Strusser and Abraham Weil both agreed that the skull found at Wisteria Cottage was undoubtedly Grace Budd's. Their conclusion was based partly on the pattern of molar development, which was consistent with that of a girl approximately eleven years old, and partly on the location of the fillings, which matched the ones marked on the dental chart that had been admitted into evidence the previous afternoon.

Several members of the Greenburgh police department who had been involved in the search of the Wisteria premises described the discovery of the skeletal remains, and Medical Examiner Amos Squire bolstered the state's case by testifying that the bones were those of a preadolescent girl approximately fifty-two inches tall.

The rest of the day was taken up with the presentation of three more of Fish's confessions—the ones he had made to Acting Captain John Stein, head of the Missing Persons Bureau; to P. Francis Marro, Assistant District Attorney of New York County; and to Frank Coyne, the former Westchester D.A.

Prosecutor Gallagher read each of the statements to the jury over the vehement objections of James Dempsey, who called for a mistrial on the ground that the recitation of four separate confessions (including the one Detective King had read the previous day) was "of a prejudicial nature" and had been done for no other purpose than "to inflame and arouse the jury against this defendant." Like all of Dempsey's motions for a mistrial, this one was denied.

At one point, Dempsey and Justice Close engaged in a heated exchange. "I object at this time to four different witnesses testifying to the same confession," Dempsey declared.

"Object to them when they are offered," said Justice Close.

"I object to four confessions going in. I don't object to any proper evidence."

Justice Close's voice grew stern. "I am the judge of what is proper."

"I have the right to protect this defendant," Dempsey protested. "His life is at stake."

"I am not objecting to your objections, but I object to your speeches."

"I am making my objection."

"You don't make objections," said the judge. "That is the trouble. You make speeches."

"I object to your Honor's remarks in that respect."

Justice Close leaned back in his seat and made a little waving motion with one hand. "All right. Now, go on."

But Dempsey wasn't ready to drop the subject. "I submit that I have to protect my client's interests here."

"He will be protected," answered the judge.

Dempsey had good reason to be concerned. By the time Gallagher had completed the confessions, more than one reporter felt that Fish's insanity case had suffered, as one of them put it, a devastating "body blow." At several places in the statements—when he told Captain Stein, for example, that he "would have given anything to have her back again" five minutes after murdering Grace Budd—Fish had professed to feelings of remorse. Other admissions, too—that he had done his best to avoid the police after the killing, for instance—seemed to reveal very clearly that Fish knew the difference between right and wrong.

In spite of the damage that had been done to his defense, the bizarre old man seemed to perk up for the first time while the statements were being read. He lowered his left hand from his eyes, nodded appreciatively, and chuckled to himself every now and again, as though his confessions were filled with the most delightful bons mots.

The State rested its case at 11:34 on Friday morning after a few final witnesses had been called to the stand, including Professor Dudley Morton, the anatomist who had made a thorough examination of the victim's remains in his lab at the College of Physicians and Surgeons. As *The New York Times* reported, Professor Morton "clinched the State's proof of the corpus delecti" by testifying that the bones were those of a "female individual" approximately eleven years old and just over four feet tall—the same age and height as Grace Budd had been at the time she had disappeared forever.

It was time for the defense to begin its case. After asking for a directed verdict of insanity "on the ground that the People by their own evidence have repudiated the presumption of sanity" and having his motion promptly denied, James Dempsey called his first witness to the stand—Fish's despised and estranged oldest son, Albert Fish, Jr.

Until this point, the evidence in the trial had focused exclusively on the specifics of the Budd crime. The State's case had been a relatively uncomplicated affair, a matter of establishing that the bones recovered at Wisteria Cottage were Grace Budd's remains and of proving, largely through Fish's various confessions, that the killing had been the coldly premeditated act of a man who was fully aware of the heinous nature of his crime. In effect, Gallagher had spent the past four days leading the jury on a systematic, step-by-step re-creation of the murder, from Fish's initial visit to the Budds' apartment to Grace's awful final moments and the disposal of her butchered corpse in the woods behind Wisteria.

During the next few days of the trial, Dempsey would take his audience on a journey, too, though it would be a far less straightforward one: not a tracing of the path leading from the Budds' doorway to Grace's death site, but an expedition into the dizzying blackness of Albert Fish's mind—a trip that was truly (in the language of the old man's favorite author, Edgar Allan Poe) a descent into the maelstrom.

A slight, delicately featured man who looked much younger than his thirty-five years, Albert Fish, Jr. delivered his testimony without so much as glancing at his father. His voice, though soft, was full of bitterness.

At Dempsey's prompting, he began by recalling the time he had spotted his father standing on the hilltop behind their rented bungalow, shouting "I am Christ!" That had been in 1922, when Fish was fifty-two years old, five years after Anna Fish had abandoned her family and run off with her lover, John Straube. By then, Gertrude was married and settled in Queens, and Fish had taken the rest of his children and moved to the bungalow in the Westchester town of Greenburgh, where he had been hired to paint the exterior of a church. Just a few hundred yards down the road from the rented bungalow stood the house that the locals called Wisteria Cottage.

Next, the young man gave a graphic account of the episode that had occurred the summer before his father's arrest, when he had returned unexpectedly to the apartment on Amsterdam Avenue he shared with his father and discovered the old man beating himself with a nail-studded paddle. He also described the time in 1929 when he had stumbled upon the two bloody paddles stashed behind the kitchen sink of the Brooklyn apartment he and his father were occupying at the time.

And then there were the needles. Albert Jr. testified that he had known about his father's habit of shoving needles into himself for many years. He had first learned about it from his younger brother John, who had spied their father performing this grotesque ritual on himself as early as 1925.

Albert himself, however, had not encountered any evidence of this weird practice until the summer of 1934, not long after the paddle incident, when he had come upon a collection of sewing needles tucked away on a shelf in the Amsterdam Avenue apartment. There were fourteen of them altogether, threaded through a packet of newspaper clippings dealing with subjects like nudism and enforced sterilization. Later, the young man found a small box containing ten more needles in a fishbowl on the mantelpiece.

Dempsey asked the young man if he had said anything to his father about the needles.

Albert Jr. nodded. "I asked my father who used the needles and he said, 'I did.' I said, 'Are they your needles?' He said, 'Yes, they are.' I asked him what he used them for, and he told me he got certain feelings that came over him, and every time he did that, he would have to go into a bedroom or some place and stick those needles into his body."

"Did your father say anything about sticking them in other people?"

"Yes, sir, he did," the young man said in his soft but emphatic voice. "He told me, 'When I can't stick them in myself, I like to torture other people with them.'"

One of the most unusual stories related by the younger Fish involved a black cat that his father had developed an obsession with during those same, bizarre months in the summer of 1934. What was particularly strange about the old man's obsession was that, as far as his son could tell, the animal was purely imaginary.

Sometime that August, the young man testified, his father had approached a man named Hoffman, the owner of the buildings they had been hired to superintend, and asked him "if he would please get a bag of lime, that he needed it, and Mr. Hoffman asked him what he wanted it for. He told Mr. Hoffman that there was a great big black cat that used to run in front of him every now and then, and he wanted the lime to kill the cat with. Well, Mr. Hoffman thought it was curious, but he said, 'All right.'"

Fish had sprinkled the lime all around the basement floor. Apparently unsatisfied with this measure, however, he set about constructing an elaborate booby trap, which the younger Fish described to the jury as a wooden contraption resembling a "chicken coop or a fox trap. And he put a whole lot of boards across it, heavy beams and everything. He told me that when the cat goes in there it would hit a certain piece of wood that held the rest of the boards up, the entire weight, and when the board fell from underneath, this heavy timber would fall down and kill the cat."

"What did your father have to say about the cat while you were looking at this contraption?" Dempsey asked.

"Well, we spoke together about ten minutes, and he suddenly turned around quick, and he said, 'There it goes now! Did you see it? Look at the size of it!' I said, 'Pop, there is no cat in front of you.'"

"Was there any cat there at all?" Dempsey asked.

"No, sir. No black cat."

The part of Albert Jr.'s testimony that created the biggest splash in the tabloid press, however—and that gave rise to yet another lurid epithet for the old man—had to do with his father's eating habits. The younger Fish testified that, whenever the moon was full, a wild look would come into the old man's eyes, his face would grow flushed, and he would demand raw steak for dinner.

"Tell us in your own words the discussion you had

with your father about this raw meat business in July, 1934," Dempsey said.

"That was pay day," Albert Jr. began, "and I came home with the intention of having a good supper. I got home and sat down to eat. As I did, I noticed a piece of raw steak and a box of Uneeda biscuits."

"What did you say to your father?"

"I asked my father if that is all we had for our supper, and he said, 'Yes. Why?'"

"What was said by him with respect to the meat being raw?" Dempsey asked.

"He told me, 'That is the way I like my meat, and you eat it the way I eat it.'"

That night, Albert Jr. testified, he went outside for a breath of air and noticed that the moon was full. Returning to the apartment, he saw his father resting on the couch. "His face was awful red," Albert said, "and it seemed funny because he was not out in the sunshine that day."

"What else did you notice about your father at that time?" Dempsey asked.

"The expression in his eyes."

"Tell us about that."

"It looked as though he had seen something and was frightened. Just like someone was chasing him."

Within twenty-four hours, writers for the *Daily Mirror* and the *Daily News* had checked the Weather Bureau records from 1928 and discovered, as Norma Abrams reported, "that the moon was at its fullest on June 3, 1928, when the Budd child was killed and her body dismembered." And Fish, who had already been tagged with a string of sensational labels—the Thrill Vulture, Vampire Man, Ogre of Old Wisteria—was rechristened with a new tabloid nickname: The Moon Maniac.

Albert Fish, Jr., was followed on the witness stand by Dr. Roy Duckworth, the roentgenologist who had supervised Fish's pelvic X-rays at Grasslands Hospital in late December, 1934. Two months after that session, Duckworth had brought Fish in for an additional set of X-rays, which had revealed the presence of two more needles in the old man's lower body, bringing the total up to twenty-nine.

Using a shadow box set up at the front of the courtroom facing the jury, Duckworth pointed out the precise location of each of the needles—in the groin, close to the back wall of the rectum, slightly above the transverse section of the colon, near the bladder, clustered around the tip of the spine. Judging by their eroded condition, some of the needles had been in Fish's body for "quite a number of years," Duckworth explained. Others had apparently been inserted through the perineum as recently as six months before.

The last witness of the day, Mrs. Gertrude DeMarco—Fish's favorite child—wept sporadically as she testified to the old man's paternal devotion.

She began by recounting the details of her mother's desertion. Mrs. DeMarco had been a girl of thirteen when, on the afternoon of January 19, 1917, Anna Fish had given each of her children some change and sent them off to the movies. When they had returned, their mother was gone, along with the boarder, John Straube, and every stick of furniture in the house.

Searching through the empty rooms, they found a few pennies in the bathtub, and a note advising them to send a telegram to their father, who was living in White Plains while he finished a painting job for the Second Presbyterian Church in Tarrytown.

Fish had hurried home to Queens that very evening. He brought Gertrude and the others to their aunt's house in Flushing for a few nights, then moved them up to Westchester, renting some rooms in Elmsford for himself and the children while he completed his job at the church.

"And from that time on until the children were married or grew up, what did your father do with respect to the children?" Dempsey asked.

"He always went to work and provided for them. He was very good."

"Did your father ever strike you?"

"Never."

"Did he ever strike any of the children?"

"Never."

"What did your father say to the children, if anything, if they struck any animals? You always had a dog around, didn't you?"

"Oh, he would say, 'Don't do that. You will hurt the poor little dog.'"

What his daughter described as Fish's undeviating kindness even extended to his errant wife. About three months after Anna Fish ran off, Mrs. DeMarco's older sister received a letter from their mother "saying that the man she went away with was beating her and starving her."

"What did your father do when he heard that?" asked Dempsey.

"Well, my father said, 'The poor creature. Send her a letter and tell her to come home.'"

The letter was dispatched, and Anna Fish returned to her family, seemingly contrite. One week later, however, John Straube had shown up at the door, pleading with his paramour to take him back. Fish himself was away at work again. Mrs. Fish invited her lover inside and hid him in the attic, where he continued to live. "She used to bring food up to him, unbeknown to my father," Mrs. DeMarco explained.

Before long, however, Fish had found out about Straube. Though he was willing to forgive his wife, he insisted that Straube had to go. But Anna Fish refused to give up her lover and ran off again, this time for good.

All this was not to say that her father, kind and forgiving as he was, did not have his small eccentricities. Mrs. DeMarco recalled the time in 1931 when Fish was living with her family in Astoria, Queens. They had just finished lunch when Fish began squirming in his chair. "And I says, 'What's the matter, pop, is your rupture bothering you again?' Because he had a rupture and was operated on, and I thought maybe it had come back to him. He says, 'Oh no, no. You see, not so long ago I put three more of those needles in me.' I didn't know what to think. I says, 'Well, what did you do that for, pop?' He says, 'Well, you see, there is a mood that comes over me and I just can't help myself.'"

Dempsey nodded as he listened to this anecdote, then asked, "What can you say about your father's habits generally?"

"He never smoked, never drank." Mrs. DeMarco sniffed back some tears. "He had very good habits."

At 4:45 P.M., Justice Close, after apologizing to the jury for having to "detain them over the weekend," recessed court until 10 A.M. the following Monday. The murder trial of Albert Fish had reached its exact midpoint.

33

∽∾∾∾∾∾∾∾∾∾∿

"We all thought Papa Fish was a funny kind of man, but we were all so young and countrified that we just assumed that men from New York were all like that."

MARY NICHOLAS

Except for juror number nine, Louis S. Hirsch—who was granted a two-hour visit to his Scarsdale home on Saturday afternoon because of the death of his seventy-five-year-old mother-in-law, Mrs. Anna Brainin—the Fish jury spent the weekend confined in the Roger Smith Hotel. Room windows open to the unseasonable warmth, which reached a record-breaking seventy-four degrees on Saturday, the men passed the time playing pinochle and bridge, reading novels, and poring over the newspapers. All the articles about the Fish trial had been scissored from the papers, but there was still plenty to read about, from the latest celebrity gossip to at least one event of genuinely world-shaking significance.

From the Midwest came a report that aviator Wiley Post had failed in his second attempt to set a nonstop, coast-to-coast record when a sudden oxygen loss in his cockpit had forced him to bring down his weather-beaten plane, the Winnie Mae, at the Cleveland Airport. Down in St. Petersburg, Babe Ruth, wearing the uniform of the Boston Braves, made his debut against his former team-mates. (The Braves beat the Yankees by a score of three to two, though the Bambino contributed little to the victory, having been held to a single hit.) In London, Woolworth heiress Barbara Hutton—whose personal fortune was estimated at $42,000,000—confirmed rumors of her impending divorce from Prince Alexis Mdivani.

These stories, however, were trivia compared to the stunning news from Berlin, where Adolph Hitler effectively tore up the Versailles Treaty over the weekend by announcing the reinstitution of military conscription in the Reich. A few days later, at a rally in Cologne, Nazi propagandist Jules Steicher made an impassioned speech comparing Hitler to Christ.

As shocking as the testimony had been so far, it wasn't until day six of Albert Fish's trial—Monday, March 18—that Justice Close found it necessary to ban female spectators from the courtroom. Up to then, the jurors had heard various references to the extravagant perversity of Fish's obscene correspondence. On Monday, they finally began hearing the fulsome details of the old man's sexual pathology from witnesses who knew about it firsthand.

Grace Shaw was a married, middle-aged wife and mother, who, in September, 1934, had placed a classified ad in *The New York Times* Sunday edition offering to care for elderly or invalid boarders at her home in Little Neck, Queens. Several days after the ad appeared, she received a letter supposedly written by a movie director named Robert E. Hayden—one of Fish's favorite masquerades—who claimed that he was due back in Hollywood and needed a place to board his disabled son Bobby. The letter, which Dempsey read to the jury as soon as the courtroom was cleared of women, was one of Fish's standard sadomasochistic concoctions. "Here is the case," he had written.

When 5, Bobby fell down the cellar stairs. Sustained a brain concussion. Has never been really normal since. Though going on 20, good looking, well built, fully developed, he has the mentality of the age when he fell. Every part of his body has grown but the brain. He is harmless and just as easy to spank or switch as a child of 5 . . . He gets cross & cranky at times and don't always mind. I am now trying out European treatment in such cases. Prof. Cairo of Vienna Austria recommends it. He says when he gets a spell *he must be whipped.* They are having great success with it over there in such cases. So you see, as his own father I would sooner have him whipped than have him lose his reason entirely. . . . Should you take him in charge, on the first occasion he shows temper *spank him* same as you would a small boy and don't hesitate to use the cat-o-nine tails on his bare behind.

When Mrs. Shaw wrote back to say that she had consulted her twenty-year-old daughter and both of them were willing to care for Bobby in the style "Hayden" had described, she received a warm response by return mail. "Just got home and found your letter," Fish had written. "Am so glad you are interested. Before I call on you, will you kindly advise me—Are you a widow? And if so would you consider another marriage?"

Mrs. Shaw replied that she was indeed married, though her husband's presence, she hastened to add, would not in any way interfere with the regimen recommended by the eminent Professor Cairo of Vienna. Apparently, Fish was somewhat crestfallen by the news of Mrs. Shaw's marital status. Clearly, she was a woman after his own heart. But he was happy to have lucked upon her nevertheless and immediately sent a reply:

My Dear Mrs. Shaw

Just got your very nice letter. I am much pleased to know that you are not one bit ashamed to strip Bobby naked and bathe him. Am also glad you spoke to your daughter and she is willing to aid you in taking care of him. There is no good reason why either of you should be ashamed. You know *times* have changed and so have the *people.* What in times past was considered immodest is now very commonplace. Then again look at what young girls training to become nurses *see* and *touch* in hospitals. Now with so many brothers and sisters, you should be highly proficient in bathing. Not to speak of the fine art of spanking. You know in Bobby's case *whipping* is to be your pass word. In your efforts to earn a living for yourself and daughter, you are fortunate in having a girl old enough to assist her mother in using a paddle or the cat-o-nine-tails on Bobby's bare behind. You say she gives her OK and is willing to do her part. I shall be very glad to *compensate* her for spanking or switching him. Bear this in mind, both of you. It is for *his own good* that he is to be whipped. So don't let your heart stay your hand. Do you know that I feel that in part I am to blame for the condition Bobby is in. My conscience says that for being careless I should be well whipped *in the same manner (and place)* both of you will whip Bobby. Some day I hope you will accommodate *me.* I would give a nice new $100 bill for a good old fashioned spanking and a taste of the switch. There is a place on 42 St., Fleishman's Baths, where naked men are rubbed *all over* by women. White—Black—Chinese. I could go there and be well whipped. Most women would get a kick out spanking a naked man. But I prefer some privacy—a home. Let your daughter read this letter. I am a man of the world and she can get knowledge of the world through it.

I feel that we shall be fast friends.

Again, Mrs. Shaw conveyed her willingness to perform the prescribed services. With that, Fish commenced a month-long relationship with the Queens housewife, conducted mostly by mail, that grew progressively more perverse. Fish wrote to her regularly, sometimes twice a day, describing in ever more graphic detail the corporal punishments Bobby's mental health required. At one point, he even enclosed a helpful little diagram, representing the ideal position for a spanking—belly-down, spread-eagle, ankles and wrists secured to the corner bedposts, bare buttocks ready for the whip. And to all these proposals Mrs. Shaw gave her unqualified consent.

According to her courtroom testimony, Mrs. Shaw was simply stringing her correspondent along until she had gathered enough evidence to bring to the postal authorities—though under cross-examination, she admitted that she had, in fact, been willing to perform the proposed "duties" on Bobby for the substantial sums "Hayden" had promised.

In any event, she did a good job of convincing Fish that he had found the dominatrix of his dreams. Eventually he contrived to meet Mrs. Shaw in person, hoping to receive, as he put it in another letter, "some good home cooking with a good spanking thrown in."

But—though he had been paving the way for this possibility from the very start ("some day I hope you will accommodate *me*")—the old man decided, for whatever reason, not to show up in the guise of Hayden. Instead, he invented another identity for himself, a "friend and ward" of Hayden's named James Pell, whom he introduced in a letter dated October 7, 1934. "Last night," Fish had written:

I thought of a good way to *test your ability at Spanking*. Now Mr. James W. Pell is a friend & ward of mine. He has been declared incompetent and I have $32,500 of his money in trust. He is without a living relation and I don't see why you can't earn some of his money. Two of his sons were blown to pieces in the War. At times he imagines he is a boy at school, has been naughty and must be spanked for it . . . The least I have in mind is this. You have told me that I need not worry about you being ashamed to strip Bobby naked and spank his bare behind. If you are not ashamed of Bobby, you won't be of Jimmy. So when you meet him, take him upstairs, undress him, give him a bath, then *spank him good*. He will say teacher whip me. You might as well let your daughter acquire the art of spanking by beginning on Jimmy.

The very next day, Fish sent Mrs. Shaw another letter containing additional details about Pell. "In 1928 he was operated on for a hernia. When you have him stripped you will see the mark of the incision. Look on his left groin, from his penis to his hipbone. He was prepared for another operation ten days ago. All hair shaved off. That is why he looks like a *picked chicken*. . . . Jimmy has a habit of painting his behind red or gold. When you strip him you will see."

Mrs. Shaw agreed to meet Pell. And so, on a Sunday afternoon in late October, Fish—carrying a letter of introduction, supposedly written by Hayden, plus a small, newspaper-wrapped package—rode the bus to Glenwood Avenue and Northern Boulevard, where he was met by Mrs. Shaw. Surprised at the shabby appearance of the withered old man, Mrs. Shaw led him along the quiet suburban streets to her home. In response to his question, she explained that her husband was away on an errand and not expected back for at least one hour.

Ushering him into the living room, she introduced him to her daughter, who offered him a cup of coffee. While the young woman went off to prepare it, Fish handed Mrs. Shaw the paper-wrapped package and letter. She carried them into another room and tore each of them open in turn.

Inside the package was a length of rope that been soaked in brine. The letter, as she testified at the trial, contained detailed instructions for whipping the old man with the rope. The language of the letter, said Mrs. Shaw, "was of such a nature that I could not go through with it."

Shaken, Mrs. Shaw returned to the living room and pulled up a chair in front of the old man. "Mr. Pell," she said, "there is no reason why I should have to whip you. There is no need for it. You are not a patient of mine. Were I to do such a thing and you dropped dead, I would be held for murder."

By then, Mrs. Shaw had become convinced that she had been made the victim of a hoax, that there was no wealthy movie director named Robert Hayden—only this shriveled old deviant with his drooping moustache and painted ass. She allowed him to finish his coffee and then sent him on his way.

The next day, she made copies of all the letters she had received from "Hayden" and mailed them to *The New York Times*. Within a week, the material had been passed along to the proper authorities and, in early November, a postal inspector named R. H. Kemper was assigned to the case.

Acting under Kemper's instructions, Mrs. Shaw continued to correspond with "Hayden." Indeed, she made the tone of her letters markedly more personal, addressing him for the first time as "My dear Robert." The increased intimacy of her letters sent Fish into rapturous flights of utterly degraded fantasy. "My Dearest Darling Sweetest Little Girlie Grace," Fish wrote to her on November 9. "Just got your letter calling me dear Robert. Dear Honey Heart of mine, you have *captured me*. I am your Slave and *everything I have is yours*. Prick—Balls—Ass *and all the money you want*. . . . If you were my own sweet wife, you would not be afraid of me. O girlie of my heart would I love you—and how. Hug-Kiss-Squeeze you, spank you, then KISS *just where* I spanked! *Your nice-pretty-fat-sweet ass*. . . . You won't need toilet paper to wipe your sweet pretty fat Ass as I shall eat all of it, then *Lick* your sweet ass *clean with my tongue*. . . ." And so on.

Following Kemper's directions, Mrs. Shaw answered these ravings by asking "Hayden" to her home for Thanksgiving dinner, an invitation which he immediately accepted. When the holiday arrived, several post-office inspectors plus a New York City police detective were waiting at her home to arrest the old man.

But he never showed up.

Helen Karlsen, the Brooklyn landlady who, in 1927, had been another recipient of Fish's unwelcome attentions, also testified on Monday. Unlike the forthright Mrs. Shaw, she blushed at having to discuss such sordid business. No amount of coaxing by Dempsey could get her to describe the precise contents of the letters Fish had slipped under her bedroom door.

"Do you recall the substance of the letters?" Dempsey asked.

"Well, I do but I don't want to say anything about it."

Dempsey finally prevailed on her to summarize one of the less unmentionable parts of Fish's first letter. "He told me he was going to a lodge," Mrs. Karlsen said, her voice barely above a whisper, "and he expected to have a lot of things done to him, and one of the principal things would be he would be tarred and feathered, and he wanted me to help him next day to remove all this. He said the lodge allowed him twenty dollars for this procedure and he would double it to forty dollars if I would help him."

"The other two letters," asked Dempsey. "Were they of similar character?"

"Yes, only worse than that."

Mrs. Karlsen went on to describe the bloody, nail-studded paddles she had discovered in the attic after Fish's eviction, though she shied away from characterizing the "little mess" she had found on his bedroom floor.

"What do you mean by a little mess?" asked Dempsey.

"I don't like to say just what it was," Mrs. Karlsen replied. "He just made some dirt and left it behind the door."

"Can you say what kind of dirt it was?"

"Human dirt."

"Number Two?" asked Dempsey, resorting to playground euphemism.

"Yes."

Without doubt, the day's weirdest testimony came from the person described by reporters as a "surprise defense witness." This was Mary Nicholas, Fish's seventeen-year-old "step kiddie" to whom he'd written from Eastview, promising her "18 good hard smacks" on her bare behind for her birthday and describing the voyeuristic opportunities available at the Y.M.C.A. Dempsey had brought her to White Plains from her home in Bartlett, Ohio, to testify on behalf of the old man she continued to refer to as "Papa."

A plain-featured high school freshman with a pug nose and round, wire frame glasses, Mary struck the street-savvy newsmen at the press table as the epitome of Midwestern innocence. Reared in rural Ohio, the youngest of seven children of Mrs. Myrta Nicholas—one of the three women Fish had wed illegally in 1930—the dark-haired teenager seemed as naive as a nursery schooler as she told of the bizarre doings that had taken place in her home shortly after Fish's arrival.

It had been in January, 1930, when Mary was twelve, that Fish had traveled to the Nicholases' little house in Bartlett to meet Mary's widowed mother, whose name he had gotten from a matrimonial agency. He spent the first night getting acquainted with the family and describing his train trip from New York.

On the second night, he offered to teach the children some games.

"What games?" Dempsey asked.

"Buck-Buck, How Many Hands Up," Mary said pleasantly.

Speaking in the tone of voice grown-ups tend to use when conversing with very young children, Dempsey asked her to explain how the game was played.

"He went into his room," said Mary, "and he had a little pair of trunks, brown trunks, that he put on. He took everything else off but those. He put those on and came out into the front room, and he got down on his hands and knees, and he had a paint stick that he stirred paint with."

"About how big a stick was that?"

"It was about that long," Mary said, holding her hands approximately two feet apart. "And about that wide," she said, moving her palms to within six inches of each other.

Dempsey asked her to continue.

"He would give the stick to one of us, and then he would get down on his hands and knees and we would sit on his back, one at a time, with our back facing him, and then we would put up so many fingers, and he was to tell how many fingers we had up, and if he guessed right, which he never did, why, we weren't supposed to hit him. Sometimes he would even say more fingers than we really had. And if he never guessed right, why, we would hit him as many fingers as we would have up."

Justice Close leaned toward the witness. "Was your mother there when you played that?" he asked.

"Yes."

"How long would you play that game?" Dempsey asked. "For hours?"

"Oh, no," Mary said. "We wouldn't play it very long, just about an hour at a time every evening."

Occasionally, Mary went on to explain, they played the game with a hairbrush instead of a stick. For variety's sake.

"Which end of the hairbrush would you hit him with?" Dempsey asked.

Mary shrugged. "Sometimes the side with the bristles on, sometimes the other side, just whichever way we happened to pick it up."

"And all he had on was this little pair of trunks?"

"Yes, and they were very thin."

When Dempsey asked if she and her siblings had played anything else with their elderly guest, Mary said, yes, a game called "Sack of Potatoes Over." And how was that one played? inquired Dempsey.

"He put on those little trunks, and then he would throw us up on his shoulder, and we would slide down his back, and we would scratch him with our nails. By the time we would get through playing, why, his back would be red."

Fish had also tried to introduce his new little friends to another of his favorite activities, but this time he had met with some resistance. "He brought a package of pins with him," Mary explained, "and he told my sister and I one evening to see if we could stick those pins in our fingernails right up there just as far as they could get, and he gave my sister and I one, and before we even had any stuck into our fingers, he stuck a pin in his finger, too."

"In how many fingers did he stick it?"

"All of them."

"How far up did he shove the pins?"

"As far as it would go."

"What did you notice about his fingers after he had the pins stuck all the way in?"

"They bled," Mary said simply.

Fish seemed disappointed that Mary and her sister weren't as enthusiastic about this pastime as they had been about "Buck-Buck, How Many Hands Up" and "Sack of Potatoes Over." "He asked us how come we didn't stick the pins in our fingers, too." But when the children explained the reason—"we told him it hurt"—he behaved very understandingly and "never said anything more."

Apparently, no one in the Nicholas household saw anything wrong with Fish's little games. They couldn't help noticing, however, that the old man did have a few habits that seemed peculiar even to them. "Every night after we would get through playing the games," Mary continued, "why, he would go to the toilet, and he took all the paper off the roll and lit it, and he had a big fire. The first night we noticed it, I just happened to be outside and seen smoke coming out the door and I ran back and told my mother. We went down there, and there he was, he had a fire in the middle of the floor. She told him to put it out, and he wouldn't do it, he wouldn't help put it out, so we got some water and put it out."

"Did the fire do much damage?" asked Dempsey.

"No."

"Did it burn the floor?"

"No. He done that every night."

"He set a fire every night?" Dempsey asked, his tone tinged with incredulity.

"Yes, every night."

"In the center of the floor there?"

"Yes."

Apparently, however, Fish's virtues—whatever they

were—outweighed his shortcomings in the eyes of Mary's mother. Ten days after the old man showed up in Bartlett with his paint stick and matches and package of pins, he and the widow Nicholas were married.

Several members of Fish's immediate family added their contributions to the never-ending catalogue of Fish's eccentricities. His son Henry described the time the old man had spent three days trying to fill some cracks in the front stoop of their house by pouring several sackfuls of uncooked oatmeal down them.

Mrs. Anna Collins, Fish's oldest daughter, recalled a night in 1917 when Henry—then a child of three—had asked her for a glass of water. Walking downstairs to fetch it, she had found her father lying on the floor, completely rolled up in the living-room carpet. Only his head was visible, from the nose up. "Pop," she had admonished him. "Go on up to bed. You will never get any rest that way." The next morning, when Anna came downstairs to fix breakfast, Fish was just unrolling himself from the carpet. When the girl asked him why he had chosen to sleep that way instead of upstairs in his bed, Fish had replied, "St. John the Apostle told me to."

Fish's pretty, eleven-year-old granddaughter Gloria— the apple of the old man's eye—recalled a summer day, four years earlier, when she had come inside her house for a glass of water and found her grandfather bent over the living-room sofa, spanking himself with a stick.

Eugene Fish, the last of Fish's children to testify, told of the time he had discovered his father standing nude by the front window of an apartment the old man had been hired to paint, running a dry brush over the window casing. A particularly poignant moment in the trial occurred toward the end of Gene's testimony, when he was asked about an incident that had taken place in April, 1928, when he, his brother John, and their father were sharing an apartment on East 81st Street in Manhattan.

"One night," Gene began, "I returned home from work about 5:15 or 5:30. We lived on the top floor. The kitchen was in between the front room and the back bedroom. As I came into the kitchen, I noticed a light in the bedroom. The kitchen was dark. So I walked into the bedroom"—here, Gene's voice cracked slightly—"and I saw my father sticking needles into himself."

"What happened at that time?" Dempsey asked gently.

"I asked him why he was doing it," Gene answered, his lower lip beginning to tremble, "And he said he had a message from Christ." With that, the young man buried his face in his hands and broke into sobs.

The psychiatric testimony began early on Tuesday, March 19, when Fredric Wertham took the stand. He remained there for the rest of the day and was back the following morning.

Of all Dempsey's witnesses, Dr. Wertham was by far the most important. His testimony cast far-reaching light on Fish's psychopathology, illuminating for the first time the terrible depths of his madness. To be sure, there were large, shadowy areas of the old man's life and mind whose dark secrets Wertham had not been able to penetrate. Fish's sexual history stretched back over half a century and was so steeped in iniquity that even he had lost track of his crimes.

Still, the story Wertham told that day—the seventh of the trial—provided the most shockingly detailed picture of Albert Howard Fish that the world would ever get. Once again, Justice Close ordered all women spectators from the courtroom. The twelve male jurors, who had begun to seem slightly numbed by the week-long barrage of horror, were jolted to life by Wertham's testimony, looking visibly dismayed throughout much of the day. Fish's children, sitting on the bench behind their father, repeatedly covered their eyes and wept.

Wertham began by sketching Fish's family history. In two generations (meaning, Wertham explained, Fish's "brothers and sisters and the brothers and sisters" of his parents), the doctor had discovered no less than seven cases of extreme psychopathology, including a paternal uncle who suffered from a religious psychosis, a half-brother who was confined to a state hospital for the insane, a younger brother who died of hydrocephalus ("water on the brain," as Fish called it), and a sister who, in Fish's words, "had some sort of mental affliction." Fish's mother, too, was regarded by her neighbors as "very queer, inasmuch as she heard noises on the street and saw things."

Fish's father, Randall, had been seventy-five-years old when the boy was born. Fish claimed to have distinct memories of how the old man looked. Beyond that, he recalled only one detail, the nickname his father had given him—"Stick in the Mud."

Randall Fish died when his youngest son was five, and the boy was shipped off to St. John's Orphanage in Washington, D.C. The years he spent in that institution were the stuff of nightmares, a brutal induction into a life of petty crime and routine depravity. It was there that he first learned to associate pleasure with pain.

"Now the experience in the orphanage is very important," Wertham explained.

Because he dates his earliest sexual abnormalities to this time. He described to me very vividly that in that place not only did the inmates commit all sorts of sensory acts with each other, in which he joined, but it made the greatest impression on him. One of the guardians there, a sister or teacher, had the habit of frequently whipping the boys and taking six at a time and having them strip and having one see what happened to the others. And he remembers very vividly seeing the other boys whipped, and he recalls that before the age of seven, he had his first sexual feeling.

"And what did he get that feeling from?" asked Dempsey.

"From being whipped himself and from seeing other boys whipped and screaming."

As a young child, Wertham continued, Fish had displayed "a number of early neurotic traits," including enuresis—bedwetting—which he experienced until he was eleven. He was also a high-strung and inordinately "sensitive" child. "I can give you one example of that," said Wertham, going on to explain that Fish's real first name was Hamilton. He had changed it as a teenager, however, because his schoolmates used to tease him by calling him "Ham-and-Eggs," and "he couldn't stand it." The name he adopted, Albert, had originally belonged to his younger brother, the one who had died of brain disease.

At this point, Wertham proceeded directly to what he called "the outstanding fact" of Fish's life, a fact, he said, which could be summed up in a single sentence. "I can tell you that, to the best of my medical knowledge, every sexual abnormality that I have ever heard of this man has practiced—not only has he thought about it, not only has he daydreamed about it, but he has practiced it."

To begin with, said Wertham, Fish was a sadist of "incredible cruelty . . . All his mind was bent on eliciting responses of pain in someone else." In addition, he was a homosexual. "All through his life, women were just a substitute," said Wertham. "An entirely secondary choice and secondary pleasure."

Fish's third "outstanding" abnormality, Wertham went on, was what was known technically as pedophilia. His "prime sexual interest," the doctor explained, "has only been children from the age of about five to fourteen or sixteen."

There were more abnormalities, of course. Indeed, Wertham had provided Dempsey with a list of no less than seventeen perversions or paraphilias that Fish had practiced throughout his life. For the moment, however, Wertham was only interested in focusing on Fish's three "main abnormalities" and the strategies he had relied on to satisfy them:

> He started his sexual career, so to say, at the age of seventeen, at the time he became a painter. Now, that profession of painter this man has used as a convenience. He worked in many different institu-

tions. He worked in Y.M.C.A.'s, he worked in homes for the tubercular, he worked in any kind of home where there were children, where he thought he could get children. In all these places, he made his headquarters the basement or the cellar. And he had the habit of wearing a painter's overalls over his nude body, which gave him two advantages. First of all, he was nude in a moment. And secondly, he would be seen by his victims only in his painter's clothes, and if they later met him on the streets or in his other clothes, they wouldn't recognize him.

There was another benefit to the painter's trade, too. It allowed Fish to move easily from one locality to another. His basic equipment was highly portable. All he needed to do was pack up his brushes and tarps and leave, though sometimes, Wertham explained, Fish had found it necessary to depart in such a hurry that he had simply abandoned his belongings and disappeared.

As Wertham spoke, a terrifying picture came into focus of Fish as a creature of fiendish cunning, a prowler in the darkness, emerging from his netherworld to snare his young prey. "Now this man has roamed around in basements and cellars for fifty years," said Wertham. "There were so many innumerable instances that I can't begin to give you how many there are. But I believe to the best of my knowledge that he has raped one hundred children. At least."

After committing one of his outrages, Fish would promptly pick up and move, sometimes to a different neighborhood, sometimes to a different city. And sometimes, "after a particularly brutal episode," to a different state. Fish had been "in no less than twenty-three states, from New York to Montana," said Wertham. "And in every state he has had something to do with children."

Here Wertham glanced over at Justice Close. "The story becomes a little more repugnant as we go along." This remark turned out to be a significant understatement.

Though many details of Fish's past remained hazy,

Wertham had learned that, in his teens, Fish "had been a homosexual prostitute, a boy who stood around on corners and went with other men for money." As a young man in his twenties, he had also made a trip overseas to Brussels, where he had visited brothels specializing in flagellation and other sadomasochistic acts. There, Fish had "practiced oral perversions on the rectums of men and women. He was also extremely interested in urine." After his return to America, Fish began to "do all of these things" to his child victims.

"The terrible thing of it all," Wertham continued, "is that his interest was not so much to have sexual relations with these children as to inflict pain on them."

Wertham explained Fish's method. He would entice his little victims into a basement with small bribes of candy or pocket change. Once there, he would bind them, rape them, and beat them—or worse. Sometimes he would gag them, "although he preferred not to gag them, circumstances permitting, for he liked to hear their cries."

Many of his victims, Wertham explained, "came from poorer classes. He told me he selected colored children especially because the authorities didn't pay much attention when they were hurt or missing."

The doctor went on to describe an instance in which Fish had "kept a colored boy in a shack by the Potomac in Washington for a number of weeks. He undressed this boy, took his clothes away, and kept him as a captive. He told me that he intended to kill this boy, but somehow or other it didn't work out."

In another instance, Fish had taken a young boy, bound him, and whipped him violently "on both sides of his body." Fish had eventually let this little victim go, but the boy's genitals were bleeding so badly that Fish became frightened and fled the city.

The most appalling incident of all the atrocities that Wertham recounted that day was the so-called Kedden episode, which had taken place in 1911. At the time, Fish was forty-one and living in St. Louis.

Kedden, a handsome but slow-witted nineteen-year-old who looked even younger, had "bummed his way from the South on a banana train." There had been five black men in the boxcar along with him, and the six of them had spent the trip engaging in "all kinds of sexual activities, mostly fellatio and homosexuality."

Fish "picked the boy up somehow" and brought him to his room. Kedden was covered with lice. Fish bought a patent hair remover and "stripped all the hair off his body, including the hair off his pubis." Then, for a period of two to three weeks, "they carried on all kinds of mutual sadistic and masochistic activities."

"He had this boy whip him and he played all sorts of games—one was the father and one was the child, one was the teacher and one was the child. He forced the boy to urinate on him." Fish drank the boy's urine and ate his feces, then "forced the other one to eat and drink these things, too."

Their games began to grow more frenzied. At one point, Fish "cut the boy's buttocks with a razor blade and attempted to drink the blood." Eventually, Fish tied the boy up, stimulated him to erection, and began to cut off his penis with a pair of scissors. Before he could finish the job, however, he experienced a sudden change of heart. "The boy had such an agonized look that Fish couldn't stand it," Wertham explained. Binding the bleeding wound, Fish left a ten dollar bill on the bed for the mutilated boy and ran away to another city.

Wertham paused while the jurors, some of whom looked seriously shaken, readjusted themselves in their seats.

"All right, go ahead, sir," Dempsey said after a moment.

"I might mention here some other very strange abnormality in his sex life," Wertham said, and proceeded to describe a perversion that was not simply "very strange" but apparently unique in the annals of *psychopathia sexualis*.

"He has on a number of occasions taken flowers, taken roses, and inserted these roses into his penis. Then he would stand before the mirror and look at himself. He would get sexual gratification from that. In the end, he would eat the roses."

Next, Dempsey asked Wertham about Fish's relationships with women. After all, the man had been married for many years and had fathered six children. Wouldn't that seem to indicate a capacity for "normal relationships"?

Wertham shook his head. "All his relationships with women were just as abnormal as his relationships with men. In all his marriages he practiced these things with his wives. In fact, he selected them for that particular purpose. He married his wife when she was nineteen years old and he was in his thirties. He made sure before he married her that she was interested at least to some extent in the things he was doing, and his relations with her were entirely abnormal."

As for the other women he had married, "he made sure first, from the letters, that they would fall in with all these things."

Very simply, Fish was incapable of experiencing "love for any mature person. He never had any feelings of friendship for any mature person." Wertham sketched a picture of Fish as a hopelessly stunted personality. "I might say I have never seen a man who was so interested in merely infantile and childish desires. After all, a child would be cruel to an insect, and a child does not know the difference between man and woman, and a child would play with urine and feces without knowing what that means. But I have never seen a man who did all these things up to the age of sixty-five, as this man has."

As pathological as Fish's entire life had been, it took an even darker turn sometime in his mid-fifties. It was then that he began to manifest the signs of full-blown psychosis. Among other things, he became obsessed with the notion of castrating and killing a young boy as a form of penance for his own sins.

"He had always been very much interested in

religion," Wertham explained. "He told me very proudly that religion was his great point." Indeed, as a young boy Fish had dreamed of becoming a minister.

His religious preoccupations became markedly more intense—and dangerous—during his mid-fifties. "At that time he became interested in ideas of atonement or punishment," said Wertham. In his deranged imagination, Fish dwelled obsessively on the story of Abraham and Isaac, persuaded that he, too, should attempt to sacrifice a young boy, "and if it wasn't right, then an angel would stop him at the last moment."

At other times, he had visions of Christ and heard mumbled words—"stripes," "rewardeth," "delighteth," "chastiseth"—that he interpreted as divine commandments to torment and kill. Fish would organize the words into quasi-Biblical messages: "Blessed is the man who correcteth his son in whom he delighteth with stripes, for great shall be his reward." or "Happy is he that taketh Thy little ones and dasheth their heads against the stones."

On at least one occasion prior to the Budd incident, he had tried to carry out his sacrificial plan. He had lured a fourteen-year-old boy to a preselected spot in the country, where he intended to bind him, castrate him, whip him until he was unconscious, and then leave him to bleed to death. But "at the last moment, an automobile came by, so he saw this was too dangerous and gave it up."

Originally, he had lined up Edward Budd for the same purpose but had been discouraged both by the boy's size and the presence of his friend, Willie Korman. And so Fish had settled for Edward's little sister. Grace, of course, was a girl, but a prepubescent one, her body lithe and boyish. In the frenzied moments of the murder, Fish had actually perceived her as a young boy (as he had mentioned during one of his confessions). Citing Freud, Wertham later explained that, in beheading Grace, Fish was performing a symbolic castration.

Fish's religious mania also accounted, at least in part, for his practice of inserting needles into his body.

Though he obtained masochistic gratification from torturing himself in this way—he invariably achieved a sexual climax during each of these episodes—he also "did it in response to his idea that God wanted him to punish himself so as to atone for all these sins he had committed."

Wertham also explained that, in addition to shoving needles so far inside himself that they couldn't be extracted, Fish had on countless occasions stuck them only part way in and then removed them. As a result, the X-rays revealed only "a very small part of what this man has suffered."

Many times, Fish had "tried to insert them into his testicles." But the pain had been unbearable—even for him—and he had ceased trying.

By now, it was late afternoon. Before the day ended, Dempsey wanted to make sure that Wertham had a chance to testify on one last, critical matter. "Now, was anything said about cannibalism or eating human flesh?"

"He told me that for a long time, many, many years, he had been interested in the subject of cannibalism," Wertham replied.

He told me that he had read with great pleasure all sorts of accounts where this was supposed to have happened. For instance, he claims he read about the Perry expedition, that on a ship they had to kill three sailors and eat them, something that was discussed in the newspapers. He read other incidents of that sort, where explorers in Africa or somewhere had killed somebody. He said his brother had told him certain stories, how in China during a famine people had eaten human flesh and that he himself was consumed with the desire to eat human flesh. He definitely told me that he ate the flesh of Grace Budd.

Wertham went on to describe the stew Fish had made from the little girl's body and the "absolute sexual excitement" he had known while consuming it. But there was another dimension to the experience, too, for even here, Fish's religious mania had played a part.

Unbelievable as it seemed, this ultimate outrage had been a sacramental as well as a sexual act for Fish. In his insanely disordered mind, the drinking of the child's blood and the eating of her flesh had been "associated with the idea of Holy Communion."

On Wednesday morning at nine A.M., Wertham was back on the witness stand. It was time for Dempsey to present the "hypothetical question" that he and his associates had spent the previous evening putting together.

A legal device dictated by the rules of evidence, this question was a detailed recapitulation of all the evidence presented so far—cast, however, as hypothesis instead of fact and culminating in a question mark.

Gallagher insisted on examining the question before Dempsey presented it. The lawyers spent the next two hours closeted with Justice Close. It was nearly 11:15 when the three men finally emerged from the judge's chambers and Dempsey began reading the question to Wertham.

"Now, Doctor, assuming that on or about the 19th day of May, 1870, a male child was born in Washington, the youngest of twelve children upon his father's side and the youngest of seven children on his mother's side," Dempsey began. He proceeded to relate Fish's biography from his boyhood in the orphanage to his life as a family man and devoted father, prefacing each part of the narrative with the same formulaic phrase—"Now assume further, Doctor . . ."

Dempsey went on to describe Anna Fish's desertion and the increasingly weird behavior Fish's children had observed in their father in the ensuing years. Eventually the lawyer arrived at the Budd murder itself, describing it yet again in graphic detail. Then came the series of bizarre episodes that followed—Fish's obscenity arrests and bigamous marriages, his visit to the family of Mary Nicholas, his dealings with Grace Shaw, the things that Albert Jr. had witnessed while living with the old man.

"Assume, further, Doctor, that in the year 1934 the defendant was residing at 1883 Amsterdam Avenue in the City of New York and was seen in his bedroom jumping up and down looking back at himself and hitting himself with a paddle. Assume further that he was hitting himself on the backside and his face had a very red color."

On and on the question went, describing the letter Fish had mailed to the Budds, his arrest and confessions, his obsession with cannibalism, the clippings on nudism and sterilization found among his belongings, the needles in his body and burn scars on his gluteal cleft, the letters he had written from prison.

The entire question, 15,000-words long and covering forty-five typewritten pages, took an hour and fifteen minutes to read. It was nearly 12:30 P.M. when Dempsey finally reached the end. "Now, Doctor, assuming the truth of the facts as stated in the foregoing hypothetical question, what, in your opinion, is the mental condition of this defendant today?"

Wertham needed only three words to answer: "He is insane."

Following the lunch recess, Gallagher cross-examined Wertham for several hours, pressing him on the question of Fish's ability to distinguish right from wrong. Didn't Fish's cunning both in the commission of the crime and in his attempts to conceal it afterward indicate that he did, in fact, know the difference?

Wertham responded that Fish was certainly intelligent enough to understand the consequences of his crime and to take precautions against discovery and arrest. But to really know right from wrong requires a "certain emotional sympathy," Wertham explained. "You have to *feel* what is right and wrong. This defendant is suffering from a mental disease. He is so mixed up about the question of punishment, of sin, of atonement, of religion, of torture that he is in a particularly bad state to know the difference between right and wrong. He is even worse off than that, because he actually has a perverted, a distorted, if you will, an insane, knowledge of right and wrong."

At another point, the prosecutor asked whether much of what Fish had told Wertham might not have been fantasy. Referring to the needles in the old man's groin, Wertham replied that he had never seen a fantasy that showed up on an X-ray. "And if the attorney will permit me to say," Wertham added, "the child is dead, after all. I mean, it was no fantasy when he told me he killed this girl."

It was late afternoon when Wertham left the stand. Determined to have the case in the hands of the jury by week's end, Justice Close ordered an evening session, the trial's first. After recessing for supper, the court reconvened at 7:30 P.M. to hear the testimony of Dempsey's two remaining expert witnesses, Doctors Smith Ely Jelliffe and Henry A. Riley, a professor of neurology at the College of Physicians and Surgeons, who had been brought in to bolster the insanity defense shortly before the trial began.

The two physicians corroborated Wertham's findings, adding a few new details. Riley's testimony stressed Fish's religious delusions, describing the old man's hallucinations or, as Fish called them, "visitations": "He would see the face of Christ or the whole body of Christ garbed in various kinds of raiment, showing the marks of the nails in the hands and the feet," Riley explained. "Often he said he could see blood actually coming out of the side of Christ. And usually when these visitations occurred, he could see the lips of Christ moving, and they would be saying things to him, giving him definite messages."

One of these messages shed additional light on Fish's motives for murdering Grace Budd. "He told me," said Riley, "that he had received a direct command that he should take a virgin and sacrifice her so that she shouldn't become a harlot."

Jelliffe confirmed that the "whole killing of the Budd girl took on the character of a religious ritual." He also repeated Fish's revised account of the crime—an account which contradicted, in one key respect, the old man's previous confessions.

In his initial statements to the police, Fish had steadfastly denied any sexual dimension to the murder. To Jelliffe, however, he admitted otherwise, revealing that, while kneeling on her chest and choking the struggling girl, "he had had two emissions."

34

~~~~~~~~~~~~~

*He shall have judgment without mercy, that hath
showed no mercy.*

JAMES 2:13

Commenting on the trial years later, Frederic
Wertham had trouble keeping the scorn out of his voice
when he referred to the witnesses Gallagher put on the
stand on Thursday, March 21, to rebut the defense
psychiatrists. All four of these men, Wertham charged,
offered "extraordinary statements under oath." Their
testimony made for one of those questionable parades of
expert opinion "so often said to give a black eye to
psychiatry . . . especially forensic psychiatry."

Dr. Menas S. Gregory, former head of the Bellevue
Psychiatric Department, was the first to testify that
morning after the defense had rested its case. Gallagher
questioned him briefly, asking him to describe the examinations Fish had undergone during his thirty-day observation period in late 1930. Dr. Gregory then read the
report he had prepared in which he had diagnosed Fish
as "abnormal" but sane.

Dempsey's cross-examination was considerably more
intense. Fulfilling his pledge to blame the Bellevue staff
for "turning Fish back on the streets," Dempsey ham-
mered away at Gregory, his tone growing more scathing
as he went on. Put on the defensive, Gregory angrily
maintained that Fish was no different from millions of
other people.

"Is it a common sort of thing, Doctor, for people to

have sexual abnormalities with respect to urine and human excretion?" Dempsey inquired.

"Well, it is much commoner than you think."

Dempsey arranged his features into a "do tell" look. "Do you call a man who drinks urine and eats human excretion sane or insane?"

"Well, we don't call them mentally sick."

"That man is perfectly all right?" asked Dempsey incredulously.

"Not perfectly all right," Gregory said, making an effort to subdue the angry tremor in his voice. "But he is socially perfectly all right." Indeed, said Gregory, countless people suffered from the very same perversion. "Not only that, they are very successful people, successful artists, successful teachers, successful financiers."

A few moments later, as Dempsey continued to attack Gregory's handling of Fish's case, the psychiatrist became so agitated that he half-rose from his seat, shouting, "In a city hospital, you have to do the best you can!"

"And very often, the best you can is none too good," answered Dempsey, his voice heavy with scorn. "Isn't that right?"

"No!" shouted Gregory. "It is very excellent, and you can't show many mistakes!"

Justice Close leaned toward the witness. "Don't get excited, Doctor," he said soothingly.

"I am not excited," Gregory answered, but his voice was trembling so badly that the judge called a five-minute recess until the witness could compose himself.

Dr. Perry M. Lichtenstein, who had served as the resident physician in the Tombs prison for nearly twenty years, was the next witness. Before he began testifying, Dempsey spent a good deal of time questioning Lichtenstein's psychiatric qualifications. And for valid reasons, since Lichtenstein had never had a day's formal training in psychiatry. By his own admission, his knowledge of the field came almost entirely from his "personal studies of individuals." He had also read a number of books on the subject. Dr. Lichtenstein proudly maintained that from these sources, as well as from his long acquaintance with many qualified alienists, "I did learn a whole lot in psychiatry."

"I submit, if your Honor please," Dempsey said, turning to the bench, "that in questioning Dr. Lichtenstein's qualifications, we have a man here who upon his own admission has never had any hospital or institutional experience in the study of psychiatry, nervous or mental diseases. His education has been acquired in the Tombs during these twenty years, and it is an absolute fact that his connection with the Tombs has been that of an attending physician as distinguished from a psychiatrist. I therefore challenge the qualifications of Dr. Lichtenstein."

Gallagher was ready with an answer. "I want to state here," the prosecutor declared, "that the doctor stated he has drawn his experience from practical life, and that Abraham Lincoln never went to college."

"Abraham Lincoln never testified as a psychiatrist, as I know of," Dempsey replied dryly.

Nevertheless, Justice Close overruled Dempsey's objection and allowed Lichtenstein to proceed, leaving "the question of the weight of his testimony to the jury."

Unlike Dr. Gregory, Lichtenstein remained perfectly unflappable during his time on the stand. Though Dempsey battered away at his testimony for more than an hour, he could not shake the doctor's serene insistence that Fish's mind "was perfectly sound and that he knew what he was doing" when he murdered Grace Budd.

At one point Dempsey asked Lichtenstein if he recalled Fish's "statement that at the time of the killing he thought it was a boy."

"Yes, sir, I remember that," Dr. Lichtenstein said.

"Does that indicate to you that there was any confusion of ideas or that the defendant was laboring under any mental disturbance?"

Lichtenstein shook his head. "Not at all."

"In other words," Dempsey said, raising his eyebrows, "that does not indicate to you that there was any question in the defendant's mind at that time as to whether he knew what he was doing?"

"In my opinion," the doctor said calmly, "at that time

he had in mind that he wanted to take the boy originally, and while he perpetrated the act upon the girl he had a mental picture of the boy." Lichtenstein gave a little shrug. "It was nothing abnormal."

Lichtenstein also had a unique explanation for Fish's self-tormenting activities. "Assume, Doctor," Dempsey asked at one point, "that a man takes alcohol and puts it on cotton and puts that into his person and sets fire to it. Does that indicate an aggravated mental condition?"

"That is not masochistic," Lichtenstein declared. "He is only punishing himself and getting sex gratification that way." Of course "getting sex gratification" from being punished is the textbook definition of masochism. But Lichtenstein never noticed the self-contradiction.

Dr. Charles Lambert, the next psychiatric witness called in rebuttal, testified that, during his three-hour interview with Fish, the old man had been "frank, friendly, and talked freely in an orderly way." Fish had confessed to having violated "as many as twenty-five or thirty boys and girls" every year. His victims, according to Lambert, numbered in the hundreds. Like the two men who preceded him, Lambert declared that Fish was sane, defining him as a 'psychopathic personality without a psychosis."

"Doctor," said Dempsey, looking hard at the witness. "Assume that this man not only killed this girl but took her flesh to eat it. Will you state that that man could for nine days eat that flesh and still not have a psychosis and not have any mental diseases?"

"Well, there is no accounting for taste, Mr. Dempsey," Lambert replied breezily.

At a later point, Dempsey returned to the question of coprophagy. Lambert's response was much the same as Dr. Gregory's had been.

"Tell me how many cases in your experience you have seen of people who actually ate human feces, of your own knowledge," Dempsey inquired.

"Oh, I know individuals prominent in society," Lambert answered in his characteristically off-hand manner.

"One individual in particular that we all know," he added.

"That actually ate human feces?" Dempsey demanded.

"That used it as a side dish in his salad," Lambert replied, projecting the perfect nonchalance of the psychiatric investigator whose experience of human behavior had made him immune to surprise.

Dempsey had no more success in getting the final witness, Dr. James Vavasour, to admit that Fish's multiple perversions were a sign of psychosis. He did, however, manage to raise certain doubts about the alienist's impartiality, pointing out that in the five years Vavasour had been professionally associated with the Westchester District Attorney's office he had never once declared a defendant insane.

Like Lambert, Vavasour confided that one of his patients, "a very prominent public official," enjoyed dining on human feces. When Dempsey asked whether such behavior was common among psychopaths, Vavasour replied that it "was not uncommon."

Dempsey shook his head. "I have learned there are a lot of common things in this case I never knew about before," said the lawyer, undoubtedly speaking for many others in the courtroom for whom the trial had been a crash course in sexual psychopathology.

Minutes later, the state rested its case. Justice Close recessed the court until the following day at nine A.M. "Keep your minds open," he admonished the jurors. "Do not form or express any opinion until you hear the summation of counsel and the charge of the Court, when you will retire to deliberate with your fellow jurors."

As the day's session ended, Fish handed Dempsey a small scrap of paper on which he had scrawled a short, cryptic message—"Before you sum up, read to the jury Jeremiah, Chapter 19, 9th verse."

It is impossible, of course, to know what the old man was thinking when he made this suggestion. Perhaps, in his derangement, he hoped to impress the jury with his knowledge of the Bible. Or perhaps he was offering Scriptural justification for his deeds.

In any case, it seems unlikely that Dempsey would have helped his client's case by taking his advice.

The passage, involving the Lord's threats of punishment against the sinning kingdom of Judah, reads: "And I will cause them to eat the flesh of their sons and the flesh of their daughters, and they shall eat every one the flesh of his friend in the siege and straitness, wherewith their enemies, and they that seek their lives, shall straiten them."

Each of the summations lasted about two hours. Dempsey spoke first, rising to address the jury shortly after 9:15 A.M. on Friday, March 22, the tenth and final day of the trial.

Dempsey delivered an eloquent speech on behalf of the defendant whose crimes, by the lawyer's own admission, had been "fiendish, brutal, inexcusable." In selecting the jury, Dempsey explained, he had aimed for a group made up mostly of fathers because "I don't believe that in Westchester County any jury composed of eleven fathers can convict another father of six children who loved his children. And I don't believe that any jury of eleven fathers will believe that a man could do the deed that this man is charged with doing unless he was out of his mind."

Dempsey accused the police of deliberately "soft-pedaling the evidence" by neglecting to ask Fish about cannibalism. "Why? Why didn't they ask that question? Why do you suppose, gentlemen, that not a single police official and not anyone of the two prosecutor's offices who have questioned this man asked why he took that girl's head outside and left it in the privy" and why, after dismembering the body, "he kept the fleshy parts?"

The reason, Dempsey proclaimed, was simple: "When they came to the end of a long trail, six and one-half years, they found a maniac, and it is significant to me that the district attorney has been trying to keep down some of the actual horror."

He also continued his attack against Bellevue "for having such a man as this down there for a period of three or four weeks" and then "turning him out on the streets."

If Bellevue could not do a better job of diagnosing "people that are suspected of having mental aberrations," Dempsey charged, "then I say to you, gentlemen, that there is very little protection afforded to law-abiding citizens by the psychiatric ward of Bellevue from maniacs and such people."

Dempsey also laid part of the blame for the tragedy on Grace's parents—a charge that no one had ever made before, at least not publicly. "Now I appreciate, as you do, the sorrow that this case has brought to Mr. and Mrs. Budd," Dempsey said.

But I honestly do believe, gentlemen, that one of the reasons why Mr. and Mrs. Budd feel so badly is because they permitted that little child—whom God had given to them for protection and care during her infancy and childhood—they permitted that little girl to be taken off by this defendant. This is not a case, gentlemen, where the man takes the little girl off the street or by force. This is a case where the man took the child with the consent and permission of the parents.

Now, whether they appreciated it or not, the fiend that this man was, he was, after all, a total stranger to them. And I say to you advisedly that there is no feeling of protection, in the animal sphere or in the human sphere, no feeling of protection such as a mother gives to her child. I submit that some of the responsibility must go to that family for permitting that little girl to go with an absolute stranger on that particular Sunday.

Mostly, however, Dempsey stuck to a single theme, returning time and again to the one, bedrock issue on which he had built his defense—how could a man who had spent a lifetime committing such atrocities possibly be in his right mind?

Dempsey's voice grew more impassioned as he reviewed the outstanding facts of the case and posed the same crucial question about each of Fish's acts—Would a sane man have behaved that way? "Does a sane man go out, just decide he is going to kill someone, and it doesn't make any bit of difference who it is?" Would a sane man have taken his victim "right up next door to where he had lived" in the "broad light of a mid-afternoon in June," killed her "alongside the window that was nearest the adjoining house," then walk outside to clean his hands in the grass "in the afternoon sun, in the light of day?"

Would a sane man have neglected to take such an elementary precaution against arrest as shaving off his moustache? Or written such a letter as the one Fish had mailed to Mrs. Budd? Could a sane man have practiced "the most repulsive indulgences a human mind can conceive of" for over fifty years?

And how could any man eat human flesh and be in his right mind?

There was no doubt, Dempsey acknowledged, that Fish had proceeded with diabolical cunning and deliberation,

But every maniac, every insane person plans and connives. Every animal, gentlemen, plans and connives. Plans are in all existence, whether human or animal, whether the mind is intact or not. The squirrel plans for the winter and brings the nuts so that he might tide himself over the barren winter months. All animals plan. And there is, I daresay, more planning, conniving, and scheming of people behind the walls of Matteawan than any other place. The fact that a man can connive and plan an outrageous, dastardly, fiendish crime like this is no indication of the fact that a man is in his right mind.

Dempsey ended with a flourish—a final, impassioned plea meant to impress on the jurors the full weight of the "fearful responsibility" that now lay before them. "So I ask you gentlemen," Dempsey said solemnly,

I ask you to bear with me for a moment. Tell me now, each man answering in his own heart, now that you have heard all the evidence for the People and all of the evidence for the defense, tell me now: Do you believe before[msp311] God that Albert Fish was sane on June 3, 1928? Do you believe on that day he knew the distinction between right and wrong?

Unless you believe that, gentlemen, if you later find him guilty, it will be on mere breath, not upon evidence. Recall the answer in your heart when you get to the jury room. Record that answer man for man when you cast those ballots for life or death. The voice of one man, gentlemen, saves Albert Fish's life. It takes twelve ballots of guilty to send him to death. And before you make that answer, I have but one more request to make of you, and having made it under these circumstances, you cannot, gentlemen, you will not forget it.

In the course of human nature ten of you twelve men will die in full possession of your reason and memory. When that hour comes, when the blood begins to congeal and the breath to fail, when death snaps one by one the strings of life, when you look back to the past and forward to judgment, remember Albert Fish, that when he was helpless and defenseless and pleaded with you for his life, that you said, 'Let him live,' or 'Let him die,' and if you said 'Let him die,' may He who breathed into your nostrils the breath of life judge you more mercifully than you judged this maniac.

Though Edward Budd had been present in the courtroom throughout the trial, his parents had not attended since the day of their testimony. Today, all three of them sat together on a bench not far from the defense table, listening expressionlessly as Dempsey summed up his case. Directly across the narrow aisle sat Fish's six children, dry-eyed except for Gertrude, who clutched a handkerchief to her tear-streaked face.

Throughout the trial there had been virtually no

communication between the members of the two families, though at one point, during a short recess, Gertrude had approached Edward Budd in the hallway outside the courtroom and tearfully apologized for her father's dreadful crime.

Fish himself sat up during Dempsey's summation and, for one of the few times since the start of the trial, actually seemed to be paying attention. When the lawyer made his final appeal, the old man lifted his gnarled hands in a small, pathetic gesture of supplication, then let them drop helplessly into his lap. Then, as Dempsey begged mercy for the poor, "defenseless" old man who sat before the jury, pleading for his life, Fish's eyes filled with tears and he began to weep silently for himself.

In contrast to Dempsey's impassioned summation, Gallagher's was largely a cut-and-dried recap of the case. His tone suggested that the prosecution had no need for oratory, that the facts spoke for themselves, that no reasonable man, confronted with the evidence of Fish's dreadful crime, could possibly fail to find the old man guilty.

Indeed, his most emotional comment was his first one. "Mr. Dempsey in his closing remarks asked you to remember certain things about the defenseless Mr. Fish," he said, his voice turning harsh as he spoke the old man's name. "Gentlemen, I want you to remember the defenseless little innocent Grace Budd as she kicked and screamed in the springtime of her life and said she would tell her mamma."

Gallagher took time to answer Dempsey's charges against Bellevue Hospital and Grace Budd's parents, arguing that those accusations were simply "a smoke screen, an attempt on the part of the defense to kick up some dust here and throw it into your eyes to get away from the true issues of this case."

Those issues could be stated very simply: Had Grace Budd been killed by Albert Fish and, if so, had the old man been in full possession of his senses at the time of the murder?

As for the first of these issues, Gallagher reminded the

jury that he had "produced in this case an array of over forty witnesses to prove the People's case" beyond "any doubt." He then provided a step-by-step synopsis of the evidence, paying particular attention to the proof of the corpus delecti.

The second point, Fish's sanity, had been established by the expert witnesses the state had put on the stand—a more trustworthy bunch, Gallagher suggested, than the trio who had testified for the defense. "I think so far as the array of alienists is concerned, ours showed a more friendly attitude, they told you from their own minds and hearts what this defendant told them, they did not shift about in the chair and quibble about little points."

Acknowledging that Fish was "sexually abnormal"—a "conniving and scheming sexual pervert" who had "engaged in revolting practices with women and children" —Gallagher nevertheless insisted that Fish was not suffering from "a disease of the mind." He scoffed at the idea that Fish had been motivated by a "divine command." "There was no divine hallucination or divine command when he purchased this pot cheese can or these tools with which to carry out this nefarious plan. And when he sent the telegram there was not any divine command. And when he went there that day, there was no divine command to go to the house.

"Don't put any stock, gentlemen, in this divine command business. That is merely a smoke screen again." Every step of Fish's crime spoke of "premeditation and design," directed toward the fulfillment of a clear-cut goal—"to satisfy his own sexual gratification."

"And so, gentlemen, the People leave this case in your hands, knowing that whatever you do, you will do the right thing by the People of this County, of this State, and by the defendant."

On that flat, even perfunctory note, Gallagher brought his summation to a close.

Justice Close began his charge to the jury at precisely 1:50 P.M., immediately following the lunch recess. Standing beside his chair in accordance with local custom, he presented an orderly and lucid summary of the issues, explaining the six possible verdicts that might be rendered in the case, ranging from acquittal to first-degree murder as charged. He proposed a systematic way for the jurors to proceed in their deliberations and recited several relevant sections of the Penal Code, including the ones pertaining to the legal definition of insanity.

One section in particular "may have some bearing upon the evidence in this case," the judge explained, then read it aloud to the jury. "A morbid propensity to commit prohibited acts, existing in the mind of a person who is not shown to have been incapable of knowing the wrongfulness of such acts, forms no defense to a prosecution thereof."

It was a point that the judge clearly felt was worth repeating. "Well, now, gentlemen," he stressed. "If you find that this man through his own perversion has so weakened his will that an irresistible impulse comes upon him to satisfy his sexual passions, that would not excuse him from the consequences of his act. He must have been suffering from such a defect of reason as not to know the nature and quality of his act or to know that it was wrong when he performed it, or he must answer for the consequences of his act."

At 3:01 P.M., the judge completed his charge, dismissing the alternate juror, Thomas Madden, with the thanks of the Court. As the jury retired to begin its deliberations, a flock of newsmen surrounded Madden, who created a stir by declaring that the psychiatric testimony had been completely confusing to him. Had he been called on to take part in the final deliberations, he would have simply disregarded the opinions of the alienists and relied on his own judgment. As far as he was concerned, Fish was insane.

Taking an informal poll among themselves, the reporters came up with the same verdict.

At 6:00 P.M., the jury recessed for dinner at the Roger Smith Hotel, resuming their deliberations at 7:30. Slightly less than one hour later, at precisely 8:27 P.M., the twelve men filed back into the courtroom, having agreed upon a verdict.

John Partelow, the foreman, rose to deliver it.

"And how do you find the defendant, guilty or not guilty?" intoned the clerk.

"We find the defendant guilty as charged in the indictment," Partelow declared solemnly.

The reporters hurried to the nearest phones to file the news. Albert Fish had been found guilty of murder in the first degree. The verdict carried a mandatory sentence of death in the electric chair at Sing Sing.

Fish, sitting with his hands folded tightly in his lap, slumped at the news, though he stood with his shoulders squared and his back straight as two guards led him up to the clerk's table, where he delivered his pedigree in a soft but steady voice.

At Dempsey's request, Justice Close deferred the formal sentencing until Monday morning at 10:00 A.M.

Fish's children, waiting tensely in the hallway, heard the news from a reporter. The old man's sons flinched but said nothing. Fish's two daughters broke into violent sobs and were led from the courthouse by their husbands.

Mrs. Budds's reaction was jubilant. "Good for him!" she exclaimed. "Just what I expected."

Her son Edward concurred. "I'm glad of the verdict. It won't bring Gracie back. But it was what he deserved."

Only Mr. Budd seemed struck by the gravity of the verdict. "I had a funny feeling when I heard it," he told reporters. "It hit the top of my head when I realized he would go to the electric chair. It put a tremor through me." He paused for a moment, then echoed his wife and son. "But he deserves it. Insanity was the bunk!"

As guards led the dazed-looking Fish past a crowd of reporters and photographers, several of the newsmen shouted out to him, asking how he felt about the verdict. "I feel bad," he murmured. "I expected Matteawan."

Dempsey, too, was asked for his reaction. "The man is insane," he said, shaking his head. "I can't conceive how twelve intelligent men in the face of this overwhelming evidence of perversion, which makes him an incredible pervert even among perverts, could decide he was sane."

As it happened, the majority of the jurors wouldn't necessarily have disagreed with Dempsey. Buttonholed

DERANGED

by reporters on the sidewalk outside the courthouse, one of the jurors revealed that most of them had, in fact, thought Fish was insane. But they felt he should be electrocuted anyway.

Later that night, a report began to circulate that made its way into the next day's papers. According to this story, Fish's attitude toward the outcome of his trial had undergone a significant change once he'd had a chance to think it over. He still believed that the verdict "wasn't right" and he felt especially sorry that "my family will have no one to guide them."

But the more he considered the prospect of his own execution, the less unhappy about it he felt. Indeed, as Norma Abrams wrote in the *Daily News,* "his watery eyes gleamed at the thought of being burned by a heat more intense than the flames with which he often seared his flesh to gratify his lust."

"What a thrill it will be to die in the electric chair!" Fish was quoted as saying. "It will be the supreme thrill—the only one I haven't tried!"

35

~~~~~~~~~~~~~~

> *"We do not even know if, when animals tear each other to pieces, they do not experience a certain sensual pleasure, so that when the wolf strangles the lamb, one can say equally well, 'he loves lambs' as that 'he hates lambs.'"*
>
> THEODOR LESSING

The tabloid headlines trumpeting the news of Fish's sentence seemed to be the fitting climax of the long, lurid affair. But there were more shocks to come.

In the days following the end of the trial, Fish was back on the front pages as a result of several new confessions. To be sure, these confessions merely confirmed what the authorities had believed for months. But they were no less sensational for that.

The first took place on Sunday evening, March 24, in Warden Casey's office, where—to a group that included Elbert Gallagher and his boss, District Attorney Walter Ferris—Fish admitted that he had, in fact, kidnapped and slain four-year-old Billy Gaffney in February, 1927.

The old man had already written out the details of that killing in a letter to James Dempsey—and if the atrocities Fish described in that letter were true, then, for sheer ghastliness and depravity, the Gaffney crime had surpassed even the Budd outrage.

"There is a public dumping ground in Riker Ave., Astoria," the letter began. "All kinds of junk has been thrown there for years . . . I will *admit* the motorman *who positively identified* me as getting off his car with a small boy was *correct*. I can tell you at that time I was looking for a suitable place to do the job." Then he proceeded to the specifics:

Not satisfied there, I brought him to the Riker Ave. dumps. There is a *house* that stands alone, not far from where I took him. A few yrs. ago I painted this house for the man who owns it. He is in the auto wrecking business. I forget his name but my son Henry can tell you, because he bought a car from him. This man's father lives in the house. Gene, John, Henry helped me paint the house. There were at that time a number of old autos along the road.

I took the G boy there. Stripped him naked and tied his hands and feet and gagged him with a piece of dirty rag I picked out of dump. Then I burned his clothes. Threw his shoes in the dump. Then I walked back and took trolley to 59 St. at 2 A.M. and walked from there home.

Next day about 2 P.M., I took tools, a good heavy cat-o-nine tails. Home made. Short handle. Cut one of my belts in half, slit these half in six strips about 8 in. long.

I whipped his bare behind till the blood ran from his legs. I cut off his ears—nose—slit his mouth from ear to ear. Gouged out his eyes. He was dead then. I stuck the knife in his belly and held my mouth to his body and drank his blood.

I picked up four old potato sacks and gathered a pile of stones. Then I cut him up. I had a grip with me. I put his nose, ears and a few slices of his belly in grip. Then I cut him thru the middle of his body. Just below his belly button. Then thru his legs about 2 in. below his behind. I put this in my grip with a lot of paper. I cut off the head—feet—arms—hands and the legs below the knee.

This I put in sacks weighed with stones, tied the ends and threw them into the pools of slimy water you will see all along road going to North Beach. Water is 3 to 4 ft. deep. They sank at once.

I came home with my meat. I had the front of his body I liked best. His monkey and pee wees and a nice little fat behind to roast in the oven and eat. I made a stew out of his ears—nose—pieces of his face and belly. I put onions, carrots, turnips, celery, salt and pepper. It was good.

Then I split the cheeks of his behind open, cut off his monkey and pee wees and washed them first. I put strips of bacon on each cheek of his behind and put in the oven. Then I picked 4 onions and when meat had roasted about ¼ hr., I poured about a pint of water over it for gravy and put in the onions. At frequent intervals I basted his behind with a wooden spoon. So the meat would be nice and juicy.

In about 2 hr. it was nice and brown, cooked thru. I never ate any roast turkey that tasted half as good as his sweet fat little behind did. I eat every bit of the meat in about four days. His little monkey was as sweet as a nut, but his pee-wees I could not chew. Threw them in the toilet.

While the police announced plans to search the Riker Avenue dump on the chance of turning up evidence of Fish's professed butchery, newsmen traveled to Brooklyn to get Mrs. Gaffney's reaction.

Eight years after her son's disappearance, Elizabeth Gaffney still refused to believe that her boy was gone for good. On Christmas days, she continued to set a place for him at the family table. Somewhere, she insisted, her son was alive and well.

"I know in my heart and soul that Billy will come back to me," she told the reporters. "I have never felt he is dead. I cannot get it out of my head that a woman took Billy away. He was nice-looking and well-liked."

As for Fish's confession, Mrs. Gaffney declared that she would not believe it until she had heard the details from the old man's own lips and satisfied herself that he was telling the truth.

Inspector John Lagrene, in charge of Brooklyn detectives, promptly announced that Mrs. Gaffney would have her chance to confront her son's confessed murderer as soon as Fish was transferred to his new accommodations in Sing Sing.

On the morning of Monday, March 25, Albert Fish was brought before Justice Close, who sentenced him to die in the electric chair at Sing Sing during the week of April 29.

Dressed in dark trousers and a gray coat, his sunken cheeks stubbled with white, the old man heard the sentence in silence, then gave a friendly little wave and piped, "Thank you, judge!"

Elsewhere in the courthouse, Lawrence Clinton Stone —the so-called furnace killer of five-year-old Nancy Jean Costigan—was receiving his sentence at the same time. After pleading guilty to a charge of second-degree murder, Stone was given a sentence of fifty years to life by Justice William Bleakley.

Fish and Stone were manacled together. Then, guarded by Warden Casey and Chief Deputy Sheriff Frederick Ruscoe, the two prisoners were driven off to Sing Sing, which, in the words of one reporter, "opened its gates to receive both scions of Revolutionary families at the same time."

Inside the prison, the paths of the two men—who had not exchanged a word during the entire ride—diverged. Stone was given convict number 90,273 and taken to the cell he would occupy for the next half century, while Fish—number 90,272—was led off to the death house.

Before the day was over, the old man would drop another bombshell, admitting that, in 1924, he had murdered eight-year-old Francis McDonnell, the Staten Island policeman's son. Fish confessed that he had lured the little boy into the woods, strangled him with the child's own suspenders, and was about to dismember the body when he thought he heard someone approaching and fled.

The following morning, the *Daily Mirror* declared that Fish's latest disclosures certified his status as "the most vicious child-slayer in criminal history." Occupying the center of the front page was a large photograph of Fish as he was being led off to Sing Sing. Above it, the caption read, "PARENTS WILL BREATHE EASIER."

In the end, no one would ever know the precise number of murders the old man had committed, though one reliable source—a Supreme Court justice who had gotten the information from police investigators—told Frederic Wertham that Fish had probably been responsible for the torture-killings of at least fifteen children.

Three days after his transfer to Sing Sing, on Thursday, March 28, Albert Fish was served a pork chop dinner in his cell on death row. When the tray was removed, the guard failed to notice that one of the pork bones was missing from the plate.

During the night, Fish—repeating the procedure he had employed in Eastview—sharpened the bone against the floor of his cell. The next day, he used it to carve an eight-inch cross on his abdomen.

Keeper Daniel Maloney spotted Fish as he was in the act of mutilating himself, entered the cell, and took the bone away from the old man. When Warden Lewis Lawes asked Fish why he had wounded himself, the old man explained that he was "in pain" from the needles inside his body, and "I thought maybe I could relieve it that way."

On a mild Sunday afternoon in early spring, Mrs. Elizabeth Gaffney traveled to Sing Sing prison to have her face-to-face meeting with Albert Fish. Accompanying her were Inspector John Lagarene, Sergeant Thomas Hammill, and Detective William King (who, just a few months later, would receive the Rhinelander Medal for outstanding detective work from Mayor Fiorello LaGuardia during a gala ceremony at City Hall).

Fish was led from his cell to the counsel room in the death house by his lawyer, James Dempsey, and Principal Keeper John Sheehy.

Once inside the room, however, the old man announced that he would not see or speak to Mrs. Gaffney. He began to weep bitterly and demanded to be left alone.

Standing in the doorway, Mrs. Gaffney attempted to

put various questions to Fish through Dempsey—
questions about the clothing Billy had been wearing on
the day of his disappearance and other details that only
his abductor would be likely to know. But Fish refused to
answer.

Two hours later, Mrs. Gaffney finally gave up and
headed back to Brooklyn, still unpersuaded that Albert
Fish was the person who had stolen her son.

It was April 3 when Mrs. Gaffney made her visit. By
then, Dempsey had already filed his appeal and Fish's
execution had been stayed.

36

~~~~~~~~~~

The memory of the just is blessed; but the name of the wicked shall rot.

PROVERBS 10:7

Dempsey pleaded for a reversal of Fish's conviction on several grounds, including the prosecutor's literally bone-rattling display of the corpus delecti and the judge's "definite hostility towards the defense." Primarily, however, Dempsey based his appeal on the seemingly self-evident argument that there was "reasonable doubt . . . as to Albert H. Fish's sanity."

Among the evidence he cited to support his case was the list of Fish's "abnormalities" that Dr. Wertham had prepared for the trial. This list, Dempsey asserted, included "every known sexual perversion and some perversions never heard of before":

1. Sadism.
2. Masochism.
3. Active and passive flagellation.
4. Castration and self-castration.
5. Exhibitionism.
6. Voyeur Acts.
7. Piqueur Acts (jabbing sharp implements into oneself or others for sexual gratification).
8. Pedophilia.
9. Homosexuality.
10. Fellatio.
11. Cunnilingus.

299

12. Anilingus (oral stimulation of the anus).
13. Coprophagia (eating feces).
14. Undinism (sexual preoccupation with urine).
15. Fetishism.
16. Cannibalism.
17. Hypererotism (abnormal intensification of the sexual instinct).

Fish was a "psychiatric phenomenon," Dempsey declared. "It is noteworthy that no single case-history report, either in legal or medical annals, contains a record of one individual who possessed all of these sexual abnormalities."

Dempsey ended his appeal on a characteristically fervent note. "Albert H. Fish's insanity was disregarded by the jury, undoubtedly through passion and prejudice. *His conviction proves merely that we still burn witches in America.*"

On November 26, 1935, the Court of Appeals unanimously decided to uphold Fish's death sentence. The execution was rescheduled for the week of January 13, 1936.

On a bitterly cold day in early January, Dempsey—accompanied by several of his associates, five of Fish's children, and Dr. Fredric Wertham—traveled to Albany in a last-ditch attempt to save Albert Fish from the chair. The lawyer had arranged a hearing with Governor Herbert Lehman to plead for a commutation of the death sentence.

Wertham made the lengthiest and most impassioned speech, appealing to the governor "not on behalf of Mr. Fish—who doesn't mind the electric chair anyway, in his distorted ideas of atonement. He is, in my opinion, a man not only incurable and unreformable but also unpunishable. I am appealing on behalf of the many victims, past and future, of men such as Fish."

Fish was manifestly a sick man, and to execute him, Wertham argued (resorting to the same analogy Dempsey had employed) was "like burning witches. The time will come when psychiatrists will be as little proud of their role in these procedures as the theologians of the past."

On the other hand, with Fish committed to an institution, science would have a chance to study the man's psychology and learn something that might help prevent future crimes against children. "Science is prediction," Wertham asserted. "The science of psychiatry is advanced enough that with proper examination such a man as Fish can be detected and confined before the perpetration of these outrages, instead of inflicting extreme penalties afterwards."

Throughout Wertham's speech, Governor Lehman remained perfectly impassive, though his counsel, sitting directly to the governor's left, seemed responsive to the psychiatrist's arguments, smiling and nodding in approval and even, on several occasions, looking seriously moved. Wertham was encouraged to believe that his appeal was getting through.

He was wrong. The moment Wertham finished speaking, Governor Lehman rose from the table, nodded slightly, and left, unimpressed by the arguments and unwilling to reverse the court's judgment.

On the morning of their final days, condemned men at Sing Sing were transferred from their cells to a wing of the death house that the inmates called "the dance hall." It was there, on Thursday, January 16, 1936, that Albert Fish ate his last meals. For lunch, he had a T-bone steak from which the bone had been removed. The same precaution was taken with the roast chicken he requested for dinner. By the time his dinner arrived, however, he had largely lost his appetite and ate only a few mouthfuls.

Sometime around 10:30 P.M., the Reverend Anthony Petersen, Protestant chaplain of the prison, arrived to pray with Fish, who had spent much of his time during the preceding weeks poring over his Bible. Shortly before 11:00, two guards entered the cell. One of them knelt before Fish with a knife and deftly slit the old man's right trouser leg.

Then, flanked by the guards and followed by Reverend

Petersen, the old man shambled down the corridor toward the execution chamber. The time was 11:06 P.M.

Throughout the day, Warden Lawes—one of America's most distinguished criminologists and a staunch opponent of capital punishment—had waited close to his phone, hoping for a reprieve. But it never came. When a reporter asked Lawes how he felt about Fish's imminent execution, he replied, "I am not supposed to feel. I am just part of the apparatus."

At the sight of the electric chair, Fish did not quail, as even the hardest men often did, though he did not seem like someone who was looking forward to the "supreme thrill" of his life, either. Hands clasped in prayer, he lowered himself into the chair and allowed the straps to be adjusted around his arms, legs and torso.

His face looked very pale in the instant before Robert Elliott, the gaunt, gray-haired executioner, slipped the black death mask over it. The leather cap with its electrode was fitted to the old man's close-shaven head. After fastening the chin-strap, Elliott stooped to secure the second electrode to Fish's right leg beneath the trouser-slit. Then he stepped to the control panel.

Afterward, stories circulated that the needles in the old man's body had produced a burst of blue sparks when the electricity was activated. But this was simply part of the folklore that grew up around Fish in the following years. There were no pyrotechnics. Fish died like other men.

When the current hit, his body surged, his neck cords bulged, his clenched fists turned a fiery red. Eventually, the body subsided.

At precisely 11:09 P.M., the attending physician stepped up to the body, cupped his stethoscope against the motionless chest, and declared that Albert Fish—the oldest man ever executed at Sing Sing—was dead.

For the Budds, the end was like the beginning—a stranger came knocking at the door.

This time, it was a reporter for the *Daily News,* who showed up at the Budds' 24th Street apartment shortly after midnight. He rapped on the door, waited, then rapped again. It was a full ten minutes before Mrs. Budd trudged from her bedroom, opened the door, and peered outside.

Albert Fish was dead, the reporter informed her. He paused expectantly, pen and notepad at the ready.

But if he was hoping for a juicy quote or dramatic response, he was disappointed. Mrs. Budd heard the news in silence, without a flicker of emotion on her face.

A few moments later, her husband's thin voice came drifting through the apartment, calling her back to sleep. Without a word to the reporter, Mrs. Budd pushed the door closed and returned to her bedroom, shuffling heavily through the familiar darkness.

Acknowledgments

A few years ago, I wrote a book called *Deviant* about the Wisconsin ghoul Edward Gein, who served as the model for *Psycho's* Norman Bates. While researching the book, I wrote to Robert Bloch, author of the novel upon which Hitchcock's classic terror film was based, to ask, among other things, why he thought so many people continued to be fascinated by Gein. Bloch replied, "Because they are ignorant of the activities of . . . Albert Fish."

Intrigued by the answer, I began digging into Fish's incredible case, and the result is the present book. My acknowledgments, then, must begin with a word of thanks to Robert Bloch for his initial (if unwitting) inspiration.

I owe a very large debt of thanks to James Dempsey, Albert Fish's defense lawyer. Still active at eighty-nine, this remarkable gentleman shared his memories of Fish with me and gave me access to documents which proved invaluable in my reconstruction of the case. Without his help, this project would have been infinitely more difficult to complete.

Many other people helped along the way. For various forms of assistance I am grateful to: Greg Albanese, Jim

ACKNOWLEDGMENTS

Donna, Fred Ellwick, Dr. John Frosch, Una Vavasour Grazelski, Sergeant Donald J. Haberski, Andrew Hill, Jay Klinik, Mr. and Mrs. Charles Marks, Eneta McAlister, Joe McCormack, Catherine Ostlind, John Padraki, Jerry Perles, Faigi Rosenthal, Len Rubin, John Sheridan, Charles Sullivan, Mark Tulis, and Mike Wilk.

I would also like to thank all the people who were kind enough to answer my call for information concerning Fredric Wertham: Christopher Beall, Monte Beauchamp, Thomas Cole, Emily Essex, Dana Gabbard, Edith Goodman, Ian Gordon, William Kaplan, Sylvia Pollack, Richard Roffman, Natalie Shainess, Ralph Slovenko, Herman Steinberg, Arthur Stern, Jane Strompf, Miriam Wallace, and Bill Zavatsky.

Linda Marrow has been a wonderful editor and an even better friend. For those reasons, this book is dedicated to her.

READ ABOUT
THE *SHOCKING* AND *BIZARRE*
CRIMES OF OUR TIME
FROM POCKET BOOKS

- ☐ LIFE WITH BILLY
  Brian Vallée ....66549/$3.95
- ☐ BROTHERHOOD OF MURDER Thomas Martinez
  with John Guinther...67858/$4.95
- ☐ TED BUNDY: THE DELIBERATE STRANGER
  Richard Larson ....72866/$4.95
- ☐ CARELESS WHISPERS
  Carlton Stowers ....68348/$4.95
- ☐ COPS Mark Baker ....68551/$4.95
- ☐ DEVIANT: THE SHOCKING TRUE STORY OF
  THE ORIGINAL "PSYCHO"
  Harold Schechter ....64482/$3.95
- ☐ DERANGED
  Harold Schechter ....67875/$4.50
- ☐ FOR LOVE OF MONEY Mary Walton ....63879/$3.95
- ☐ HUNTING HUMANS
  Elliott Leyton ....65961/$4.50
- ☐ THE LAST DAYS OF THE SICILIANS
  Ralph Blumenthal ....68277/$4.95
- ☐ ALL HIS FATHER'S SINS:
  THE SHOCKING TRUTH ABOUT CALIFORNIA'S
  MOST GRUESOME SERIAL KILLER
  Lt. Ray Biondi & Walt Hecox ....67265/$4.50
- ☐ MICHIGAN MURDERS
  Edward Keyes ....73480/$5.95
- ☐ HACKSAW Edward R. Jones ....67877/$4.95
- ☐ SUFFER THE CHILD
  Judith Spencer ....66852/$4.95
- ☐ TROOPER DOWN Marie Bartlett ....67610/$4.50
- ☐ THE VALACHI PAPERS
  Peter Maas ....63173/$3.95
- ☐ WISEGUY Nicholas Pileggi ....68350/$4.95
- ☐ WASTED
  INSIDE THE ROBERT CHAMBERS
  JENNIFER LEVIN MURDER
  Linda Wolfe ....70900/$4.95

POCKET BOOKS

Simon & Schuster Mail Order Dept. TCD
200 Old Tappan Rd., Old Tappan, N.J. 07675

Please send me the books I have checked above. I am enclosing $_____ (please add 75¢ to cover postage and handling for each order. Please add appropriate local sales tax). Send check or money order— no cash or C.O.D.'s please. Allow up to six weeks for delivery. For purchases over $10.00 you may use VISA: card number, expiration date and customer signature must be included.

Name_____

Address_____

City _____ State/Zip _____

VISA Card No. _____ Exp. Date _____

Signature _____ 175-16

INNOCENCE LOST

The True Story of a Quiet Texas Town and The Coldblooded Murder Committed by Its Kids

Carlton Stowers

Midlothian was a traditional, God-fearing town, but then a young undercover cop was murdered in a desolate field, and his execution exposed a terrifying subculture of rampant drug use, youth violence, and Satanic worship deep in the heart of Texas.

An unflinching look at the shocking true story behind the chilling headlines of murder in Texas.

**Available In Hardcover
From Pocket Books In July**

POCKET
B O O K S